Edmondo de Amicis, Pedro Mantellini González

The heart of a boy = Cuore

Edmondo de Amicis, Pedro Mantellini González

The heart of a boy = Cuore

ISBN/EAN: 9783744735544

Printed in Europe, USA, Canada, Australia, Japan

Cover: Foto ©Thomas Meinert / pixelio.de

More available books at **www.hansebooks.com**

THE HEART OF A BOY
(CUORE)

A STORY

BY
EDMONDO DE AMICIS

From the One Hundred and Sixty-sixth Italian Edition

BY
PROF. G. MANTELLINI

ILLUSTRATED

CHICAGO
LAIRD & LEE, PUBLISHERS

CONTENTS

OCTOBER: PAGE

   The First Day of School, ... 9
   Our Master, ... 11
   An Accident, ... 12
   The Calabrian Boy, ... 13
   My Classmates. 15
   A Noble Action, ... 16
   My School Mistress of the Upper First, ... 18
   In an Attic, ... 20
   The School, ... 22
   The Little Patriot of Padua, ... 23

NOVEMBER:

   The Chimney Sweep, ... 25
   All Souls' Day, ... 27
   My Friend Garrone, ... 28
   The Charcoal Man and the Gentleman, ... 30
   My Brother's School-Mistress, ... 31
   My Mother, ... 33
   My Companion Coretti, ... 35
   The Principal of the School, ... 39
   The Soldiers, ... 40
   The Protector of Nelli, ... 42
   The First of the Class, ... 44
   The Little Vidette of Lombardy, ... 46
   The Poor, ... 51

DECEMBER:

   The Trading Boy, ... 53
   Vanity, ... 54
   The First Snow Storm, ... 56
   The Little Mason, ... 58
   A Snow Ball, ... 59
   The School-Mistress, ... 62
   In the Home of the Wounded Man, ... 63

	PAGE
The Little Florentine Writer,	65
Will,	72
Gratitude,	74

JANUARY:

The Substitute,	75
Stardi's Library,	77
The Son of the Blacksmith,	78
A Nice Visit,	80
The Funeral of Vittorio Emanuele,	82
Franti Expelled from School,	83
The Sardinian Drummer Boy,	85
The Love of Our Country,	93
Envy,	95
Franti's Mother,	97
Hope,	99

FEBRUARY:

A Well-Awarded Medal,	101
Good Resolutions,	103
The Little Railway Train,	104
Pride,	106
The Wounds of Work,	108
The Prisoner,	110
Papa's Nurse,	113
The Workshop,	122
The Little Clown,	124
The Last Day of the Carnival,	128
The Blind Boys,	131
The Sick Master,	137
The Street,	139

MARCH:

The Evening Schools,	140
The Fight,	142
The Boy's Relatives,	144
Number 78,	146
The Little Dead Boy,	148
The Eve of the Fourteenth of March,	150
The Distribution of Prizes,	151
A Quarrel,	156
My Sister,	158

CONTENTS

	PAGE
Blood of Romagna,	160
The Little Mason Seriously Ill,	168
The Count Cavour,	170

APRIL:

Spring,	172
King Umberto,	173
The Infant Asylum,	178
At the Gymnasium,	182
My Father's Teacher,	185
Convalescence,	194
The Friend of the Workman,	196
Garrone's Mother,	198
Giuseppe Mazzini,	199
Civic Valor,	201

MAY:

The Children with the Rickets,	206
Sacrifice,	208
The Fire,	210
From the Apennines to the Andes,	214
Summer,	248
Poetry,	249
The Deaf and Dumb Girl,	251

JUNE:

Garibaldi,	258
The Army,	260
Italy,	262
Thirty-two Degrees Centigrade,	263
My Father,	265
In the Country,	266
The Distribution of Prizes to the Workmen,	269
My Dead School-Mistress,	272
Thanks,	274
A Shipwreck,	275

JULY:

The Last Page from My Mother,	282
The Examination,	283
The Last Examination,	285
Farewell,	287

AUTHOR'S PREFACE.

This book is particularly dedicated to boys of the elementary schools, between the ages of nine to thirteen years, and it might be called, "History of a School Year, by a pupil of the Third Grade of a Public School in Italy."

By saying that it was written by a pupil of the third grade, I do not wish to convey the idea that it was written by him entire, or as it appears in print. The boy noted down successively in a copy-book, what he knew, what he saw, what he felt, thought and experienced inside and outside the school; and his father, at the end of the year, wrote these pages from those notes, endeavoring not to alter the thought but to preserve, as near as possible, even the words used by his son. The latter, however, four years later, having entered the High School, re-read the manuscript and added to it something of his own, drawing upon his memory, still fresh, of the people and things.

Now read this book, boys. I hope it will please you and do you some good.

THE HEART OF A BOY

OCTOBER

THE FIRST DAY OF SCHOOL

Monday the 17th.

This is the first day of school. My three months spent in the country passed like a dream. This morning my mother took me to the Baretti school to have me entered for the third elementary grade. I was thinking of the country and went reluctantly. The streets were swarming with boys; the booksellers' shops crowded with fathers and mothers who were buying bags, portfolios, and copybooks; and so many people thronged in front of the school that a janitor and policeman had a very hard time keeping the entrance clear.

Near the door, some one touched me on the shoulder; it was my teacher of the second elementary. Always cheerful, he said:

"Well, Enrico, are we separated forever?"

I knew it too well, still those words pained me.

We made our way through the crowd with difficulty. Ladies, gentlemen, women of the middle class, workingmen, officers, grandmothers, servants, each leading a boy with one hand and holding the books of promotion with the other, were crowding the entrance and the stairway, making such a buzzing that it seemed like entering a theatre. I saw with pleasure the large hall on the ground floor with the doors of the seven class rooms where I had passed nearly every day for three years. There was a crowd of school mistresses coming and going. She who had taught me in the first upper class saluted me from the door of her room and said:

"Enrico, you go upstairs this year, I shall not even see you pass!" and looked at me with sadness. The principal had around him mothers in distress because there was no room for their children, and it seemed to me that his beard was a little whiter than it was last year. I also noticed that some of the boys had grown taller and stouter.

On the ground floor, where the divisions had already been made, there were children of the first and lowest grade who did not want to enter the class-room and who balked like donkeys; it was necessary to push them in; some escaped again from their benches; others, seeing their parents leave, commenced to cry, and the father or mother would return to offer consolation or take them home again, and the teachers were in despair.

My little brother was to enter the class of Mistress Delcati; I was put in that of Master Perboni up on the first floor.

At ten o'clock we were all in the class-room; fifty-four of us: only fifteen or sixteen of my class-mates of the second grade, among whom was Derossi, the one who always wins the first prize. The school-room seemed small and sad to me. I was thinking of the woods and mountains where I had spent the summer. I was also thinking of my teacher of the second class; he was so good and always laughed with us, and so small that he seemed like a companion, and I was sorry not to see him there with his bushy red hair. Our present teacher is tall, with long hair and no beard, and he has a straight wrinkle across his forehead. His voice is heavy and he looks at us fixedly, as though to read our inmost thoughts; I do not think he ever laughs. I was saying to myself: "This is the first day. Nine more months. How much work, how many monthly examinations, how much fatigue!" I felt the need of finding my mother at the close. I ran to her and kissed her hand. She said: "Courage, Enrico! we will study together," and I returned home happy. But I no longer have my master with his kind and cheerful smile, and the school does not seem so pleasant to me as it did last year.

OUR MASTER

Tuesday the 18th.

My new teacher pleases me since this morning. While we were coming in, he stood at his post, and many of his pupils of last year peeped in through the door to salute him: "Good day, Signor teacher," "Good day, Signor Perboni;" some would enter, touch his hand and run away. It was plain that they liked him and would have been pleased to remain with him. He answered: "Good day," shook the hands that were tendered him, but looked at no one, and at every salute remained serious, with the straight wrinkle on his forehead, turning his head toward the window and looking at the roof of the house opposite. Instead of enjoying those salutations he seemed to suffer from them. Then he looked at us, one after the other, attentively. While dictating, he came walking down between the benches, and seeing a scholar whose face was all red with pimples, he paused, took the boy's face between his hands and looked at him; asked the cause of the trouble and felt his forehead to see if it were warm. In the meanwhile, the boy behind him stood up on the bench and began to play the marionette. Our master turned around suddenly; the boy sat down quickly and awaited his punishment. The teacher placed his hand on his head and said: "Do not do it any more!" and returned to his desk. When he had finished dictating, he looked at us silently for a moment, and then said very slowly, in his heavy yet kind voice:

"Listen, we have a year to pass together, let us seek to pass it well. Study and be good. I have no family. You may take the place of my family. I had a mother last year but she is dead. I have no one else in the world now but you.

I have no other affection, no other thought than you. You must be my sons; I love you; you must love me. I do not want to be obliged to punish any one. Show me that you are boys with good hearts, and our school will be a family and you will be my consolation and my pride. I do not ask a promise of you, I am sure that in your hearts you have already told me 'yes' and I thank you."

At that moment the janitor came in to announce that the class was over, and we left our desks very quietly. The boy who had stood up on his bench approached the master and said to him in a trembling voice:

"Signor master, will you forgive me?"

The master kissed his forehead and said: "Go, my son."

AN ACCIDENT

Friday the 21st.

The year has commenced with an accident. Going to school this morning, I was repeating the words of the teacher to my father, when we beheld the street thronged with people who were crowding in front of the school. My father said: "An accident! the year commences badly."

We entered with some difficulty. The large hall was so crowded with relatives of the boys that the teachers could hardly reach their class-rooms, and all were turned toward the principal's room and we could hear them saying, "Poor boy." "Poor Robetti!"

Above the heads at the further end of the room, which was thronged with people, one could see the helmet of a policeman and the bald head of the principal; then a gentleman with a silk hat entered and they all said: "It is the doctor." My father asked a teacher what was the matter, and he answered: "A wheel passed over his foot." "It crushed his foot," said another. "It is a boy of the second grade, who, when coming to school through the street Dora Grossa, saw a child of the first grade, who had run away from his mother, fall in the middle of the street only a few steps from an omnibus which was coming upon him. He ran and caught up the boy and put him in safety, but not being quick enough to withdraw his own foot, the omnibus had passed over it. He is the son of an artillery captain." While they were telling us this, a lady entered the room looking like a crazy woman, breaking her way through the crowd. It was the mother of Robetti, for whom they had sent. Another lady ran to meet her and threw her arms around her neck, sobbing; it was the mother of the child who had been saved. Both ran into the room and a desperate cry was heard: "Oh, my Giulio, my child!"

At that moment a carriage stopped in front of the door, and the principal appeared with the boy in his arms, the sufferer's head leaning upon his shoulder, with a white face and closed eyes. All were silent, and one could hear the mother sobbing. The principal stopped a moment, raised the boy with both arms and showed him to the people. Then masters, mistresses, parents and boys murmured together: "Bravo, Robetti! Bravo, poor boy!" They threw kisses at him, and the mistresses and boys who were near him kissed his hands and his arms. He opened his eyes and said: "My satchel!" The mother of the boy who had been saved showed it to him and said: "I will bring it for you, you angel, I will bring it for you." In the meantime she was sustaining the mother of the wounded boy, who covered her face with both hands. They went out, laid the boy in the carriage, which was driven away. Then we all entered the class room silently.

THE CALABRIAN BOY

Saturday the 22nd.

Last evening, while the teacher was giving us the news of poor Robetti—who will be compelled to walk on crutches for a time—the principal entered the class room with a new pupil, a boy with a brown face, black hair, big black eyes, and with thick eyebrows which met between his eyes. He was dressed in dark clothes with a black leather belt around his waist. The principal, after whispering into the ear of the master, left the boy with him. He looked at us with his big black eyes as though he were frightened. Then the master took him by the hand, and said to the class: "You must congratulate yourselves. To-day there enters the school a little Italian boy, born at Reggio di Calabria, more than five hundred miles away from here. You must love your brother who comes from so far. He was born in that glorious country which has given to Italy many illustrious men, that still gives her strong workers and brave soldiers; where there are great forests and high mountains; one of the finest parts of our land, inhabited by people full of talent and courage. Do love him in a way that will make him forget that he is far away from the place where he was born. Demonstrate to him that an Italian boy, no matter in what Italian school he may be placed, will find brothers there." After saying this, he arose and pointed out on the wall map of Italy the place where Reggio di Calabria is situated. Then he called:

"Ernest Derossi," the one who always gets the first prize. Derossi stood up.

"Come here," said the master. Derossi left the bench and went and stood by the desk opposite the Calabrian boy.

"As the first in the school," said the master, "give a welcome to your new companion, the welcome of a boy of Piedmont to the son of Calabria."

Derossi embraced the Calabrian boy, saying with his clear voice, "Welcome!" and the latter kissed him on both cheeks with impetuosity. All clapped their hands. "Silence!" cried the master; "one does not clap hands at school;" but one could see that he was happy; the Calabrian boy was also happy.

The master assigned him his place and accompanied him to his desk, then he said:

"Remember what I am about to tell you. In order that a Calabrian boy might be at home in Turin, and that a boy of Turin be welcome in Reggio di Calabria, our country fought for fifty years and thirty thousand Italians died. You must respect each other, love each other, and any one who would offend his class mate because he was not born in our province would rende. himself ever unworthy to raise his eyes when the flag of our country passes."

As soon as the Calabrian boy was seated in his place, his neighbors presented him with some pens and a picture, and another boy from the last bench sent him a rare Swedish postage stamp.

MY CLASSMATES

Tuesday the 25th.

The boy who sent the postage stamp to the Calabrian boy is the one I like best. He is called Garrone; is the tallest of the class, and is almost fourteen years old. He has a large head and broad shoulders. He is good, one can see that when he smiles, but it seems to me that he is all the time thinking like a man. I already know the names of my classmates. There is another one I like; his name is Coretti, and he wears a knitted chocolate colored coat and a cat-skin cap. He is always jolly; he is the son of a huckster of wood, who was a soldier in the war of '66, in the army of Prince Humbert, and I have heard he has three medals. There is little Nelli, a hunchback, a frail boy with a pale face. There is one very well dressed, who wears fine velvet and who is called Votini. On the bench near me there is a boy whom they call "The Little Mason" because his father is a mason. His face is round like an apple, his nose is like a ball, and he has a particular skill for making the "hare's face." He wears a little soft hat which he doubles up like a handkerchief and puts in his pocket. Next to the

Little Mason, there is Garoffi, a tall, thin fellow with a nose like an owl's beak and very small eyes. He is always trading marbles, pictures, match boxes, and stamps. He writes his lessons on his nails to read when the teacher is not watching him. There is also a little gentleman called Carlo Nobis. He looks as though he were rather proud, and he sits between two boys whom I like very much; one is the son of a blacksmith ironmonger. He wears a big coat which reaches down to his knees, seems fearful of saying much and never laughs. The other is a lad with red hair who has a withered arm which he carries in a sling suspended from his neck. His father has gone to America, and his mother goes around selling green vegetables.

Stardi, my neighbor on the left, is a curious type. He is a little fellow, heavily built, a grumbler who never speaks to any one and seems to understand very little. He pays attention to the teacher without winking, with his forehead wrinkled and his teeth shut tight. If spoken to while the master speaks, the first and second time he does not answer, but the third time he kicks. He has next to him a boy with a shrewd face. His name is Franti, and he has already been expelled from another school. There are also two brothers who look as much alike as two drops of water. They both wear hats Calabrian in style with a pheasant feather stuck in the top. But the handsomest and most talented one of all, he who will surely be the first this year, is Derossi; and the teacher, who has already comprehended this, questions him all the time. However, I like Precossi, the son of the blacksmith ironmonger, the boy who wears the long jacket, and who looks so scared; they say his father beats him. He is very timid, and every time he questions or touches any one, he says "Excuse me," and looks up with his sad, gentle eyes. But Garrone is the bravest and the best.

A NOBLE ACTION.

Wednesday the 26th.

Garrone made himself known this morning. When I

entered the school (a little late, as I had been stopped by my old teacher of the first grade, who asked me at what time she might come to see us at home) the teacher had not yet arrived, and three or four boys were tormenting poor Crossi, the one with red hair, who has a paralyzed arm and whose mother sells green vegetables. They would poke him with rulers, throw chestnut burrs in his face, and call him "cripple" and "monster," mimicking him as he appeared with his withered arm suspended by the sling from his neck. He was all alone at his end of the bench looking like a dead person, and was listening, looking first at one and then at another with supplicating eyes, beseeching them to let him alone, but they ridiculed him still more and he commenced to tremble and redden with rage. All of a sudden Franti, the one with the ugly face, jumped on the bench, pretending that he was carrying two baskets on his arms, aping Crossi's mother as she used to come and wait for her son at the door; for now she is ill. Many began to laugh loudly. Then Crossi lost his head, and grasping an ink-stand he threw it with all his might at the head of Franti, who dodged it, and it struck the chest of the teacher, who was just entering the school room. The boys all scampered to their places and were silent and frightened.

The teacher, pallid, ascended to his desk and in an altered voice asked:

"Who did it?"

No one answered.

The teacher looked again, raising his voice, and demanded: "Who did it?"

Then Garrone, moved with pity for poor Crossi, rose with a dash and said, resolutely: "It was I."

The teacher looked at him, and then at the other pupils, as though stupified, and said in a tranquil voice: "No, it was not you."

After a moment, he added: "The guilty one will not be punished; let him rise."

Crossi rose and said, crying: "They were beating me, they were insulting me, and I lost my head and threw——"

"Sit down," said the teacher. "Those who provoked him rise up."

Four arose with bowed heads.

"You," said the teacher, "you have insulted a companion who did not provoke you; you have marked an unfortunate boy, tormented a weak one who could not defend himself. You have committed one of the lowest acts, one of the most shameful that can stain a human creature. Cowards!"

Having said this, he descended among the benches, put a hand under Garrone's chin, who sat with his head down, making him raise his face; he looked straight into his eyes and said: "You are a noble soul!"

Garrone, profiting by the moment, murmured something in the ear of the master, who turned toward the guilty ones and said: "I forgive you."

MY SCHOOL MISTRESS OF THE UPPER FIRST

Thursday the 27th.

My old teacher has kept her word. She called at the house to-day, just as I was going out with my mother to take washing to a poor woman mentioned in the paper. It was a year since we had seen her in our home, and we all greeted her cheerfully. She is not changed; still the same little woman with a large green veil around her head, plainly dressed and her hair carelessly arranged. She has no time to make herself look nice. She has a little less color than she had last year, has some white hair, and coughs all the time. My mother said to her:

"Dear teacher, you do not take good care of yourself."

"Oh, never mind," she answered with a pleasant, but melancholy smile.

"You strain your voice so," suggested my mother. "You do too much for the boys."

It is true one can always hear her voice. I remember when I was going to her school, she always spoke so that the boys would not become inattentive, and she would not remain seated for a moment. I was very sure she would come because she never forgets her pupils. She remembers their names year by year, and on the days of the monthly examination, runs to the principal to ask how many points they have made. She waits for them at the exit and has them show their compositions to see whether they have made progress. Some of the boys from the high school, who wear long trousers and carry a watch, still come to see her. To-day she was returning, all out of breath, from the Pinacoteca (picture gallery) where she had taken her boys. Last year she took her pupils every Thursday to a museum and explained everything to them. Poor mistress; she has grown thinner than of old, but she is still lively. She always becomes animated when any one speaks to her of the school. She wished to see again the bed where she beheld me sick two years ago, and which is now my brother's; she looked at it for awhile and could not speak. She could not stay long as she had to go and visit a boy of her class who is sick with the measles, the son of a saddler close by. Besides, she had a bundle of papers to correct, an evening's work, and two private lessons in arithmetic to give to a woman who keeps a shop, before night came.

"Well, Enrico," she said to me when going, "do you still love your mistress, now that you are able to solve a difficult problem and can write a long composition?" She kissed me and called up from the bottom of the stairs: "Do not forget me, Enrico!"

Oh, my good mistress, never, never will I forget you. When I am a big fellow, I will still remember you and will go to see you among your boys, and every time I pass near a school and hear the voice of a mistress, it will seem to me that

I hear your voice, and I will live over again the two years which I spent in your school, where I learned many things; where I saw you so many times so sick and tired, yet always so cheerful, so intelligent, and in despair if one acquired some bad way of holding the pen; trembling when the examiner questioned us, happy when we made a good showing; always good, always loving like a mother. Never, never, will I forget you, my mistress!

IN AN ATTIC

Friday the 28th.

Last evening, my mother, sister and I went to take some clothes to a poor woman recommended for charity by the newspaper. I carried the parcel and Silvia had the newspaper with the initials of her name, and the address. We went up under the roof of a high house, through a long corridor with many doors. My mother knocked at the last one and a woman opened it; she was a blonde, still young but thin. It occured to me at once that I had seen her somewhere before with that same blue handkerchief worn on her head.

"Are you the woman mentioned in the newspaper as so and so?" asked my mother.

"Yes, Signora, I am."

"Well, we have brought you some clothes." Then the

woman began so thank and bless us without end. In the meanwhile, I saw in a corner of the bare, dark room, a boy kneeling before a chair with his back turned toward us; he looked as though he were writing, and he was, indeed, writing, with his paper on the chair.

"How can he write in the dark?" While I said this to myself, I suddenly recognized the red hair and jean jacket of Crossi, the boy with the paralyzed arm, the son of the vegetable vender. I told it softly to my mother, while the woman was putting away the clothes.

"Hush," said my mother. "Maybe he is ashamed to see you because you bestow charity on his mother; do not call him."

At that moment, Crossi turned around and I felt embarrassed; he smiled, and my mother gave me a push to make me run and embrace him. I did so, and he arose to his feet and took my hand. Then his mother said:

"I am here all alone with this boy; my husband has been in America for six years; besides, I am sick so that I cannot go around selling green vegetables and earn a few *soldi*. I have not even a table left, upon which my poor little Luigino can do his work. When I had a bench down at the door, he could at least write on that; but even that has been taken away, and he has not even a little light by which to study without ruining his eyes. It is fortunate for me that I can send him to school, as the municipality provides him with books and copy-books. Poor little Luigino, who would study so willingly. Miserable woman that I am."

My mother gave her the contents of her purse and kissed the boy, who almost cried when we left. She did right to tell me: "Look at the poor boy, how he is obliged to work; and you, you have all the comforts and still study seems hard to you. Ah, my Enrico, there is more in one day of his work than in a year of yours. Such pupils ought to be given the first prize."

THE SCHOOL

Yes, dear Enrico, study is hard, as thy mother tells thee. Yet, I do not see thee go to school with that resolute mind and smiling face, as I would like. Thou art still stubborn; but, listen, think a little how miserable and despicable thy days would be if thou didst not go to school! At the end of a week thou wouldst ask with clasped hands to return again, wearied by annoyance and shame, tired of thy new toys, and of thy own existence. Everybody studies now, Enrico. Think of the workmen who go to school in the evening, after having worked all day; of the women and girls of the laboring class, who go to school on Sunday, after having worked all week; of the soldiers who take up their reading and writing books after they return tired from their drilling; think of the deaf and dumb boys and of the blind, who also study; even prisoners learn to read and write. Think in the morning, when thou goest out, that on that very morning, in thy own town, there are thirty thousand boys, going like thyself, to shut themselves in for three hours in order to study. Then again! Think of the innumerable crowds of boys who go to school about the same hour in all countries. Think of them—in thy imagination, while they are going—going through village by-ways, through noisy streets, along the shores of the sea and of the lakes, through the mist or under the burning sun; in little boats, in countries where there are canals, on horseback through great prairies, in sleighs over the snow, over mountains and hills, through woods and across torrents, up through solitary paths of the mountains; alone, in couples, in groups, in long files; all with books under their arms, clothed in a thousand different costumes, speaking a thousand different tongues; from the remotest schools of Russia, almost lost in the ice, to the remotest schools of Arabia shaded with palm trees; millions and millions, all going to learn the same things in a hundred different ways. Imagine these vast multitudes of boys from hundreds of nations, this immense movement of which you form a part. And know that if this movement were to cease, humanity would fall back into barbarism. This *movement is the progress, the hope, the glory of the world. Have courage then, thou little soldier of this immense army. Thy books are thy weapons, the whole world thy field of battle; and the victory is human civilization. Do not be a cowardly soldier, my Enrico.* *Thy Father.*

THE LITTLE PATRIOT OF PADUA

(MONTHLY STORY.)

Saturday the 29th.

No, I will not be a "cowardly soldier," but I would go to school more willingly if the teacher would tell us a story every day like the one he told us this morning. He says he will tell us one every month. He will give it to us in writing, and it will always be a tale of noble and true acts performed by a boy. "The Little Patriot of Padua" is the title of this. Here it is:

A French steamer left Barcelona, a city in Spain, for Genoa. There were on board Frenchmen, Italians, Spaniards, and Swiss. There was among the others a boy of eleven, apparently quite alone, who kept himself aloof like a savage. And no wonder he looked at every one with forbidding eyes. Two years previous to this, his father had sold him to the master of a company of mountebanks, who after having taught him to perform tricks by dint of beatings, kicks and fasting, had taken him across France and Spain, abusing him very often and never giving him enough to eat.

Arriving at Barcelona, no longer able to stand the ill-treatments and hunger, reduced to a pitiable state, he had run away from his tormenters and had gone to ask protection of the Consul of Italy, who moved with pity, had put him on board that steamer, giving him a letter to the chief of police in Genoa, who was ordered to send him back to the parents who had sold him like a beast.

The poor boy was ragged and sickly looking. They had given him a second-class cabin. All looked at him, some questioned him, but he did not answer, and seemed to hate and despise everyone. So much privation and so many blows had irritated and spoiled him. Three of the passengers, however, by insisting with their questions had succeeded in making him loosen his tongue, and in a few rough words, a mixture of Venetian, Spanish and French, he told his story. Those three passengers were not Italians, but they understood him, and partly from compassion, more because excited by wine, they gave him a few soldi, joking, jesting, and urging him to tell them more. Several ladies having entered the salon at that moment, two or three of them, for the purpose of making a show of themselves, gave him some more money, crying: "Take this, take that," and making the money sound upon the table.

The boy pocketed everything, thanking them in a subdued voice in his brusque manner, but with a look for the first time smiling and affectionate. Then he climbed up to his berth, pulled the curtains, and remained thinking of his own affairs. With that money he could enjoy a good meal on board, after two years of starvation! He could buy himself a jacket, as soon as he landed in Genoa. For two years he had gone dressed in rags! He could also take some home, and be received by his father and mother a little more humanely than if he arrived there penniless. It was a little fortune for him. He was thinking of all this and taking comfort in his thoughts behind the curtain of his cabin, while the three passengers were talking, seated at the dining table in the middle of the second-class salon. They were drinking and talking about their travels and of the countries they had visited, going from one topic to another. At last, they began to discuss Italy. One commenced to complain about the hotels, another about the railroads; and then, growing warmer, they all began to abuse everything. "One would prefer to travel in Lapland," said one; another, "had found in Italy none but swindlers and brigands." The third added that Italian officials did not know how to read.

"An ignorant people," repeated the first.

"A filthy people," quoth the second.

"Rob———" exclaimed the third, meaning to say robbers, but could not finish his word. A tempest of soldi and half-lire fell upon their heads and shoulders and leaped upon the table and floor, making a great noise. All three arose at once, looking up, and received another handful of coin upon their faces

"Take back your soldi," said the boy disdainfully, looking out between the curtains of his berth, "I do not accept alms from those who insult my country!"

NOVEMBER

THE CHIMNEY SWEEP

Tuesday the 1st.

Last evening, I went to the girls' school building, next to our own, in order to give the story of the boy from Padua to Silvia's teacher, who wanted to read it. There are seven hundred girls in this school! When I arrived, they were just coming out, all happy on account of the vacation of All Souls' day, and something beautiful took place before my eyes. In front of the door of the school, on the other side of the street, a chimney sweep stood, leaning with his head on his arm against the wall. He was a very small lad, all black in the face, with his bag and scraper, and he was crying and sobbing as though his heart would break. Two or three of the girls of the second grade approached him and asked:

"What is the matter with you? Why do you cry in this way?" But he did not answer and kept on crying.

"But tell us, why do you weep?" repeated the girls. Then he raised his head from his arm, showing the face of a baby, and said, weeping: "I have been in many houses to sweep the chimneys and earned thirty soldi; but I have lost them, they slipped through a hole in my pocket," and he showed the pocket which had a rip in it. He further said that he did not dare go home without the money.

"The master will beat me," he sobbed, and again dropped his head on his arm, as though he were in deep despair. The girls stopped a moment and looked at him sorrowfully. In the meanwhile, other girls had gathered around him, rich and poor, with their satchels on their arms. One, who had a blue feather in her hat, pulled from her pocket two soldi and said:

"I have nothing but two soldi, let us make a collection."

"I also have two soldi," said another dressed in red, "we will be able to find thirty among all of us," and they began to collect, calling aloud: "Amalia! Luigia! Annina! A soldo! Who has any soldi? Here are the soldi."

Some of them had soldi with which to buy flowers and writing books, and they gave them. Others, smaller ones, gave some centesimi, and the one with the blue feather collected everything and counted in a loud voice:

"Eight, ten, fifteen;" but more was needed. Then, one of the largest of them appeared; she looked like a young lady, and gave a half-lira, and all began to cheer her. Still five soldi were lacking.

"Now some of the fourth grade are coming, and they have

some," said one. Those of the fourth class came, and the soldi fell down in a shower. They all hurried forward eagerly. It was a fine sight to see that poor chimney sweep in the midst of those girls, dressed in so many different colors; it looked like a whirl of feathers, ribbons and girls. The thirty soldi had been collected, and more were giving; the little ones who had no money would make their way among the larger ones, throwing him their bouquets of flowers in order that they might give something. All of a sudden the janitress came out crying:

"The signora directress!" The girls scampered away on all sides like a flock of birds, and, at that moment, the little chimney sweep was seen standing alone in the middle of the street, wiping his eyes. He was happy with his hands full of money, and he had in the button holes of his jacket, in his pockets, and on his hat, bouquets of flowers, and there were some on the ground at his feet.

ALL-SOULS DAY

Wednesday the 2d.

This day is consecrated to commemorate the dead. Dost thou know, Enrico, to whose death you boys should dedicate a thought on this day? To those who have died for you—for boys and for all children. How many have died, and how many are continually dying! Hast thou ever thought how many fathers have worn out their lives by toiling? How many mothers have descended into their graves before their time, used up by privation to which they had condemned themselves for the sake of sustaining their children? Dost thou know how many men put a knife in their hearts, in despair, rather than see their children in misery, and how many women drown themselves, or die of grief, or go insane because they have lost a child? Think of all these dead ones on this very day, Enrico. Think, too, of the many schoolmistresses who have died young, who were consumed by the fatigues of the school, for the love of children, whom they had not the heart to leave. Think of the many physicians who have died from contagious diseases, having courageously sacrificed themselves to cure children. Think, too, of all those who have perished in shipwrecks, in fires, in times of famine, who in the supreme moment of danger have yielded to infancy the last morsel of bread, the last hope of escape, the last place of safety, and who expire, glad of their sacrifice, since they have saved the life of a little innocent. They are innumerable, Enrico. Every cemetery contains hundreds of these sainted beings. If they could rise a moment from their graves, they would cry the name of some child for whom they sacrificed the joys of youth, the peace of old age, all affection, their intelligence, their life; young mothers of twenty, men in the bloom of youth, octogenarians, old women, young men; heroic and obscure martyrs to infancy; so many who were great and noble, that the earth does not produce flowers enough to cover their graves. Think to-day with gratitude of those dead, and thou wilt be better and more affectionate to those who live and toil for thee, dear fortunate son, who in the " Day of the Dead" hast no one for whom to weep.

Thy Mother.

MY FRIEND GARRONE

Friday the 4th.

There were only two days of vacation, and yet it seems to me such a long time since I have seen Garrone. The more I know him, the better I like him, and it is so with all the others except those who are overbearing and are not friendly toward him, because he does not allow them to indulge their oppression. Every time any one of them raises his hand over a little fellow the little fellow cries: "Garrone!" and the big boy does not strike him any more. His father is an engineer on the railroad. He commenced late to go to school because he was ill for two years. He is the tallest and strongest of the class; he can raise a bench with one hand. He eats all the time. He is good; one may ask anything of him, chalk, rubber, paper, or pen-knife; he lends or gives everything away, and he never whispers or laughs in school. He keeps quiet on his bench,—which is rather narrow for him,—with his back bent and his head bowed. When I look at him, he smiles with his eyes half closed as though he would say: "Well, Enrico, are we friends?" But he makes me laugh. Tall and big as he is, he wears a jacket, trousers, sleeves, everything too small for him; a hat that will hardly set on his head, thick shoes, a cravat tied like a string around his neck, and he has his hair clipped. Poor Garrone, to look into his face is to like him. All the little ones like to sit near him. He knows his arithmetic well. He carries his books in a pile bound with a strap of red leather. He has a knife with mother-of-pearl handle which he found last year in the field for military manœuvring, and once he cut his finger to the bone with it; but no one at school knew it and he said nothing at home for fear he might frighten his parents. He takes with good nature anything told him in jest and he is never offended; but woe to the one who tells him: "It isn't true!" When he affirms a thing, fire flashes from his eyes, and he hammers upon the desk with his fist hard enough to split it. Saturday morning, he gave a soldo to a boy of the first upper, who was in the street, because some one had stolen the boy's soldo and he could not buy himself a copy-book. Garrone has been working for three days, making a pen ornamentation around an eight-page letter for the "Saint's Day" of his mother, who often comes to take him home, and who is tall and stout like him, and looks rather pleasant. The teacher always notices Garrone and every time he comes by him puts his hand on his head. I am very fond of him. I am sure that he would risk his life to save a companion, that he would allow himself to be killed in order to defend him; one can see this so clearly in his eyes; and, although it seems as though he always grumbles with his big voice, it is unquestionably a voice which comes from a kindly heart.

THE CHARCOAL MAN AND THE GENTLEMAN

Monday the 7th.

Garrone would never have said what Carlo Nobis said yesterday morning to Betti. Carlo Nobis is vain because his father is a grand signor, a tall gentleman who always wears a full black beard, very serious looking, and who comes nearly every day to accompany his son. Yesterday morning, Nobis quarreled with Betti, one of the smallest boys, the son of a charcoal man; and not knowing how to answer him, because he was in the wrong, he said to him in a loud voice: "Your father is a worthless ragged man." Betti grew red to the roots of his hair and said nothing, but tears came to his eyes, and when he went home he repeated those words to his father; and, behold, the charcoal man, a little fellow, all black, appeared at the school in the afternoon with the lad, in order to make his complaint to the teacher. While he was telling his grievance to the master, every one was quiet. The father of Nobis, who was taking off his son's overcoat on the threshold of the door, as he usually does, hearing his name pronounced, entered and asked an explanation. The master answered: "It is this workman who comes here to complain because your son Carlo said to his boy 'Your father is a worthless ragged man.'"

Nobis' father frowned and blushed a little and then asked his son, "Did you say those words?" Carlo standing in front of little Betti in the middle of the school room, with drooping head, did not answer.

Then his father took him by the arm and pushed him further ahead, beside Betti, so that the two almost touched each other and said: "Beg his pardon."

The charcoal man tried to interfere, saying "No, no," but the gentleman paid no heed, and repeated to his son, "Beg his pardon.

"Repeat my words: 'I beg to apologize for the insulting, senseless and ignoble words which I said against your father, whose hand my father feels honored to grasp.'"

The charcoal man made a gesture as if he would say, "I will not," but the gentleman paid no heed, and his son said slowly, with a tremor in his voice, without raising his eyes from the floor: "I beg to apologize——for the insulting—— senseless——and ignoble words which I said against your father, whose hand my father feels himself honored to grasp."

Then the gentleman reached his hand to the charcoal man, who grasped it with force; and then suddenly pushed his son into the arms of Carl Nobis.

"Do me the favor to put them next to each other," said the gentleman to the teacher. The teacher placed Betti in Nobis' bench, and when he saw them in their places, the father of Nobis made a bow and left.

The charcoal man remained a few moments, standing there in thought, looking at both boys; then he approached the bench, looked at Nobis with an expression of affection and regard, as if he wished to say something, but said nothing. He stretched out his hand as if to give him a caress, but dared not, and only stroked his brow with his large hand, then started for the door, turning once more to look at him, and departed.

"Remember well what you have seen, boys," said the teacher; "this is the finest lesson of the year."

MY BROTHER'S SCHOOL MISTRESS

Thursday the 10th

The son of the charcoal man was a pupil of Mistress Delcati, who came to-day to see my sick brother. She made us laugh by telling that the mother of that boy two years ago brought to her home an armful of charcoal, to thank her because she had given a medal to her son. The poor woman persisted in leaving it and almost cried when she had to return home with her apron full. The mistress also told of another good woman, who brought her a very large bouquet of flowers inside of which there was a quantity of soldi. She amused us a great deal by telling us stories, and my brother took his medicine which before he did not want to swallow. How much patience they must have with those boys of the first grade, all without teeth like the old men, who cannot pronounce either the r's or the s's. One coughs, another has the nose bleed, and another loses his shoes under the bench. This one cries, because he has pricked himself with a pen, and that one weeps, because he has bought copy-book number two instead of number one. Fifty all in one class, who know nothing, with those little hands like butter, who have to be taught to read and write! They carry in their pockets pieces of licorice, sugar, buttons, brick dust, every kind of small articles, and the teacher is obliged to go through their pockets, but they hide these things even inside their shoes. They pay no attention; if a fly enters through the window, it puts them all in confusion. In summer, they carry horn-bugs to school, which fly around and fall into the ink-stands and stain the copy-books with ink. The mistress, who plays the part of mother toward them, must help them to dress, bandage the fingers that are pricked, pick up the caps that fall, take heed that they do not exchange their coats, or else they indulge in cat-calls and shrieks. Poor school mistress, and besides some of the mothers will go and complain: "How is it, madam, that my child has lost his pen?" "How is it that mine does not learn anything?" "Why don't you give the prize to my boy, who knows so much?" "Why don't you have the nail which has torn the trousers of my Piero taken out of the bench?"

At times, my brother's mistress gets angry at the boys, and

when she can endure it no longer, she bites her finger in order not to give a blow. She loses her patience and then she repents, caresses the child who has been scolded, sends the little rogue out of the school, and then stops her own tears. She gets angry with the parents, who, in order to punish their children, compel them to fast. Mistress Delcati is young and tall, has a dark complexion, and dresses well. She is so restless and nervous that she is affected by a mere trifle. She speaks with a great deal of tenderness.

"But at least the children are attached to you?" my mother asked. "Some are," she answered, "but when the year is over, the greater part do not look at me any more. When they are with the male teachers they are ashamed to have been with a school mistress. After two years of cares, after we have loved a child so much, it is sad to be separated from him; we say: ' Oh, I am sure of that one, he will love me. ' But, the vacation over, we return to school, we run to meet him: ' Oh, my child, my child !' and he turns his head the other way." At this point, the mistress was interrupted. "But you will not do this, little fellow?" she said; then arose with her eyes full of tears and kissed my brother, "You will not turn your head the other way, will you? You will not deny your poor old friend?"

MY MOTHER

In the presence of thy brother's preceptress thou hast failed to respect thy mother! Let this not happen again, my Enrico, never, never again! Thy irreverent words entered my heart like a steel blade. I was thinking of thy mother when, years ago, she stood a whole night bent over thy little bed to watch for thy breath, crying with anguish, and shutting her teeth in terror because she thought she was going to lose thee, and I was afraid she would lose her mind; and I felt a sense of reproof for thee. Thou hast offended thy mother! Thy mother, who would give a year of happiness to spare thee an hour of sorrow, who would ask alms for thee, who would allow herself to be killed to save thy life! Listen, Enrico, fix this thought well in thy mind. Remember that destiny has many troubles in store for thee. The greatest trouble will come the day when thou wilt lose thy mother. A thousand times, Enrico, when thou wilt be a man, strong, and hardened by all the struggles of life, thou wilt be oppressed by a great desire to

hear again for one moment thy mother's voice, to see again her open arms ready to receive thee sobbing like a poor child without protection and without comfort. Then thou wilt remember all the bitterness thou hast caused her, and with what remorse wilt thou pay for all, thou unhappy creature! Do not hope for any serenity in thy life, if thou hast saddened thy mother. Thou wilt repent, thou wilt ask her pardon, thou wilt venerate her memory, all in vain, thy conscience will not grant thee peace. The sweet and good image will always have for thee an expression of sadness and reproach which will torture thy soul. Oh, Enrico, beware! This is the most sacred of human affections; woe to him who tramples upon it! The assassin who respects his mother has still something honest and chivalrous in his heart. The most famous of men if he sadden and offend her is a vile wretch. Nevermore let a harsh word proceed from thy mouth for the one who gave thee life. And, if another such word should escape thee, let it not be the fear of thy father but the impulse of thy soul which will throw thee at her feet to supplicate her, that with a kiss of forgiveness she may erase from thy forehead the stain of ingratitude. I love thee, my son; thou art the dearest hope of my life; but I would rather see thee dead than ungrateful to thy mother. Go, and for a little time do not offer me any of thy caresses. I could not exchange them in my heart.   *Thy Father.*

MY COMPANION CORETTI

Sunday the 13th.

My father has forgiven me, but still I remain somewhat sad. My mother sent me to take a walk through the Corso, with the janitor's oldest son. Half way through, passing near a truck standing before a shop, somebody called me. I turned around; it was Coretti, my schoolmate, all in a perspiration, with his chocolate colored knitted jacket and his catskin cap, but merry, and carrying a load of wood on his shoulders. A man standing on the truck handed him an armful of wood at a time, which he would take and carry into his father's shop, where he would pile it up in a great hurry.

"What are you doing, Coretti?" I asked.

"Don't you see?" he answered, holding out his arms to take the wood. "I go over my lesson."

I laughed, but he was speaking in earnest, and, having taken his armful of wood, began saying while running: "*The conjugation of the verb consists in its variations, agreeing in number——and person——*"

And then throwing down the wood and piling it up: "*According to the time——according to the time to which the action refers——*"

It was our grammar lesson for the next day. "What would you have me do?" he said. "I make the most of my time. My father has gone away on account of his business. My mother is ill. I have to unload the wood. In the meanwhile I go over my grammar; it is a difficult lesson to-day. I do not succeed in hammering it into my head. My father will be here at seven to give you the soldi," he then said to the the truckman.

The truck moved away. "Go into the shop for a moment," said Coretti. I entered. It was a large room full of piles of wood and fagots, with a school desk on one side.

"To-day is a day of rush, I assure you," said Coretti. "I have to do my work by fits and starts. I was writing about the prepositions, and some one came to buy. I started to write again, and the truck came. I have already taken two trips to the wood market in the Piazza Venezia this morning. I am so tired I can hardly stand on my feet and my hands are all swollen; I would be in a fine fix, indeed, if I had to do my drawing task." As he spoke he began sweeping up the dry leaves and little sticks which had fallen on the brick pavement.

"But where do you do your work?" I asked Coretti. "Surely not here?"

"Come and see," and he took me into a little room behind the shop, which was used as a kitchen and dining room, with a table in the corner where he had all his books and writing material and the beginning of his lesson. "By the way," he said, "I have left out the second answer: '*With leather one makes shoes, belts,*'——now I have it——'*valises.*' And taking his pen, he started to write in his beautiful hand-writing.

"Is any one here?" some one cried at that moment from the shop. It was a woman who came to buy some fagots.

"Here I am," answered Coretti, and sprang from his place to weigh the fagots. He took the soldi, ran into the corner to register the sale in a copy-book, and returned to his work, saying: "Let's see if I can finish this paragraph," and he wrote: "*Traveling bags and knapsacks for soldiers.*" "Ah," he said, "My poor coffee is boiling over," and he ran to the stove to take the coffee-pot from the fire. "It is the coffee for mamma," said he. "I had to learn to make coffee. Wait a moment, and we will take it to her, so that she may see you; it will give her pleasure. She has been sick in bed for seven days—— Confound it! I always scald my fingers with that coffee pot. What can I add after '*knapsacks for soldiers?*' I must add something more, and I cannot think of it. Come to mamma."

He opened the door and we entered the room. There was the mother of Coretti in a large bed, with a white handkerchief tied around her head.

"Here is the coffee, mamma," said Coretti, handing her the cup. "This is my schoolmate."

"Oh, what a fine signorino," said the woman, "you have come to see the sick, isn't it so?"

In the meantime, Coretti had fixed the pillows behind his mother's shoulders, and had put up the blankets of the bed, and brightened the fire, and driven the cat away from the bureau drawers.

"Is there anything more you wish, mamma?" he asked, and took away the cup. "Did you take the two spoonfuls of syrup? When it is gone, I will go to the apothecary for more. The wood has been unloaded. At four o'clock I will put the meat on the fire, as you have told me. When the butter woman goes by, I will give her the eight soldi. Everything will go well, do not fear."

"Thanks, my son," answered the woman. "My poor son! he thinks of everything."

She asked me to take a piece of sugar, and then Corretti showed me a little picture, a photograph of his father dressed like a soldier with the medal of valor that he had won in the battle of '66, in the army of Prince Humbert. His son looks like him, with those lively eyes and that merry smile.

"I have found another," said Coretti, and he added in his copy-book, "*One can make harnesses.*" "The balance I will do this evening; I will sit up late. How happy you are to have all your time to study; and then you can go promenading besides."

He is always jolly. Re-entering the shop, he began to chop wood upon a horse and sawed it in halves, saying: "It is like gymnastics, quite different from the '*Throw your arms forward.*' I want my father to find all this wood sawed when he returns and then he will be satisfied. The worst of it is that after I have sawed the wood, I make some t's and l's which look like serpents' as the teacher says; but what else can I do? I will tell him that I had to move my arms about. What I most care for is that mamma may soon get well. Now she is better, thank heaven! I shall study the grammar tomorrow morning when the cock crows. Oh, here comes the wagon with the logs. At work again!"

A wagon loaded with logs stopped in front of the shop. Coretti ran out to speak to the man and then came back. "Now, my comrade, I cannot keep you any longer; farewell until tomorrow. You did well to come and see me. Pleasant walk to you, you lucky fellow!"

He shook my hand and ran to take the first log and began running between the wagon and the shop, with his face as fresh as a rose under that cat-skin cap, and so bright that it was a pleasure to look at him.

"Lucky fellow!" he said to me. Oh, good Coretti, no, it is you who are fortunate; you, because you study and work more than I do, because you are more useful to your father and mother, because you are better than myself, a hundred times better, and more brave than I am, my dear schoolmate.

THE PRINCIPAL OF THE SCHOOL

Friday the 18th.

Coretti was happy this morning because his master of the second elementary came to assist with the work of the monthly examination; Coatti is his name, a big man with thick crisp hair, a black beard, black eyes, and a voice that thunders. He always threatens to take the boys by the neck to the police station, and makes all sorts of frightful faces, but he never punishes any one; on the contrary, he always laughs in his sleeve. With Coatti, there are eight more masters, including a substitute, a little fellow who looks like a youth. There is a master of the fourth class, who is muffled up in a large woolen scarf, and is always complaining about his pains. He took this illness when he was master in a country school where the walls were very damp. Another master of the fourth class is an old man with white hair and beard, who has been a teacher of the blind. There is one who is always well dressed, with eye-glasses and blonde mustache; he is called "The Little Lawyer," because while he was teaching he took a lawyer's diploma, and also got up a book to teach how to read and write. The one who teaches us gymnastics is like a soldier. He has been with Garibaldi and has on his neck the scar of a sabre wound that he got at the battle of Milazzo. Then comes the principal; tall, bald headed, with a grey beard which comes down over his chest. He has golden eye-glasses, and is all dressed in black and buttoned up to the chin; he is always so good to the boys. When they enter his office trembling, having been sent there for reproof, he does not scold them but takes them by the hand and gives so many good reasons why they should not have done what they did, why they must repent and promise to be good, and he speaks in such a kind manner and with such a sweet voice that they all leave him with red eyes; they are more confused than if they had been punished. Poor principal, he is always the first one at his place in the morning; he waits for the teachers and listens to the parents, and when the teachers have started home, he keeps on the lookout to see that none of the children fall under the carriages, and that they do not stop in the street to play or to fill their satchels with sand and stones, and every time he appears at the corner of a street, tall and dark as he is, a crowd of boys scamper in all directions, stopping suddenly the games with marbles and pens, and he threatens with his index finger at a distance with a loving and sad air. "No one has ever seen him laugh," says my mother, " since his son died." The son was a volunteer in the army, and the principal always keeps his portrait before him upon the desk in his room. He wanted to leave the school after his son's death, and he wrote his resignation to the municipality and kept it constantly on his desk, waiting from day to day to send it, because he was sorry to leave the children. The other day, he seemed to be decided, and my father, who was with him in the directors' room, was saying to him: "What a pity that you go, signor principal," when a man entered to have a boy enrolled, who was coming from another school to ours because his parents had moved. When he looked at that boy, the principal seemed surprised. He looked at him for a moment and then at the portrait which he keeps on his desk and then at the boy again, and, drawing him between his knees, he made him raise his face. That boy resembled perfectly his own lost son. The principal said "All right," wrote the name, and the father left. He remained pensive. "What a pity that you should go," repeated my father. The principal took his resignation, tore it to pieces, and said: "I shall remain!"

THE SOLDIERS

Tuesday the 22d.

His son was a volunteer in the army when he died, and this is the reason the principal always goes to the Corso to see the soldiers pass. When we came out of school yesterday, an

Infantry regiment was passing, and fifty boys began to jump around the band, singing and keeping time with their rulers on their satchels and portfolios. We stood in a group on the sidewalk, looking; Garrone, squeezed in clothes too small for him, and biting a large loaf of bread; Votini, the well dressed one, who is always picking the hair from his clothes; Precossi, the son of the blacksmith, wearing his father's jacket; the Calabrian boy; "the Little Mason"; Crossi, with his red hair; Franti, with his tough face, and Robetti, the son of an artillery captain, the one who saved the boy from the omnibus and who now walks on crutches. Franti laughed in the face of a soldier who was limping. Suddenly he felt a man's hand on his shoulder. He turned around; it was the principal. "Look here" said the principal; "to jest at a soldier when he is in the ranks and can neither revenge himself nor answer is like insulting a man when he is bound up; it is a cowardly act."

Franti disappeared. The soldiers were passing four by four, perspiring and covered with dust, and their guns were gleaming in the sun. "You must always wish well to the soldiers, boys," said the principal. "They are our defenders; they would die for us, if to-morrow a foreign army should threaten our country. They are also boys—a few years older than you are, and they also go to school, and there are among them poor and rich people, as among yourselves. They come from all parts of Italy. Look at them; one can almost recognize them from their faces: the Sicilians, the Sardinians, the Neapolitans, the Lombards. This is an old regiment, one of those which fought in 1848. The soldiers are no longer the same, but the flag is. How many died for our country around that flag twenty years before you were born!"

"Here it comes," said Garrone. And, in fact, one could see at a little distance the flag which came first above the heads of the soldiers. The principal said: "Boys, make the pupil's salute with the hand to the forehead when the tricolor passes."

The flag, carried by an officer, passed in front of us; it was all torn and faded, but there were medals hanging on the staff. We put our hands to our foreheads all together. The officer looked at us, smiled. and returned the salute with his hand.

"Good, boys!" said a man behind us. We turned to look and saw an old man who had in the buttonhole of his coat the blue ribbon of the Crimean campaign; a pensioned officer. "Bravo!" he said; "you have done a noble act,"

In the meanwhile, the band turned at the end of the Corso, surrounded by a crowd of boys, and a hundred merry shouts accompanied the blast of the trumpets like a war cry. "Bravo!" repeated the old officer. "He who respects the flag when he is small, will know how to defend it when he is grown up."

THE PROTECTOR OF NELLI

Wednesday the 23rd.

Poor Nelli was also looking at the soldiers yesterday—poor little hunchback—with a look as though he were saying: "I shall never be a soldier!" He is good and studious, but he is thin and sickly looking and breathes with a good deal of difficulty. He wears a long black shining linen apron. His mother is a little blonde lady, dressed in black. She always calls for him when the school is over; as, in the confusion, he would not go out with the other boys, and she caresses him. The first days of school, as he has the misfortune to be hunchbacked, many of the boys laughed at him and beat him upon the back with their satchels; but he never turned around, and said nothing to his mother about it, because he did not wish to cause her the pain of knowing that her son was the laughing stock of his companions. When they derided him, he would cry silently, leaning his forehead on the desk.

But this morning, Garrone sprang up and said: "If any one touches Nelli, I will give him such a blow that he will spin three times around."

Franti paid no attention, and he received a blow which made him reel. Since that time no one has touched Nelli. The teacher placed Garrone near him, upon the same bench, and they have become fast friends. Nelli is very much devoted to Garrone; as soon as he enters the school room, he looks where Garrone sits, and he never goes away without saying: "Good bye, Garrone," and Garrone does the same with him. When Nelli drops his pen or book under the bench, Garrone at once bends down and hands it to him. He also helps him to put his things in the satchel and to put on his overcoat. Because of this, Nelli likes him and looks at him constantly, and when the master praises Garrone, Nelli is happy

Nelli must at last have told his mother everything about the ridicule which he suffered those first days, and also about the companion who took his part and of whom he has grown fond. Here is what happened this morning. The teacher sent me to take the programme of the lesson to the principal half an hour before the time for school to close, and I was in the office when a blonde lady, dressed in black, entered. It was Nelli's mother, and she said: "Signor principal, is there a boy in my son's class by the name of Garrone?"

"There is," answered the principal.

"Will you have the kindness to send for him for a moment, as I wish to speak to him?"

The principal called the beadle and sent him into the class;

and, after a minute, Garrone, with his thick, crisp hair, appeared at the door, looking as though he were amazed. As soon as she saw him, the lady went to meet him, threw her

hands on his shoulders and kissed him many times on the forehead, saying: "You are Garrone, the friend of my child, the protector of my dear son; it is you, dear boy, it is you!" Then she searched hastily in her purse and in her pockets, and, not finding anything, she detached a chain with a little cross, from her neck, and said: "Take it, wear it as a memento, dear boy, in memory of Nelli's mother who thanks you and embraces you."

THE FIRST OF THE CLASS

Garrone has won the affection of every one and Derossi the **admiration**. Derossi has won the first medal and will always be the first: This year there is no one who is able to compete with him. The boys all recognize his superiority in all the different branches. He is the first in arithmetic, in grammar, in composition, and in drawing. He understands everything at a glance; has a marvelous memory; succeeds in everything without making any effort. It seems as though study were mere play for him. The teacher told him yesterday: "God has endowed you very generously; you must not waste what has been bestowed upon you." Besides all this, he is the tallest and handsomest boy of the class, with a large crown of blonde curls. He is so nimble that he can jump over the bench by laying one hand upon it, and he knows how to fence. He is the son of a merchant, and always dresses in blue clothes with gilt buttons on them. He is twelve years old, always jolly, and he is polite to every one, and tries to help all the other boys at the time of examination, and no one has ever dared to play a trick upon him or call him a bad name. Only Nobis and Franti look at him askance. Votini looks at him with envy, but he does not even notice it. They all smile at him and take him by the hand when he comes around in his graceful way. He gives away illustrated newspapers and drawings—everything which they give him at home. He has drawn a geographical map of Calabria for the little Calabrian boy. He is like a grand signor and shows no favoritism.

It is impossible not to envy him and not to feel beneath him in everything. I envy him myself, like Votini. I experience a certain bitterness and spitefulness against him, sometimes when I am striving to do my work at home, and think at that hour he has already done his correctly and without fatigue. But then, when I return to school and see him so handsome, smiling, and triumphant, and hear him answer all the questions put to him, in a frank, assured way, and see how polite he is to every one, and how all look at him, then all the bitterness, all the spite goes out of my heart, and I feel ashamed of having felt such emotions. I would like to be near him always; I would like to go through all the classes with him; his presence, his voice gives me courage, and I feel a desire to work.

The teacher has given him the monthly story to copy, which will be read to-morrow. It is "The Little Vidette of Lombardy." When he was copying it this morning he seemed moved by that heroic deed. His face was all aflame, his eyes were full of tears, and his mouth trembled. I was watching him; how handsome and noble he looked? With what pleasure would I have told him frankly to his face: "Derossi, you have worked more than I have. You are a man compared to me, and I respect and admire you."

THE LITTLE VIDETTE OF LOMDARDY
(MONTHLY STORY)

Saturday the 26th.

In the year 1859, during the war for the liberation of Lombardy—a few days before the battle of Solferino and San Martino, won by the French and the Italians, united against the Austrians—on a beautiful morning in the month of June a little troop of cavalry of Saluzzo was moving slowly through a solitary path, toward the enemy, reconnoitering the country as they went. The troop was commanded by an officer and a sergeant, and all spied into the distance before them with eager eyes, silent, expecting every moment to see the white uniforms of the advance post of the enemy shimmering through the trees. They came to a hut surrounded by ash trees, in front of which was a boy about twelve years old, standing alone, removing the bark from a small branch with a knife. From the window of the house floated a large tricolored flag, but no one was inside. Having hoisted the flag, all had run away, fearing the Austrians. As soon as the boy saw the cavalrymen, he threw away his stick and took off his hat. He was a fine-looking lad with a brave face, large blue eyes, and long blonde hair. He was in his shirt sleeves and his shirt was unfastened, showing his bare chest.

"What are you doing here?" asked the officer, stopping his horse. "Why did you not run away with your family?"

"I have no family," answered the boy. "I am a foundling. I work a little for every one, and I remained here to see the war."

"Have you seen the Austrians pass?"

"Not for the last three days."

The officer sat thinking a moment, then dismounted from his horse; and, leaving the soldiers turned toward the foe, he entered the house and went up on the roof——The house was low and from the roof only a little stretch of the country could be seen. "It is necessary to climb the trees," said the officer, and came down. Just in front of the yard there was a lofty, slender ash tree, which was rocking its top in the sky. The officer stood lost in thought for a moment, looking now at the tree, now at the soldiers; then, all of a sudden, he asked the boy:

"Have you good eyesight, you rag-a-muffin?"

"I?" answered the boy. "I can see a sparrow a mile distant."

"Can you climb to the top of that tree?"

"I can do that in a minute."

"And could you tell me what you see down below from the top, whether there are any Austrian soldiers, clouds of dust, guns glimmering, or any horses on that side?"

"Surely, I could."

"What do you want me to pay you for this service?"

"What do I want?" said the boy smiling; "nothing, of course——If the Austrians asked me, I would not do it at all ——but for our own people——I am a Lombard!"

"Well, then, climb up."

"Wait just a moment for me to take off my shoes."

He took off his shoes, tightened the strap around his trousers, threw his hat on the grass, and clasped the trunk of the ash tree.

"But, look out!" exclaimed the officer, making a gesture as if to hold him back, as though seized with a sudden fear. The boy turned around to look at him with his fine blue eyes, as if to question him.

"Never mind," said the officer; "go up."

The boy went up like a cat. "Look in front of you!" cried the officer to the soldiers.

In a few moments, the boy was at the top of the tree, with his legs around the trunk among the leaves, but with his breast uncovered, and the sun shining on his blonde head made it look like gold. The officer could hardly see him, he looked so small from the ground.

"Look straight in the distance," cried the officer.

The boy, in order to see better, took his right hand from the tree and put it over his forehead.

"What do you see?" asked the officer.

The boy bent his head toward him, and, making a speaking tube of his hand, answered: "Two men on horseback on the white road."

"What distance from here?"

"Half a mile."

"Do they move?"

"They are standing still."

"What else do you see," after a moment's silence, "Look to your right."

Then he said: "Among the trees near the cemetery, there is something which glitters like bayonets."

"Do you see any people?"

"No, they must be hidden under the wheat."

At that moment, the sharp whiz of a bullet passed high through the air and died away, far off, behind the house.

"Come down, boy," cried the officer, "They have seen you. I do not want anything more, come down."

"I am not afraid," answered the boy.

"Come down," repeated the officer. "What else do you see at your left?"

"At the left?"

"Yes, at the left."

The boy pushed his head to the left, and another whiz, sharper and lower than the first, cut through the air. The boy shook all over, "Confound them!" he exclaimed. "They are aiming at me." The bullet had passed very near him.

"Down!" cried the officer in an imperious and irritated way.

"I will come down directly. The tree, however, will protect me, do not fear. To the left, you wish to know what I can see?"

"To the left," answered the officer; "but, come down."

"To the left," said the boy, turning his head that way, "Where there is a chapel, it seems as though I can see ———

A third raging whiz was heard and almost at the same time, the boy was seen coming down, holding for a moment to the trunk and to the branches, and then falling down, head first, with open arms.

"Curse them!" cried the officer, running to him.

The boy struck the ground with his back and lay there

stretched out with his arms open ; a stream of blood was flowing from his left side. The sergeant and two soldiers jumped from their horses ; the officer bent down and opened his shirt : the bullet had entered his left lung. " He is dead ! " exclaimed the officer. " No, he lives," answered the sergeant. " Our poor, brave boy," cried the officer. " Courage ! Courage ! " But while he was saying this and pressing his handkerchief over the wound, the boy rolled his eyes wearily, and let his hand fall back. He was dead. The officer turned pale and looked at him fixedly for a moment, then laid him with his head on the grass ; and, for a while, he remained looking at him. Also the sergeant and the two soldiers stood motionless and gazed at him ; the others were turned toward the enemy. " Poor boy," sadly repeated the officer, " Poor and brave boy."

Then he approached the house and took from the window the tri-colored flag and stretched it out like a funeral pall over his body, leaving the head uncovered. The sergeant picked up the boy's shoes, cap, the little stick, and the knife.

They stood in silence for a moment, then the officer turned to the sergeant and said: " We will send the ambulance for him. He died like a soldier, and we will bury him like a soldier." Having said this, he threw a kiss to the dead, and cried, " To horse." They all jumped to their saddles, the troop formed again and followed up its route; but a few hours later the little dead boy did receive the honors of war.

Towards sunset all the lines of the Italian advance post were marching toward the enemy over the same road which had been taken in the morning by the troop of cavalry. The large battalion of bersaglieri, which a few days before had valiantly stained with blood the Hill of San Martino, proceeded in two files. The news of the death of the boy had spread through the army before the soldiers had left their encampment. A stream ran along beside the path a few paces distant from the house. When the first officers of the battalion saw the little corpse, stretched at the foot of the ash tree and covered with the tri-colored flag, they saluted him with the sword, and one of them bent over the edge of the stream, which was bordered with flowers, plucked two flowers and threw them over him. Then all the battalion, as they were passing, picked flowers and threw them over the dead. In a few moments the boy was covered with flowers, and officers and soldiers all gave him a salute as they passed by. "Bravo, little Lombard!" "Goodbye, boy!" "Honor to you, little blonde!" "Hurrah!" "Glory!" "Goodbye!" One officer threw a medal of valor on him; another went to kiss his forehead; the flowers continued to shower upon his bare feet, upon his wounded chest, and upon the blonde head. And he slept there in the grass, wrapped in his flag, with a white but almost smiling face, poor boy, as if he felt the honors paid him, as though he were content to have given his life for his Lombardy.

THE POOR
Tuesday the 27th

To give one's life for his own country like the boy of Lombardy is a great virtue, but do not forget the smaller virtues, my child. When we returned from school this morning, while thou wert walking in front of me, we passed a poor old woman who held a frail and sickly baby on her knees, and who asked alms of thee. Thou didst look at her, but didst not give her anything, although thou hadst some soldi in thy pocket. Listen, my child, do not accustom thyself to pass indifferently in front of misery which stretches out its hands to thee, and much the less before a mother who asks a penny for her baby. Think that maybe the baby was hungry; think of the heartache of that poor woman. Can you imagine the despairing sobs of thy mother the day that she might have to tell thee: "Enrico, today I can give thee no bread." When I give a soldo to a mendicant and he says to me: "May the Lord preserve thee and all thy creatures!" thou canst not comprehend the gratitude that I feel toward that poor man. It seems to me, indeed, that that wish ought to preserve me in good health for a long time, and I return home content and think: "Ah,

that poor man has paid me back more than I have given him!" Let me feel that sometimes such a good wish is provoked and merited by thee; take from time to time a soldo from thy purse and let it drop into the hand of an old man without support. Give to the mother without bread and to the baby without a mother. The poor love alms from children because it does not humiliate them to receive them, and because children, needing everything, resemble them. Notice that there are always many poor around the schools. The alms of a man is a deed of charity, but that of a child is both a deed of charity and a caress. Dost thou understand me? It is as if from his hand fell a soldo and a flower. Think that thou lackest nothing and that they lack everything! that, while thou art wishing to be happy, they are satisfied not to die. Think that it is horrible that in so many places on the streets, where carriages and children dressed in velvet are passing, there should be women who have not enough to eat! Not to have anything to eat, oh my God! That boys like thee, intelligent as thou art, good as thou art, in the midst of a large city, like wild animals lost in the desert, should have nothing to eat! No, never, nevermore, Enrico, pass in front of a mother who asks alms without putting a soldo in her hand.

Thy Mother.

DECEMBER

THE TRADING BOY

Thursday the 1st.

My father wishes that on every vacation day I should either invite one of my schoolmates to come to our house or call upon one of them, in order to become little by little friendly with all. On Sunday, I am going to walk with Votini, the well dressed, one who is always brushing his clothes and is so envious of Derossi. Today, Garoffi came to the house. He is the tall, slender fellow with a nose like an owl's beak and shrewd eyes, who always seems to scrutinize everything. He is the son of a druggist, and quite an original character. He is always counting the soldi in his pocket; he counts them on his fingers quickly, and can make any multiplication without an arithmetical table. He saves money even now, and has a book in the School Savings Bank. He never spends a soldo; and, if he drops a centesimo under the bench he is likely to look a week for it. "He is like a night owl," says Derossi. He finds old pens, old postage stamps, pins and old wax matches. Everything he picks up he saves. He has been collecting postage stamps for more than two years, and has hundreds from every country, pasted in a large album, which he will sell to the stationer when it is full. In the meantime, the stationer gives him books, because he takes so many boys into his shop. At school, he is always trafficking. He makes a sale of somekind every day, gets up raffles, and trades, then he repents of having traded and wants his goods back; he buys for two and sells for four. He plays with pens and never loses; sells old newspapers to the tobacco man; and he has a little note book, full of sums in subtraction, in which he keeps a record of all his business. He studies only arithmetic, and, if he wishes to have a prize, it is only to have free entrance to a theatre of marionettes. I like him and he amuses me. We have played market together, using scales to weigh the different things. He knows the right price of everything, understands weights and measures, and can make beautiful paper bags like the shopkeepers. He says that as soon as he finishes school, he will open a store and sell some new article of commerce which he has invented. He has always been pleased when I have given him foreign postage stamps, and he has told me exactly how much each one will sell for. Today, my father, while feigning to read, stood listening to him, and was amused. Garoffi always has his pockets full of small articles of merchandise which he covers up with a long black cloak, and he looks as though he were continually thinking like a merchant. That which is the nearest to his heart is his collection of postage stamps; that is his treasure; he always speaks of it as though he expected to make a fortune out of it. His companions call him avaricious and an usurer. I do not know; I like him. He teaches me many things and he looks like a man. Coretti, the son of the wood huckster, says that Garoffi would not give away his postage stamps even to save his mother's life. My father does not believe it. He says: "Wait before you judge him; he has that passion, but he has a heart."

VANITY

Monday the 5th.

Yesterday I went to take a walk through the viale Rivoli with Votini and his father. Passing through the street Dora Grosse, we saw Stardi, the one who kicks at those who trouble him. He was standing in front of a book-seller's window, looking closely at a geographical map, and there is no knowing how long he had stood there, because he always studies when in the street. He scarcely returned our salute, the rude fellow. Votini was well dressed—too well. He wore morocco leather boots trimmed with red, an embroidered suit with silk tassels, and a white castor hat. He carried a watch and strutted; but his vanity served him ill this time. After having walked for a long time along the path, leaving his father who walked slowly some distance behind, we sat down on a stone bench next to a boy who was modestly dressed, who

looked tired and sad, and who sat with his head hanging down. A man who seemed to be his father was walking back and forth under the trees, reading a newspaper. Votini sat down between the lad and myself and he immediately remembered that he was well dressed and wished to be admired and envied by his neighbor.

He raised his foot and said to me, "Have you seen my officer's boots?" He said that in order to have the other boy look at them, but he paid no attention.

Then he lowered his foot and showed me his silk tassels and said, glancing askance at the boy, that he did not like those silk tassels; that he wanted to have them changed for silver buttons; but the boy did not even look at the tassels.

Votini then began to turn his beautiful white castor hat on the point of his finger; but the boy (it seemed that he did it purposely) did not deign to even look at the hat.

Votini was beginning to get irritated. He pulled out his watch, opened it and showed me the works, but the other boy did not turn his head. "Is it silver?" I asked him. "No," he answered, "it is gold." "But it is not all gold," said I; "there is probably some silver in it." "No, indeed," he repeated; and, in order to force the boy to look, he held the watch before his face and said, "Look and tell me, is it not all gold?"

The boy answered drily, "I do not know."

"Oh, oh!" exclaimed Votini, full of wrath. "What pride!"

As he said this Votini's father came up and heard him. He looked fixedly at the boy for a moment, and then said brusquely to his son, "Be silent." And whispering into his ear, he added: "He is blind."

Votini jumped to his feet with a shudder, and looked at the boy's face. His eyes were glassy and he had no expression in them.

Votini stood dumbfounded, with downcast eyes; at last, he muttered: "I regret —— I did not know it."

But the blind boy, who had understood everything, said, with a melancholy and sweet smile: "Oh, it does not matter."

Yes, Votini is vain, but he has not a bad heart. He did not smile again all that day.

THE FIRST SNOW STORM

Saturday the 10th.

Farewell, walks to Rivoli, here comes the children's beautiful friend! Here comes the first snow! Since last evening, it has fallen down in large flakes like jessamine flowers. It was fun this morning at school to see it fall against the windows and pile up on their sills. The teacher also looked at it and rubbed his hands. We were all content, thinking of making snowballs and of the ice which will come, and of the fire at home. There was no one but Stardi who did not look at it; he was all absorbed in his lesson, with his hand on his temple. How beautiful! What a time we had coming out! All danced down the street, shouting and gesticulating, snatching up handfuls of snow and dashing it about like poodles in the water. The parents were waiting outside the school room with umbrellas which were covered with snow, the policeman's helmet was white, and all our satchels became white in a few moments. The boys all seemed beside themselves with joy. Even Precossi, the son of the blacksmith, the little pallid lad who never laughs; and Robetti, the one who saved the child from under the omnibus, poor boy, was leaping on his crutches. The Calabrian boy who had never seen snow, made a little ball of it and began to eat it like a peach; Crossi, the son of the vegetable woman, filled his satchel; and the Little Mason made us nearly burst with laughter, when my father invited him to come and visit me to-morrow; he had his mouth full of snow and he did not dare to swallow it nor spit it out, and he stood there choking and staring at us but could not answer. Even the teachers were laughing as they ran out of the school. My teacher of the first grade was among them, poor woman, running through the slush, protecting her face with her green veil, and she was coughing. In the meanwhile, hundreds of girls from the neighboring school were passing, screaming and dancing upon that white carpet, and the teachers, janitor and policemen were shouting: "Go home! Go home!" Their mustaches and whiskers were growing white with snow, but they also laughed at the revelry of the pupils, who were enjoying the winter.

Thou art enjoying winter —— but there are boys who have no clothes, no shoes, no fire. There are those who come down to the villages from long distances, carrying in their hands—bleeding with chilblains—a piece of log to warm up the school-room. There are hundreds of schools almost buried in snow, like caves, where the children nearly suffocate from the smoke and their teeth chatter with the cold, looking with terror through the white snow-flakes which fall without ceasing, which pile up constantly upon their distant huts, threatened by the avalanche. You enjoy winter, boys! Think of the thousands of human beings to whom winter brings misery and death!   *Thy Father.*

THE LITTLE MASON

"The Little Mason" came to-day, dressed up in his hunting jacket and clothes cast off by his father, still white with lime and chalk. My father wished him to come even more than I did. How pleased we were to see him! As soon as he entered he took off the soft felt hat, which was all wet with snow, and stuck it into his pocket; then he came forward with that careless gait, like a tired workman, with his small face round like an apple and his nose like a ball, turning his eyes to look here and there; and when he came into the dining room, he cast a glance around at the furniture, and then fixed his eyes upon the portrait which represents Rigoletto, the hunchbacked buffoon, and he made the hare face.

It is impossible to keep from laughing when you see him make the hare face. We began to play with wood blocks. He is skilled in building towers and bridges, which seem to stand as though by magic, and he works at it seriously with the energy of a man. Between the building of one tower and another, he told me about his family. They live in a garret. His father goes to the evening school to learn to read and write; his mother is from Biella. His parents must love him; one can see it, because if he is dressed as a poor child, yet he is protected against the cold. His clothes are well mended, and he wears a necktie which is tied by the hand of his mother. He told me that his father is a big fellow, a giant who can hardly go through the doors, but he is kind, and he always calls his son "Hare Face." The son, however, is very small.

At four o'clock we had lunch together, seated on the sofa.

When we got up I could not understand why my father did not want me to clean the back of the sofa, where the Little Mason had made it white with his jacket, but he held back my hand, and cleaned it himself on the sly. While we were playing, the Little Mason lost a button from his hunting jacket, and my mother sewed it on again for him; and he blushed and stood looking at her so surprised and confused that he could scarcely breathe. After that I gave him an album which contained illustrations of different characters, to look at; and, unsconcious of it, he made faces so much like them that even my father laughed. He was so happy when he left that he forgot to put on his hat, and to show me his gratitude, when we got to the landing, he once more made the hare face. His name is Antonio Rabucco. He is eight years and eight months old.

Dost thou know, my son, why I did not wish thee to clean the sofa? Because, by cleaning it when thy companion would see thee was to reprove him for having soiled it; and that would not have been right; first, because he had not done it purposely, and also because he had done it with the clothes of his father, which have been covered with plaster while at work, and what one rubs against at work is not dirt; it is dust, or lime, or varnish, anything that thou will, but not dirt. Work does not make one filthy. Never say of a workman who comes from his labor: "He is filthy;" thou must say: "He has on his clothes the traces of toil." Remember this, and love the Little Mason because he is thy companion and because he is the son of a workman.   *Thy Father.*

A SNOWBALL

Friday the 16th.

And it keeps on snowing. An ugly accident happened this morning because of the snow. As we came out of the school room, a crowd of boys just entering the Corso began to throw snowballs made of watery snow, which makes balls that are as hard and heavy as stones. Many persons were passing on the sidewalk, and a gentleman cried: "Stop, you rogues!" Just at that moment, a sharp cry was heard on the other side of the street, and an old man, who had lost his hat, was seen staggering and covering his face with his hands. A boy next to him cried: "Help! Help!"

Immediately people ran to him from every side; a snowball had struck him in the eye. All the boys dispersed, running like a flash. I stood in front of the bookseller's shop that my father had entered, and saw several of my classmates who were mingled with the others near me, rush in and pretend to be looking at the show-cases. There was Garrone with a loaf of bread in his pocket as usual, Coretti, the Little Mason, and Garoffi, the one who collects postage stamps. In the meantime, a crowd had gathered around the old man, and the policemen and others were running on all sides, threatening and asking: "Who was it?" "Who did it?" "Was it you?" Tell me, who did it?" and looking at the hands of the boys that were wet with snow.

Garoffi was next to me and I noticed that he was trembling like a leaf and his face was as white as that of a corpse. "Who was it?" "Who did it?" the people continued to cry.

Then I heard Garrone saying softly to Garoffi: "Come, go and denounce thyself; it would be cowardly to allow some one else to be arrested."

"But I did not do it on purpose," answered Garoffi, still trembling.

"It matters not, do your duty," repeated Garrone.

"But I have not the courage."

"Take courage; I will accompany you."

And the others were crying still louder: "Who was it?" "Who did it?" "One of his glasses has entered into his eye! They have blinded him, the brigands!"

I thought that Garoffi would fall on the ground. "Go," said Garrone resolutely; "I will defend you," and, taking him by the arm, he pushed him forward, holding him up like a sick person. The people saw and understood immediately, and many made a dash at him with their arms lifted, but Garrone put himself before him, crying:

"You are ten against a child!"

Then they stopped, and a policeman took Garoffi by the hand and, making his way through the crowd, he led him to a baker's shop, where the wounded man had been carried. When I saw him I recognized immediately the old employee who lives on the fourth floor of our house with his little nephew. He was leaning back on a chair with a handkerchief over one eye. "I did not do it on purpose," said Garoffi, half dead with fear; "I did not do it on purpose."

Two or three persons pushed him into the shop violently. "Bow down thy head!" "Ask forgiveness!" and they threw him on the floor; but suddenly two vigorous arms put him upon his feet, and a resolute voice said:

"No, gentlemen!" It was our principal, who had seen everything. "Since he has had the courage to give himself up," he added, "no one has the right to abuse him." They all held their peace. "Ask forgiveness," said the principal to Garoffi. Garoffi burst into tears and embraced the knees of the old man, who put his hand on his head and caressed his hair, and then they all said:

"Go home, child, go home."

My father took me away from the crowd, and said on the way home: "Enrico, in a similar case, would you have had the courage to do your duty and to go and confess your guilt?" I answered, "Yes, I would."

"Give me your word as a boy of heart and of honor that you would do so."

"I give you my word, father!"

THE SCHOOL MISTRESS

Saturday the 17th

Garoffi was very much frightened to-day because he expected a great scolding from the teacher, but the teacher did not make his appearance, and, as the substitute was also absent, the signora Cromi, the oldest of the school mistresses, came to teach us. She has two large boys, and she has taught many of the ladies to read and write, who now come to the school to accompany their own boys.

She was sad to-day because she has a sick child. As soon as the boys saw her they began to make an uproar, but with a sweet and tranquil voice she said softly, "Respect my gray hair; I am not only a teacher, but a mother as well." Then no one dared to speak; not even Franti, who was satisfied with jeering her on the sly.

Mistress Delcati, the teacher of my brother, was sent to Cromi's class, and in Mistress Delcati's place they put the one whom they call "The Little Nun," because she is always dressed in black and has a small white face. She combs her hair down smoothly; her eyes are very clear, and she has such a low voice that it seems as though she were all the time murmuring prayers. "One cannot understand her," says my mother, "she is so mild and timid, with such a tremor in her voice that one can scarcely hear her; and she never cries, never gets angry." Still she holds the boys down very quietly so that they cannot be heard, and the most roguish of them will bow his head if she only admonishes him with her finger. Her school seems like a church; this is another reason why they call her "The Little Nun."

There is another whom I also like—the little school mistress of the upper number three, the young lady with the rosy face and two dimples in her cheeks; she wears a large red feather in her hat and a yellow cross on her neck. She is always happy and keeps the class merry; she is always smiling, and when she scolds with her silvery voice it seems as though she were singing, striking her little rod on the table and clapping her hands to impose silence. When they leave the room she runs behind them like a child, first to one and then another, to keep them in line. She pulls up the cap of one and buttons the coat of another so that they will not catch cold. She begs the parents not to chastise them at home. She brings lozenges for those who cough, and lends her muff to those who are cold, and she is constantly harassed by the little fellows who torment her and ask her for kisses, pulling at her veil and mantle. She lets them do it, and kisses every one, laughing, and she returns home all out of breath but happy. She is also the drawing teacher of the girls' schoo' and supports a mother and a brother with her earnings.

IN THE HOME OF THE WOUNDED MAN

Sunday the 18th.

The little nephew of the old employe who was struck in the eye with a snowball by Garoffi belongs to the class of the teacher with the red feather. We called on him to-day at the home of his uncle, who keeps him like a son.

I had just finished writing the monthly story, "The Little Florentine Writer," for next week, which the teacher gave me to copy, when my father said to me, "We will go upstairs to the fourth story to see how that gentleman is getting along with his eye." We entered a room almost dark where there was an old man sitting up in bed with a great many pillows at his back. By his bedside sat his wife, and in the corner the little nephew was playing with toys. The old man had his right eye bandaged. He was much pleased to see my father, asking us to sit down, and told us that he was getting better, that not only was his eye not lost, but that in two or three days he would be entirely recovered. "It was an accident," he added, "and I am sorry for the fright that the poor boy must have had."

Then he spoke of the physician who was to come at that time to attend him.

Just at that moment, the bell rang. "It is the physician," said the lady. The door opens —— and whom do I see? Garoffi, with his long cloak, standing on the threshold with his head bent down as though he lacked the courage to enter.

"Who is it?" asked the sick man.

"It is the boy who threw the snowball," answered my father, and the old man said: "Oh, my poor boy, walk in, you come to inquire after the wounded man, isn't that so? He is better; be easy; I am better, I am almost well. Come here."

Garoffi, very much confused, approached the bed, making an effort to keep from crying, and the old man caressed him, but he could not speak.

"Thanks," said the old man. "Go and tell your father and mother that all is well; let them not worry on my account."

But Garoffi did not move, he looked as though he had something to say but dared not say it.

"What have you to tell me? What do you want?"

"I, nothing."

"Then, farewell, boy. Go with your heart at peace."

Garoffi walked to the door, but there he stopped and turned around toward the little nephew who was following him, and looking at him, he suddenly pulled something from under his cloak and put it in the hands of the boy, saying hastily, "This is for you," and he dashed out.

The boy took the parcel to his uncle and they saw written upon it: "*I give you this as a present.*"

After looking inside, he uttered an exclamation of surprise; it was the famous album, containing his collection of postage stamps, that poor Garoffi had given him; the collection of which he always spoke and upon which he had founded so many hopes and which had cost him so many efforts; it was a treasure, poor lad, it was half of his own blood that he had given the old man in exchange for his pardon.

THE LITTLE FLORENTINE WRITER

(MONTHLY STORY.)

He belonged to the fourth elementary class. He was a pretty Florentine lad of twelve, with black hair and light complexion, the eldest son of a railroad employee, who, having a large family and a small salary, lived in straightened circumstances. The little boy's father loved him very much, and was kind to him and indulgent, except in what concerned the school. In this one respect he was exacting and showed himself severe with him because he must soon be able to obtain employment in order to help the family along, and to accom-plish this he must learn much in a short time. And, although the boy studied, the father still exhorted him to study harder. His father was advanced in years, and severe work had made him grow old before his time; nevertheless, in order to provide for the necessities of his family, besides the large amount of work which his office brought him, he undertook to do some extra work as copyist, and would spend a great part of the night at his desk. Lately he had obtained work from a publishing house which published books and periodicals, and he had to write on the wrappers the names and addresses of all the subscribers. He received three lire for every five hundred paper wrappers which he addressed. But this work tired him out, and he often complained to the family at the dinner table.

"My eyesight is going," he would say, "this night work is killing me." His son said one day: "Papa, let me work in your stead, you know that I write just as you do." But the father answered: "No, my child, you must study. Your school is of more importance than my wrappers. It would grieve me to steal an hour from you. I thank you, but I will not allow you to do it; do not speak of it again."

The son knew it was useless to argue with his father in such matters, and so he did not insist. But this is what he did. He knew that at midnight his father would stop writing, leave his working room and go into his bedroom. At times he heard, immediately after the stroke of twelve, the noise of a chair moved and the slow step of his father. That night he waited until his father had gone to bed, dressed himself very quietly, went softly into the writing room, lit the kerosene lamp, and sat down on the desk where there was a pile of white wrappers and the list of the addresses, and began to write, imitating exactly his father's handwriting. He wrote willingly and gladly, though a little frightened, and the wrappers piled up. Once in a while he would stop to rub his hands and then begin again with increased alacrity, listening intently and smiling. He wrote one hundred and sixty, "One lire;" then he stopped, replaced the pen where he had found it, and returned to bed on tiptoe.

The next day his father sat at the head of the table in good humor. He had not noticed anything. He was doing his work mechanically, measuring it by hours, and thinking of other matters, and did not count the wrappers until the day after they were written. That day he slapped his hand on his son's shoulder, and said, "Well, Giulio, your father is still a good workman, no matter what you may think. In two hours last night he did a good third more work than usual. My hand is still quick and my eyes still do their duty." Giulio was content, and said to himself, "Poor papa; besides his gain, I also give him the satisfaction of thinking himself rejuvenated. Well, have courage!"

Encouraged by his first success, the next night as soon as the clock struck twelve he got up and went to work again, and so he did for several nights, and his father did not notice anything. One night at supper he remarked, "It is strange the amount of kerosene that we use in this house of late." Giulio felt a shock, but the conversation stopped there, and the night work went on.

However, by losing his sleep every night in this way, Giulio did not rest enough, and in the morning he would get up feeling tired, and when he did his school work in the evening he had difficulty in keeping his eyes open. One evening, for the first time in his life, he fell asleep on his copybook.

"Courage, courage!" cried his father, clapping his hands. "To work!"

He shook himself and set to work again. But the next evening and the following days it was the same thing, and even worse. He dozed over his books, would get up later than usual, study his lessons in a careless way, and seemed disgusted with study. His father began to observe this, and then to worry about him, and at last to reprove him. He should never have done so.

"Giulio," said he one morning, "you disappoint me; you are no longer what you once were. This cannot go on. All the hopes of the family rest upon you. I am dissatisfied, do you hear?"

Hearing such a reproof, the first really severe one which he had ever received, the boy was troubled. "Yes," said he to himself, "I cannot continue in this way, it is true; the test must come to an end." But that same evening, his father exclaimed with much satisfaction, "Do you know that, this month, I have earned thirty-two lire more by addressing wrappers than I did last month!" And as he said this he pulled from under the table a box of candy which he had bought in order to celebrate with his children the extra profit, and which they all received with delight.

Giulio then took courage, and said in his heart: "No, poor papa, I will not stop deceiving you; I will make a greater effort to study during the day, but I shall keep on working at night for you and for the others." And his father added: "Thirty-two lire more, I am happy——but that fellow there," and he pointed at Giulio, "he displeases me." And Giulio accepted the reproof in silence, swallowing the tears which were about to fall, and feeling at the same time, a great sweetness in his heart.

He kept on working, but fatigue following fatigue, it became harder and harder for him to resist it. He worked in this way for two months. His father continued to reprove him and to look at him with more and more of a frown. One day he went to ask information of the teacher, and the latter said:

"Yes, he goes on because he is intelligent, but he has no longer the good will which he had at first; he dozes, yawns, and seems distracted. He writes shorter compositions, and his penmanship is so bad that they must have been written in haste. He could do much more."

That evening his father took him aside and talked to him more severely than he had ever done before: "Giulio, you see that I work, that I wear my life out for the family. You do not second my efforts. You do not care for me, for your brothers, for your mother!"

"Oh! no, no, do not say so, father," cried the boy bursting into tears and opening his mouth, about to confess everything. But his father interrupted him, saying:

"You know the condition of the family; you know there is

need of good will and sacrifice on the part of all; you see how I double up my work. I was counting this month on a gratification of a hundred lire at the railway office, and I learned this morning that I will not get anything!" At this news, Giulio repressed the confession which was about to escape from his lips and repeated resolutely to himself:

"No, papa, I will tell you nothing; I will maintain secrecy in order to be able to work for you; I will compensate you for the pain that I cause you; at school I will always study enough to be advanced; what is necessary now is to help you to earn your living and to lessen the fatigues which are killing you." And the boy kept up this night work continually for two months and suffered from lassitude during the day; there were desperate efforts on the part of the son and bitter reproofs from the father.

But the worst of it all was that the latter was gradually growing colder toward his boy; he spoke to him rarely, as though he were a recreant son from whom there was no more to hope, and always tried to avoid his glance. Giulio noticed this and suffered from it, and when his father turned his back, he threw him a furtive kiss, with a pitiful and sad tenderness on his face.

Owing to the sorrow and fatigue, the boy was growing thinner, was losing his color and was forced to neglect his studies. He understood too well that some day or other it would come to an end, and every evening he would say: "Tonight I will not get up;" but at the stroke of twelve, at the moment when he must keep his resolution, he felt a remorse, and it seemed to him that if he remained in bed he failed to do his duty—robbing his father and his family of a lire; and he would get up, thinking that some night his father would wake up and surprise him, or that he would find out the deceit by chance in counting over the wrappers twice, and then all would come to an end without any action on his part, but he did not feel courageous enough to tell his father what he was doing; and he kept on with his work.

But one evening at dinner, his father said something which decided him. His mother looked at him and it seemed to her that he appeared more ill and weaker than usual; she said to him: "Giulio, you are ill!" And then turning with anxiety to her husband, "Giulio is ill. Look how pale he is! My Giulio, what is the matter with you?"

His father cast a glance at him and said: "It is his bad conscience that causes him to be in poor health; he was not like this when he was a studious pupil and a boy of heart."

"But he is looking ill," exclaimed the mother.

"I don't care," answered the father.

These words were like a knife blade in the heart of the poor boy. "Ha! he did not care for him any more!" His own father, who once trembled to hear him cough! He did not love him any more! He was no longer in doubt; he was dead in the heart of his father.

"Ah, now, my father," said the boy to himself with his heart oppressed with anxiety, "this is the end, indeed; I cannot live without your affection; I want to have it back, the whole of it; I will tell you all; I will not deceive you any longer; I will study as I did before, let what will happen, if you will only love me once more, my poor father. This time I am sure of my resolution."

Nevertheless, when midnight came, he got up again from mere force of habit more than anything else, and when he was up, he wished to go and sit for a few minutes, in the peacefulness of the night, and for the last time, in that little room where he had worked so hard, on the sly, with his heart full of satisfaction and tenderness. And when he found himself at the desk with the lamp lighted and those white paper wrappers, upon which he would no longer write the names of persons and towns which by this time he knew by heart, he was overtaken by a great sadness, and with impetuosity he grasped the pen again to begin the usual work. But in stretching out his hand he pushed a book and it fell.

The blood rushed to his heart. What if his father should waken! He would certainly not surprise him in the act of doing something bad. He had resolved to tell him everything; still, —— to hear that step approaching in the darkness—to be surprised at that hour of the night, in that sillence! He must also have wakened his mother and she would be frightened—And to think that for the first time his father should experience humiliation in his presence, having discovered everything.—— All this terrified him. He put his ear to the lock with suspended breath —— he heard no noise. He went to another door of the room, but heard nothing. The whole house was asleep. His father had not heard him.

He felt tranquil and began to write again, and the wrappers were piling up fast. He heard the regular step of the policeman in the deserted street, then the noise of a carriage which suddenly stopped; then, after a while, the rattle of a file of trucks which were slowly passing; then a profound silence, broken from time to time by the barking of a dog in the distance. And he kept on writing and writing. In the mean time his father had come in and stood behind him.

Hearing the book fall, he had risen and had stood awaiting the proper moment; the rattling of the trucks had drowned his foot-steps and the creaking of the door. He stood there with his white head over the small black head of Giulio; he had seen the pen run over the wrappers; in a moment, he had guessed everything, remembered all, understood all, and a sense of despairing repentance and of immense tenderness had invaded his soul and had kept him there, riveted and suffocated behind his child.

Suddenly, Giulio uttered a piercing shriek and two convulsive arms had clasped his head. "Oh, papa, papa, forgive me! forgive me!" he cried, having become aware of his father's presence by his weeping.

"You, forgive me," answered his father, sobbing, and coving his forehead with kisses. "I understand all. I know all.

It is I! It is I who ask forgiveness from you, blessed little child of mine. Come, come with me," and he pushed him, or rather carried him to his mother who was also awake, and throwing him into her arms, said:

"Kiss this angel of a child, who for the last three months has not slept but has worked for me, while I was saddening his heart, the heart of him who earned our bread."

The mother clasped him and held him to her breast without being able to speak a word, and then said: "Go to sleep immediately, my child, go to sleep and rest. Take him to bed!" The father took him in his arms and carried him to his room and put him to bed, still breathing hard and caressing him, fixed his pillows and his bed covers.

"Thanks, papa." The boy repeated his thanks and added: "But now, you go to bed, I am satisfied; go to bed, papa." But his father wanted to see him asleep and sat by the bedside, took his hand and said: "Sleep! Sleep! my child!" And Giulio, tired out, at last fell asleep and slept many hours, enjoying for the first time in several months a peaceful sleep, enlivened by pleasant dreams; and when he opened his eyes the sun was shining, and he saw close to his breast, leaning upon the edge of the little bed, the white head of his father who had passed the night thus, and who still slept with his brow leaning against his son's heart.

WILL.

There is Stardi in my class who would have the strength to do what the little Florentine boy has done. This morning, there were two events at school: Garoffi was crazy with satisfaction because they had returned his album with the addition of three postage stamps of the Republic of Guatemala which he had been trying to get for the last three months; and Stardi won the second medal. Stardi next in the class to Derossi! It was a surprise to all. Who would have thought it would be so in

October, when his father took him to school, bundled up in his large green overcoat, and said to the master, in the presence of all the pupils: "Have a great deal of patience, because it is difficult for him to understand." Every one called him a blockhead at the beginning. But he started to work with all his might, in the day time, by night, at home, at school, or walking in the street, with his teeth shut and his fists clenched. And, surely, by dint of trampling on every one, not caring for the jeers of others, and kicking all those who disturbed him, he passed ahead of every one, that blockhead, who did not understand the first thing about arithmetic, filled his composition with mistakes, and could not commit to memory a single paragraph. Now, he solves problems, writes correctly, sings his lesson like a song. One can guess at his iron will when one sees how he is built, so thick-set with a square head and no neck, with short hands and a coarse voice. He studies even in scrap books, newspapers, and theatre advertisements, and every time he gets ten soldi, he buys a book. He has already collected quite a little library, and, in a moment of good humor, he has promised to take me to his home to see it. He never speaks to any one, never plays with any one, but is always there at his desk with his fists on his temples, sitting like a rock, listening to the teacher. How he must have struggled, poor Stardi! The master, although he was impatient and in a bad humor this morning when he delivered the medals said: "Bravo, Stardi, *he who endures conquers.*" But Stardi did not seem at all puffed up with pride, he did not even smile, and as soon as he returned to his bench with his medal, he put his two fists on his temples and sat just as still and more attentive than before. But the finest thing happened when he went out of school, where his father was waiting for him. He is a thick-set fellow, big and clumsy, with a large round face and a heavy voice. He did not expect that medal, and could scarcely believe it was true that Stardi had won it; the teacher was obliged to convince him, and then he began to laugh heartily and tapped his son on the back of the neck, saying in a loud voice: "Well done! Bravo, my little blockhead! that is the way!" and looked at him as if amazed, but smiling. And all the boys around smiled, with the exception of Stardi, who was already pondering over the lesson for to-morrow morning.

GRATITUDE

Saturday the 31st.

Thy companion, Stardi, never complains about his master, I am sure. " The teacher was in a bad humor and was impatient." And thou sayst that, in a tone of resentment. Think a little, how many times dost thou act impatiently thyself and with whom? With thy father and thy mother, towards whom thy impatience is a crime. Thy teacher is right to be impatient at times! Think how many years he has toiled for the boys, and though he has had many who were kind and devoted to him, there are always some who are ungrateful and take advantage of his kindness, who do not appreciate his efforts; and among all of you, you cause him more bitterness than satisfaction. Think that the most blessed man on earth, if put in his place, would at times be conquered by wrath. And then if thou knewest how many times he goes to teach, not feeling well and yet not ill enough to remain away from the school room. He is impatient because he suffers, and it pains him to see that you do not notice it and that you take advantage of it. Respect and love thy master, child. Love him because thy father loves and respects him, because he consecrates his life to the welfare of so many boys, who will forget him. Love him because he opens and enlightens thy intelligence and educates thy soul; because some day when thou art a man, and when neither he nor I shall be in this world, his image will often present itself to thy mind alongside of mine, and then thou wilt notice certain expressions of sorrow and of weariness in his good face which thou dost not observe now, but that thou wilt remember and that will cause thee sorrow even thirty years later; and thou will *be ashamed, and wilt experience sadness for not having loved him and for behaving badly toward him.* Love thy teacher because he belongs to the large family of fifty thousand elementary teachers scattered all over Italy, who are like intellectual fathers to millions of boys who grow up with thee; a worker scarcely recognized and badly recompensed, and who prepares for our country a people better than the present one. I am not content with the affection which thou hast for me, if thou hast not also an affection for all those who do thee good, and among these thy master, who is the first after thy parents. Love him as thou wouldst a brother of mine. Love him when he caresses thee and when he reproves thee; when he is just, and when it seems that he is unjust. Love him when he is merry and affable, and love him also still more when he is sad. Love him always, and always pronounce with reverence this word, "master," which, next to the name of "father," is the most noble and the sweetest that a man can call any man.*

Thy Father.

JANUARY

THE SUBSTITUTE

Wednesday the 4th.

My father was right; the teacher was in a bad humor because he was not feeling well. For the last three days, a substitute nas taken his place, a little fellow without whiskers and who looks like a youth. A shameful thing happened this morning. The boys had been making an uproar at school for the past two days, because the substitute has a great deal of patience and says nothing except: "Be quiet, be silent, I beg you!"

But this morning they passed all bounds. A great noise arose and his words could no longer be heard; he would admonish and beg, but it was all lost. The principal peeped through the door twice, but as soon as he was gone, the noise would increase, as it does in a market place. Garrone and Derossi in vain turned around and made some signs to their companions to keep quiet, as it was a shame. No one paid any heed. Stardi kept quiet. He sat with his elbows on the desk and his fists on his temples, probably dreaming of his famous library. Garoffi, the boy with the hooked nose and the collector of postage stamps, kept busy, drawing up a list of subscribers at two "centesimi" each for the lottery of a big inkstand. The rest of the boys chattered and laughed, played with pen points stuck on the benches, and threw pellets of paper at each other with the elastics from their garters. The substitute would grab by the arm, now one boy and now another, and shake him, but it was time and trouble wasted. The substitute no longer knew what to do, and was entreating: "Why do you act this way? Do you want me to punish you by force?" Then he would pound his fists upon the desk and cry, in a voice mingled with wrath and tears: "Silence! Silence! Silence!" It was painful to hear him.

But the noise grew every moment. Franti threw a paper arrow at him, others uttered cat-calls, some thumped each other on the head; it was a pandemonium almost beyond description, when all of a sudden the janitor entered:

"Signor Maestro, the principal calls you."

The teacher arose and left hurriedly, making a gesture of despair. Then the noise recommenced stronger than ever. But suddenly Garrone sprang up with a convulsed face and his fist closed, and shouted with a voice thick with wrath:

"Stop this, you brutes! you take advantage of him because he is good; if he were to bruise your skin you would keep as abject as dogs. You are a lot of cowards! The first one who mocks him again, I will lay for him outside and break his teeth; I swear it, even though it be under the eyes of his father!" They were all silent.

Ah! how beautiful it was to see Garrone with those eyes that were emitting flames! He appeared like a furious little lion. He looked at the boldest boys, one by one, and they bent their heads. When the substitute, with red eyes, reentered the room not a breath was heard. He stood in amazement. But, after seeing Garrone, still all aflame and trembling, he understood and said, with an accent of great affection, as if he were speaking to a brother: "I thank you, Garrone."

STARDI'S LIBRARY

Stardi lives opposite the school and I have been in his home. I felt envious, indeed, when I saw his library. He is not rich; he cannot buy many books; but he keeps with care his school books and those which his parents give him, and saves all the soldi which he gets, and puts them aside and spends them at the book-seller's; in this way he has already got a little library. And when his father discovered that he had this passion, he bought him a nice walnut bookcase with a green curtain and had many volumes bound in the colors he liked the best. When he pulls a little string the curtain runs back and one can see three rows of books of every color, all placed in good order, shining, with the titles in gold on the back. Books of stories, of travels, of poetry, and some of them are illustrated. He knows how to harmonize the colors and puts the white volumes next to the red, the yellow ones next to the black, and the blue ones next to the white in a way that they may be seen at a distance and make a nice show, and he amuses himself by changing the combinations. He has made himself a catalogue. He is like a librarian, always around his books, dusting them, turning over the leaves, and examining the bindings; you ought to see with what care he opens them with those short, thick fingers, blowing through the pages, and they all seem new. I have worn mine all out! Every new book he buys is a feast for him; he polishes it and puts it in place, taking it and looking at it in every way, and brooding over it like a treasure. He showed me nothing else in an hour's time. He has sore eyes from reading too much. While I was there his father passed through the room. He is big and clumsy and has a large head like Stardi's. He gave him two or three thumpings on the back of his head, saying with that big voice of his:

"What do you think, eh, of this thick head of bronze? It is a thick head which I assure you will succeed in doing something!"

And Stardi half closed his eyes under that rough caress, like a large hunting dog. I did not dare to jest with him. I could hardly believe that he is only one year older than I, and when he said "Goodbye" at the door, with that face which always looks ridiculous, I came very near saying to him: "Good afternoon, sir," as I would to a man. I told my father about it afterward, when I was at home: "I do not understand it; Stardi has no talent, he lacks good manners, he has a ridiculous looking face, still he imposes respect upon me." And my father answered: "It is because he has character." And I added: "In the hour that I have been with him, he has not said fifty words; he has not shown me any toy; he has not laughed once; yet, I was glad to be there." And my father answered: "It is because you esteem him."

THE SON OF THE BLACKSMITH

Yes, and I esteem Precossi also; and it is not enough to say that I esteem him. Precossi, that little thin fellow, who has languid but good eyes and a frightened look, is the son of a blacksmith. He is so timid that he says to every one, "Excuse me," but he studies almost too much. His father returns home drunk and beats him without any reason whatever; throws his books and copy-books around with a blow of the hand; and sometimes Precossi comes to school with black and blue marks on his face, and his eyes red from crying. But one can never make him tell that his father has beaten him. His companions say to him:

"It is your father who has beaten you," And he answers immediately: "No, that is not true!" in order not to disgrace his father.

"It was not you who burned this sheet of paper," the master said, showing him his lesson half burned.

"Yes," he answered "I let it fall in the fire."

Still, we well knew that his father, being drunk, had upset the lamp on the table with a kick while Precossi was writing his lesson.

He lives in the garret of our house on the other side of the stairway. The janitor's wife tells my mother everything. One day my sister Silvia heard him from the balcony crying in terror; his father had sent him headlong down the stairs because he had asked him for money to buy a grammar. His father drinks and does not work, and his family are starving all the time.

How often does Precossi come to school with an empty stomach and nibbles in secret the small loaf which Garrone has given him, or an apple which the little teacher with the red feather has presented to him; she was his teacher in the first lower class. But he never says: "I am hungry, my father does not give me enough to eat."

His father calls for him sometimes when he passes the school. He has a fierce face, with his hair over his eyes and a cap worn on the back of his head, and he is often unsteady on his legs; the poor boy trembles when he sees him coming, but nevertheless he runs to meet him, smiling, and his father acts as though he did not see him but was thinking of something else.

Poor Precossi! He mends his torn copy-books, borrows books to study the lesson, patches up the fragments of his shirt with pins. It is pitiful to see him in the gymnastic class, wearing shoes that are so large that he can dance inside them, and with those long trousers which drag on the ground when he walks, with a jacket too long for him, and those huge sleeves turned back to the elbow. He studies and does his best and would be one of the first in the class if he could quietly work at home.

This morning he came to school with the mark of a finger nail on his cheek, and all the boys said to him: "It is your father, you cannot deny it this time; it is your father who did that. Tell the principal and he will have him called before the police magistrate." But he arose and with a voice trembling with indignation, said: "No, it is not true! It is not true! My father never strikes me!"

During the lesson, the tears fell on his book, but if any one looked at him, he made an effort to smile that he might not show his feelings. Poor Precossi! To-morrow, Derossi, Coretti, and Nelli are coming to my house, to have lunch with me. I want to ask Precossi to come also. I would like to give him some books and to turn the house upside down to amuse him; and I would fill his pocket with fruit, so that I might see him happy for once. Poor Precossi, who is so kind and good, and who has so much courage!

A NICE VISIT

Thursday the 12th.

This was one of the finest Thursdays in the year. At two o'clock sharp, Derossi, Coretti, and Nelli, the little hunchback, came to my house; Precossi's father would not allow him to come. Derossi and Coretti were still laughing because they had met Crossi,—the boy with the withered arm and red hair,— the son of the green vegetable woman, in the street; he was carrying a big cabbage in order to sell it so that with the *soldo* he received he might buy a pen-holder, and he was so happy because his father has written from America that they may expect him back any day. Oh, how happy were the two hours which we passed together! Derossi and Coretti are the two jolliest boys in school, and my father fell in love with them. Coretti wore his chocolate-colored knit jacket and his cat-skin cap. He is a lively fellow, he always wants to be doing something, stirring up something, putting something in motion. He had already carried half a wagon load of wood early in the morning; still he galloped all over the house, observing everything and talking all the time, nimble and quick like a squirrel; and going to the kitchen, he asked the cook how much we paid for our wood by the "myriagramme," and said that his father sold it at forty-five centesimi. He always speaks of his father who was a soldier in the 49th regiment at the battle of Custozza, where he fought in the army of Prince Humbert. Coretti is so gentle in his manner—It does not matter that he was born and brought up surrounded by wood, he has a kind heart, as my father says. Derossi amused us very much; he knows his geography like a teacher, and he would close his eyes and say:

"Behold, I see all Italy; the Appennines which extend to the Ionian Sea, the rivers which flow here and there, the white cities, the gulfs, the blue bays and the green hills." And, he told rapidly and in order the correct names, as if he were reading them from a paper. We all stood in admiration, looking at him with that head, covered with blonde curls, held high, and his eyes closed. So straight and handsome and dressed in black with gilt buttons, he looked like a statue. In an hour, he had learned by heart almost three pages which he must recite the day after to-morrow at the anniversary of the funeral of King Vittorio. Even Nelli looked at him with admiration and affection as he wrapped the folds of his black rain-coat around him, and smiled with those clear and mournful eyes. That visit gave me much pleasure and left me something like two bright spots in mind and heart. I was also pleased, when they left, to see poor Nelli between the other two, large and strong, who carried him in their arms, making him laugh as I never saw him laugh before. Returning to the dining-room, I noticed that the picture of Rigoletto, the hunchbacked buffoon, was no longer there; my father had taken it away so that Nelli should not see it.

THE FUNERAL OF VITTORIO EMANUELE

Tuesday the 17th.

To-day at two o'clock, as soon as I entered the school, the teacher called Derossi, who went to the teacher's desk facing us and began to speak in a vibrating tone of voice, raising it by degrees and flushing in the face:

"Four years ago, on this very day, at this very hour, there arrived in front of the Pantheon in Rome the funeral car which carried the body of Vittorio Emanuele, the first king of Italy, who died after having reigned twenty-nine years, during which time the great Italian country, divided into seven different states and oppressed by strangers and tyrants, had been incorporated into one single state, independent and free—a reign which he had made illustrious with valor, with loyalty, with boldness in danger, with wisdom in triumph, and with constancy in misfortune.

"The funeral car arrived, laden with wreaths after having gone through Rome under a shower of flowers, in the silence of an immense and sorrowing multitude, which had come from all parts of Italy; preceded by a legion of generals, ministers, and others; followed by a retinue of crippled veterans, a forest of flags and the representatives of three hundred cities; by everything which embodied the power and the glory of the people; it arrived in front of that august temple where his tomb was awaiting him. In that moment, while the cuirassiers lifted the bier from the car, in that moment, Italy was giving her last farewell to her dead king; to her old king who had loved her so much; the last farewell to her soldier, to her father; the last farewell to the most prosperous twenty-nine years of her history.

"It was a great and solemn moment. The eyes, the souls of all were quivering between the bier and the flags of the eighty regiments of the Italian army, which were draped with crepe and carried by eighty officers, drawn up in a line to form a passage, representing all Italy; eighty emblems which reminded them of the dead, of torrents of blood, of our most holy sacrifices, of our most tremendous grief. The bier, borne by the cuirassiers, passed them and they all were lowered together in an act of salute; the flags of the new regiments and the old and torn flags of Goito, Pastrengo, Santa Lucia, Novara, Crimea, Palestro, San Martino, and Castelfidardo; eighty black crepes fell and hundreds of medals shook over the coffin, and that sonorous but confused uproar stirred the blood of all those present, like the sound of a thousand human voices which were saying together: 'Farewell, good king, loyal king! You will live in the hearts of your people as long as the sun shines over Italy!' After this, the flags were raised towards the sky, and Vittorio entered into the immortal glory of the tomb."

FRANTI EXPELLED FROM SCHOOL

Saturday the 21st.

There was only one boy who could laugh while Derossi spoke of the funeral of the king, and this one was Franti. I detest him. He is a coward. When the father of a boy comes to the school to reprove his son, he rejoices over it; when one cries, he laughs. He trembles in the presence of Garrone, and beats the Little Mason because he is small; he torments Grossi because he has a withered arm; he jeers at Precossi, whom every one else respects; he even sneers at Robetti, the boy of the second-class who walks on crutches from having saved a child. He provokes all those who are weaker than himself, and when he fights he grows ferocious and tries to harm his opponent. There is something repulsive in that low forehead, in those turbid eyes, that he keeps almost hidden under the front of his cap of wax cloth. He fears nothing; laughs in the face of the teacher; steals when he gets a chance; denies everything with a straight face, and is always quarreling with somebody. He takes pins to school to prick his neighbors; tears the buttons off his jacket and off the other boys' jackets and then gambles them away. His satchel and copy-books are soiled and torn, his ruler is battered, and his pen-holder is half chewed up. His nails are bitten and his clothes are covered with grease spots and with rents that he got while fighting. He hates school, hates his school-mates, and hates the teacher. At times, the teacher feigns not to notice his rascalities, and then he does even worse. When the teacher treats him kindly, the boy makes fun of him for it. Once the master said terrible words to the boy, then the latter covered his face with his hands and pretended to be crying, but he was laughing. He was suspended from school for three days, but he returned more insolent and wicked than he was before. Derossi said to him one day: "Do stop that! do you not see how that the teacher suffers?" And he threatened to stick a nail into Derossi's stomach. But this morning he was expelled from school like a dog. While the teacher was giving Garrone the rough copy of the *Sardinian Drummer-Boy*, the monthly story for January, to transcribe, Franti threw on the floor a petard which exploded, making the school-room resound as from a discharge of guns. The whole class was startled. The teacher rose to his feet and cried:

"Franti! leave the school!"

He answered: "No, it was not I!" But he laughed, and the teacher repeated:

"Leave!"

"I will not leave," he answered.

Then the teacher lost his temper and, grasping him by the arms, he tore him from his bench. He tried to resist, grinding his teeth, and was carried out by force. The teacher carried him to the principal and then returned to the class and sat at his desk, and held his head in his hands, all out of breath, with such a worn and grieved expression in his face that it was painful to look at him.

"After thirty years that I have been teaching!" he exclaimed sadly, shaking his head. No one breathed. His hands were trembling with wrath, and the straight wrinkle in the middle of his forehead was so deep that it looked like a scar. Poor teacher! They all felt sorry for him. Derossi rose and said:

"Signor master, do not be so sorrowful, we love you." And then he looked a little more serene and said:

"Let us proceed with our lesson, boys."

THE SARDINIAN DRUMMER-BOY
(MONTHLY STORY)

During the first day of the battle of Custozza, on the twenty-fourth of July, 1848, about sixty soldiers of an infantry regiment of our army went to the top of a hill to occupy a solitary house. They were suddenly assailed by two companies of Austrian soldiers, who showered on them bullets from every side. Our soldiers were hard pressed to find refuge in the house and had time only to hastily barricade the doors, after having left some dead and wounded on the outside. Having barred the doors, our men hastened to the windows on the ground floor and commenced a brisk discharge at the enemy, who approached little by little, having arranged themselves in a semi-circle, and returning the fire vigorously. The sixty Italian soldiers were commanded by two subaltern officers and a captain, an old man, tall and austere, with white hair and mustache. They had with them a little Sardinian drummer-boy, a lad a little over fourteen years old, who looked to be scarcely twelve. He had a small olive brown face, with two deep little eyes which glittered with animation. The captain from a room on the first floor commanded the defence, giving his orders like pistol shots, and no sign of emotion could be seen in that passive face. The little drummer-boy, rather pale but steady on his legs, having jumped upon a chair, leaned against the side wall and stretched his neck to look outside the window. He saw through the smoke the white uniforms of

the Austrians as they slowly advanced. The house was situated on the summit of a steep incline and had but one little high window in the roof on the side of the slope. The Austrians did not threaten the house from that side; the slope was unencumbered and the fusilade only beat the front and two sides of the house.

But it was a terrible fusilade. A shower of bullets fell outside, and inside cracked the ceilings, the furniture, the shutters and the door frames, filling the air with pieces of wood, plaster, broken glass, whizzing, rebounding, breaking everything, and making an uproar enough to burst one's skull. From time to time, one of the soldiers who were firing from the windows would fall, crashing back upon the floor, and be taken aside. Some staggered from room to room, pressing their hands over their wounds. In the kitchen there was a dead man with his forehead cut open. The semi-circle of the enemy was drawing nearer and nearer together.

At a certain point, the captain, who had been impassive until then, began to grow uneasy and was seen rushing out of the room, followed by a sergeant. After three or four minutes the sergeant came running back and asked for the drummer-boy, making him a sign to follow him. The boy rushed up the wooden ladder and entered with the sergeant into a bare attic, where he saw the captain, who was writing with a pencil upon a piece of paper, leaning upon the little window. At his feet upon the floor there was a rope which had been used to draw water from the well. The captain folded up the sheet of paper and said brusquely, looking sharply at the boy with his cold grey eyes, before which all soldiers trembled: "Drummer-boy!"

The drummer-boy put his hand to his visor.

The captain said: "Have you any courage?"

The eyes of the boy flashed.

"Yes, captain," he replied.

"Look down there," said the captain, pushing him to the little window, "down the plain, near the houses of Villafranca, where there is a glimmer of bayonets. There are our men, motionless. Take this note, grasp the rope, descend from the little window, rush down the slope, through the fields, and when you reach our men, give this note to the first officer whom you meet. Throw off your strap and your knapsack."

The drummer-boy threw off the strap and the knapsack, put the note in his breast pocket; the sergeant flung out the rope, holding one end of it fast in his hands; the captain helped the boy to get through the little window, with his back turned to the open country.

"Look out," he said, "the salvation of this detachment rests upon your courage and upon your legs!"

"Trust in me, captain," replied the boy, as he let himself down.

"Lean down on the slope side," the captain said, again clutching at the rope together with the sergeant.

"Do not falter."

"God help you."

In a few moments the drummer-boy was on the ground, the sergeant pulled up the rope and disappeared, the captain stepped impetuously to the window and saw the boy flying down the incline.

He thought he had succeeded in running without being observed, when five or six little clouds which rose from the ground in front and from behind him, warned the captain that the boy had been seen by the Austrians, who were shooting at him from the top of the hill. Those little clouds were dust cast up by the bullets. But the little drummer-boy continued to run swiftly; all of a sudden he dropped. "He is killed!" roared the captain, biting his fist. He had barely uttered these words, when he saw the boy get up again. "Ha! it is only a fall!" he mumbled to himself and breathed again. The little drummer-boy had begun to run with all his might, but he limped. "He must have turned his ankle," thought the captain. Another little cloud arose here and there around the boy, but each time at a further distance from him. "He is safe!" the captain exclaimed in triumph, but he kept on following him with his eyes, trembling; because if he did not reach the soldiers very soon with the note, asking succor, all his soldiers would be killed, or he would be obliged to surrender and give himself up as a prisoner with the others.

The boy ran quickly for a little time, then slackened his

pace and limped, then he would start to run again, each time more fatigued, and every once in awhile he would stumble and pause.

"Perhaps a bullet has grazed him," thought the captain, who was observing all his movements. Quivering and excited, he spoke to him as though he might hear him. He measured in a restless way, with a burning eye, the distance intervening between the running boy and the gleaming of the weapons, which he saw down below in the plain in the middle of the corn-fields, gilded by the sun. In the meanwhile, he heard the uproar of the bullets in the room below; the imperious and encouraging cries of the officers and of the sergeant; the lamentations of the wounded; the breaking of the furniture and the plaster. "Go on! Courage!" he cried, following with his eyes the little drummer-boy at a distance.

"Go ahead! Run! Oh, he stops, that cursed boy! Ah! he begins to run again."

An officer came to tell him, panting, that the enemy without interrupting the fusilade, were hoisting a white cloth to intimate surrender. "Let it not be answered!" he cried, without taking his eyes off the drummer boy, who was already in the plain but not running any longer, and seeming to drag himself along with difficulty. "Go ahead! Run!" said the captain, clinching his teeth. "Run, if you have to die, you rascal, but run!" and he uttered a terrible oath. "Ah! infamous child! he has seated himself, that poltroon!" The boy, whose head up to this time he had seen above the cornfield, had disappeared as if he had fallen. After a moment his head came up again, but he was soon lost behind the hedges and the captain saw him no more.

Then the captain came down impetuously; the bullets were showering, the rooms were crowded with the wounded, some of whom were whirling around like drunken men, clutching pieces of furniture; the walls and the floor were stained with blood, and bodies were lying across the doors; the lieutenant had his right arm broken by a bullet; the smoke and the dust filled everything.

"Courage!" cried the captain. "Stand to your place! Succor is coming! Keep up your courage!"

The Austrians had come nearer and nearer the house; one could see through the smoke their contorted faces, and could hear among the crashing of the firing their wild cries, which were insulting, suggesting surrender, threatening the soldiers. Some of the frightened soldiers would leave the windows, and the sergeant would push them forward again, but the firing from the defense was growing weaker. Discouragement was visible on all faces; it was no longer possible to keep up a resistance.

Suddenly, the firing of the Austrians slackened, and a thundering voice cried, first in German and then Italian! "Surrender!"—"No!" howled the captain from the window, and the fusilade re-commenced more thickly and furiously from both sides. Other soldiers fell. Already, more than one window was without defenders; the fatal moment was imminent! The captain cried in a despairing voice:

"They are not coming! They are not coming!" and ran around furiously, bending his sword with his convulsive hand, ready to die; suddenly the sergeant, rushing down from the garret, uttered a loud cry of joy, shouting to the captain:

"They are coming! They are coming!"

"They are coming!" repeated the captain joyfully.

At that cry, all those who were unhurt, as well as the wounded, the sergeant and officers rushed to the windows, and the resistance became more furious than before. In a few moments, a certain hesitation was noticed and a beginning disorder among the foe. Quickly, the captain assembled a little troop in the room on the ground floor to make an exit with the bayonet. Then he ran up to the little window again. Hardly had he reached it, when they heard a hasty tramping of feet accompanied with a formidable hurrah, and from the windows, they saw coming through the smoke the double-pointed hats of the Italian carabineers, a squadron rushing forward at great speed, and the lightning flash of blades whirling in the air and falling on heads, on shoulders, on backs. Then the captain darted out from the door with lowered bayonets. The enemy wavered and were thrown into confusion and disorder. They hastily retreated, and the ground was left unencumbered, the house was free, and two battalions of Italian infantry and two cannons occupied the hill.

The captain, with the soldiers that remained, rejoined his regiment, fought again and was slightly wounded in his left hand by a ricochet bullet during the last assault with the bayonet. The day ended with a victory for our men.

But the day after, having recommenced the fight, the Italians were overpowered, in spite of a valorous resistance, by the overwhelming numbers of the Austrians; and, on the morning of the 26th, they had to retreat sadly toward the Mincio river.

The captain, although wounded, made his way on foot with the soldiers, tired and silent, and arriving toward sunset at Goito, on the Mincio, looked immediately for his lieutenant, who had been taken up with his broken arm by our ambulance and who had arrived there before him. Some one had shown him the church where a field hospital had been improvised. He went there. The church was filled with wounded, lying in two rows on beds and mattresses stretched on the floor. Two physicians and several nurses were coming and going, busily occupied, and one could hear suppressed groans and cries. As soon as he entered, the captain halted and looked around for his officer.

At that moment he heard himself called by a faint voice very near him: "Captain!"

He turned around; it was the little drummer-boy.

He was stretched on a cot bed, covered up to the breast with a rough window curtain in red and white squares, and with his arms out; pale and thin, but with his eyes still sparkling like two black gems.

"Is it you?" asked the captain rather sharply, although amazed. "Bravo, you did your duty."

"I did all that was possible," answered the boy.

"Are you wounded?" asked the captain, looking for his officer in the beds near by.

"What could I do?" said the boy, who gained courage by speaking, while feeling the satisfaction of having been wounded for the first time; under other circumstances he would hardly have dared to open his mouth in the presence of that captain. "I did my best to run bending down; they saw me at once. I would have arrived twenty minutes sooner if they had not hit me. Fortunately I soon found a captain of the staff and gave him your note. But it was a very hard matter to run after that caress. I was dying with thirst; I was afraid that I would never arrive, and was crying with rage, thinking that every minute delayed was sending another soul to the other world. But that is enough; I have done what I could; I am satisfied. But, with your permission, look at yourself, captain, you are losing blood."

And truly, from the badly bandaged hand of the captain some drops of blood trickled down through his fingers.

"Do you wish me to tie up your bandage, captain? Hold out your hand a minute."

The captain held out his left hand and stretched the right one to assist the boy in untying the knot and tying it again; but the boy, raising himself from his pillow with difficulty, grew pale and had to lean his head back again.

"Enough, enough," the captain said, looking at him and drawing the bandaged hand away that the boy wanted to hold. "Attend to your own affairs instead of those of others; things that are not severe may become serious."

The drummer-boy shook his head.

"But you," said the captain, looking at him attentively,

"You must have lost a great deal of blood to be as weak as you are."

"Lost much blood?" replied the lad with a smile. "I have lost more than blood. Look!"

And he pulled down the cover that was over him.

The captain started back and stopped, horrified. The lad had but one leg left, the left one had been amputated above his knee and the stump was bandaged with bloody cloths.

At that moment the military surgeon, a little fleshy fellow in short sleeves, passed by. "Ah! captain," said he quickly, pointing to the drummer-boy, "a most unfortuate case. A leg that might have been easily saved if he had not forced it in that foolish way; a cursed inflammation; it had to be cut off away up here. Oh! but he is a brave lad, I assure you; he has not shed a tear; he has not uttered a cry. I was proud that it was an Italian boy while I was performing the operation; upon my honor, he belongs to a good race, by heavens!" And he went away.

The captain frowned and looked fixedly at the boy, putting the cover back over him; then slowly, as though unconsciously, raised his hand to his head and took off his cap.

"Captain!" exclaimed the astonished boy, "what are you doing, captain, and that for me?"

And then that rough soldier, who had never said a mild word to one of his subalterns, answered, with an indescribably affectionate and sweet voice: "I am nothing but a captain, you are a hero!"

Then he threw himself with open arms on the drummer-boy and pressed him three times upon his heart.

THE LOVE OF OUR COUNTRY

Tuesday the 24th.

As the story of the little drummer-boy has shaken thy heart, it ought to have been easy for thee this morning to write a good

composition for the examination: " Why Do You Love Italy?"
Why do I love Italy? Did not a hundred answers present themselves to thee? I love Italy because my mother is Italian, because the blood which runs in my veins is Italian, because the dead, whom my mother mourns and whom my father venerates, are buried in this soil, because the city where I was born, the language

that I speak, the books which educate me, because my brother, my sister, and all my companions, and the great people among whom I live, the beautiful country which surrounds me, and all that I see, that I love, that I admire, is Italian. Thou canst not yet entirely feel this affection. But thou wilt fully do so when thou art a man; when, returning home from a long trip abroad, after a long absence, leaning over the bulwarks of the ship, thou wilt see on the horizon the blue mountains of thy country; thou wilt feel it then, *in the impetuous flood of tenderness which will fill thine eyes with tears, and which will wring from thine heart a cry. Thou wilt feel it in some distant city, in the impulse of thy soul which will push thee in an unknown crowd toward an unknown workman from whom thou hast heard, in passing, a word in thy native tongue. Thou wilt feel it in that proud and painful moment when, with indignation which brings the blood to thy forehead, thou wilt hear thy country insulted by a stranger. Thou wilt feel it more strongly and valiantly the day on which hostile people shall raise a tempest of fire upon thy country. Then thou wilt behold arms on every side, and the young men running by legions, and the fathers kissing their sons and saying: "Courage!" and the mothers saying good-bye to the youths, crying: "Conquer!" Thou wilt feel it as a divine joy, if thou shouldst ever have the fortune to see entering thy city the lessened regiment, ragged, terrible, with the splendor of victory in their eyes, and their banners torn by bullets, followed by a crowd of brave fellows, with their bandaged heads and their stumps of mutilated limbs, in the midst of a throng which will cover them with flowers, with blessings, with kisses. Thou wilt then understand what is love for thy country. Thou wilt feel it then, Enrico. It is such a great and sacred thing that, if one day I should see thee returning home safely from battle fought for thy country; thee, safe! thou, who art my flesh and soul! if I should know that thou hadst preserved thy life, that thou hadst fled from death, I, thy father, who receive thee with a cry of joy when thou returnest from school, I would receive thee with a cry of anguish, and could no longer love thee, and I would die with that poignard in my heart.*

Thy Father.

ENVY

Wednesday the 25th.

It was Derossi who wrote the best composition on "The Love of Our Country." And Votini thought he was sure of getting the first medal! I like Votini very much, although he is too vain and poses too much, but he displeases me, since sitting near his desk, I notice how envious he is of Derossi. He would like to compete with him, but he cannot do it, for Derossi is ten times as clever in every way, and Votini bites his fingers with rage. Carlo Nobis also envies him; but he is so proud that he will not show it. Votini, on the other hand, embitters himself. He complains of the difficulties at home, and says that the teacher is unjust; and when Derossi replies to questions so promptly and well, as he always does, Votini's face clouds over, he bends his head, pretends not to hear him, and makes an effort to laugh; but it is a bitter laugh. All the boys know how he feels, and when the teacher praises Derossi, they all turn around and look at Votini, who swallows his venom, and the Little Mason makes the hare face at him. This morning, for instance, things went wrong with him; the teacher entered the school room and announced the result of the examination: "Derossi, ten-tenths and first medal." Votini gave a loud sneeze. The teacher looked at him; it was easy to understand the matter.

"Votini," he said, "do not let the serpent of envy enter into your heart. It is a serpent which gnaws the brain and mars the soul."

All looked at him except Derossi; Votini tried to answer but could not.

He sat there as though paralyzed, with his white face bent down.

Then, after the teacher began giving the lesson, he commenced to write in large letters upon a small piece of paper: *I am not envious of those who gain the first medal through deceit and favoritism.* It was a note that he wished to send to Derossi. In the meanwhile, I saw that Derossi's neighbors were plotting among themselves, whispering to each other, and one of them cut with his penknife a large paper medal upon which a black serpent had been drawn. Votini also noticed this.

The teacher left the room for a few minutes; suddenly, all the boys near Derossi got up and left their desks to go and present the medal to Votini in a solemn way. The whole class was prepared for a scene.

Votini trembled like a leaf.

Derossi exclaimed: "Give it to me!"

"So much the better," they replied, "it is you who ought to give it to him."

Derossi took the medal and tore it into many pieces. At that moment, the teacher returned and the class resumed the lesson. I kept my eyes on Votini, he had become as red as a burning coal; he took the little note and slowly, as if absent minded, rolled it into a ball, put it into his mouth, chewed it for a while, then spit it out under the desk.

Coming out of school and passing in front of Derossi, Votini, who was a little confused, dropped his blotting paper. Derossi kindly picked it up, put it in Votini's satchel, and helped him to fasten his strap. Votini did not dare to raise his head.

FRANTI'S MOTHER

Saturday the 28th.

However, Votini is not yet changed. Yesterday, during the lesson in religion, in the presence of the principal, the teacher asked Derossi if he knew by heart the two verses in the Reader, beginning with

"Where'er I turn my gaze,
'Tis Thee, great Lord, I see."

Derossi answered "No," and Votini quickly said: "I know them," with a smile as though to taunt Derossi.

But he was balked, as he was not able to recite the chapter; for suddenly Franti's mother, followed by the principal, entered the room, with her grey hair disheveled, all out of breath, and all wet with snow. She was pushing forward her son who had been suspended from school for eight days. What a sad scene we had to witness! The poor woman threw herself almost on her knees in front of the principal, clasping her hands in a supplicating manner:

"Oh, signor principal, grant me this favor, allow my boy to be readmitted to the school! I have kept him hidden at home for three days; the Lord knows what may happen if his father discovers everything. He may kill him. Have mercy, as I know not what to do! I beg you with my whole soul!"

The principal tried to take her out, but she resisted, all the time begging and crying:

"Oh! if you knew the grief and care that this son has caused me, you would be moved to pity! I hope he may change. I have not long to live, signor principal. Death is near me; yet I should love to see him improve before I die, because" — and she burst into tears — " it is my child; I love him; I would die in despair; take him back once more, signor principal, in order that such misfortune may not come to the family. Do it for charity to a poor woman!" and she covered her face with her hands and sobbed.

Franti, impassive, stood with bowed head. The principal looked at him, remained in thought for a moment and then he said:

"Franti, go to your place."

The woman was consoled. She took her hands from her face and began saying: "Thanks, thanks," without giving the principal a chance to talk, and started toward the door, wiping her eyes, and saying hastily: "My child, I warn you. May all have patience. Thanks, signor principal; you have done an act of charity. Good bye, my child. Good day, boys. Thanks, until I see you again, signor teacher, and do forgive a poor woman."

Casting, from the door, another supplicating glance at her son, she left, pulling up her shawl which was trailing after her, pale, bent down, her head trembling, and we could hear her cough as she was going down the stairs. During the silence of the class, the principal looked fixedly at Franti, and then said in an accent which made one shiver:

"Franti, you are killing your mother!"

All turned around to look at Franti, and that detestable boy was smiling.

HOPE

Sunday the 25th.

"It was very beautiful, Enrico, the impetuosity with which thou hast thrown thyself upon the heart of thy mother, upon your return from the religious school. The teacher has told thee many great and consoling things. God has thrown us into the arms of each other; therefore, he will not separate us; when I die, when thy father dies, we will not say to each other those terrible, despairing words: mamma, papa, Enrico, I will see thee no more! We will see each other again in another life, where he who has suffered in this life will be recompensed, where he who has loved much upon earth will find again the beloved souls in a world without faults, without tears, and without death; but we must render ourselves worthy of that other life. Listen, my child, every one of thy good actions, every one of thy loving thoughts for those who love thee, every courteous act toward thy companions, every kind deed, is a step toward that world; so is every sorrow and every grief, for every grief is an atonement for a fault, every tear erases a stain. Resolve to be better each day and more loving than the day before. Say every morning to thyself: "To-day I will do something that my conscience will approve of, and with which my father will be satisfied; something which will make me beloved by my companions, by my teacher, by my brother, and by others." And ask that God may give thee strength to carry out thy resolutions: "Lord, I wish to be good and noble, courageous, kind, and sincere; do help me to improve every opportunity, so that when my mother gives me her last kiss at night, I

may be able to tell her: ' Thou kissest this evening a child more worthy and more honest than the one you kissed yesterday.'' Have always in thy mind the other Enrico, immortal and blessed, so that you may live after this life, and do pray. Thou canst not imagine the sweetness that I experience, how much better thy mother feels when she sees her child with hands clasped

in prayer. When I see thee praying, it seems impossible that no one can look or listen to thee. I believe then more firmly that there is a Supreme kindness and an Infinite pity; I love more, I work with more ardor, I suffer with more courage, I forgive with all my soul, and think serenely of death. Oh! God is great and kind. To hear once more the voice of thy mother, to meet again my children, to see again my Enrico, my blessed and immortal Enrico, to clasp him in an embrace which shall never be ended, never, never, through all eternity! Oh, do pray, let us pray, let us pray, let us love each other, let us be good, let us endure with heavenly hope in our souls, my adored child.

Thy Mother.

FEBRUARY

A WELL AWARDED MEDAL

Saturday the 4th.

This morning the superintendent of schools came to deliver the medals. He is a gentleman with a white beard, dressed in black. He entered with the principal a few moments before the class was over, and sat next to the teacher. He questioned many, then he gave the first medal to Derossi; but, before bestowing the second medal, he paused a few moments to listen to the teacher and the principal, who were speaking to him in a low voice. All the boys were asking each other:

"To whom will he give the second medal?"

The superintendent then said aloud: "The second medal, this morning, is earned by the pupil Pietro Precossi, who has deserved it because of his work at home; because of his lessons; because of his penmanship, and owing to his behavior in general."

They all turned to look at Precossi, and it was evident that they were pleased. Precossi arose, so confused that he did not seem to know where he was.

"Come here," said the superintendent. Precossi left his bench and went to the teacher's desk. The superintendent looked attentively at that little wax-colored face and that little body, clothed in those ill-fitting garments, at those sad eyes, which avoided his gaze but which told their story of suffering.

Then he said to him, in a voice full of affection, while attaching the medal to his breast.

"Precossi, I give you this medal. There is no one more worthy of wearing it than you. I award it not only to your intelligence and good will, I award it to your heart, to your courage, to your character, to a brave and good child. Is it not so?" he added, turning toward the class, "that he has merited it on this account?"

"Yes, yes," they all answered in one voice.

Precossi made a movement as though swallowing something, and turned his eyes toward the benches, expressing great gratitude.

"Good, dear boy," the superintendent said to him, "may God protect you!"

It was the hour to go out; our class left before the others. As soon as we were outside the door, whom did we see there in the large hall at the entrance? The father of Precossi — the blacksmith — pale, badly clad, with an ugly look, with his hair over his eyes, his cap awry, and unsteady on his legs.

The teacher saw him at once and whispered something to the superintendent; the latter looked in haste for Precossi, and, taking him by the hand, moved toward his father. The boy trembled. The boy and the principal approached the father and many of the pupils gathered around the group.

"You are the father of this boy, are you not?" asked the superintendent of the blacksmith, with a cheerful air, as if they were friends; and, without waiting for an answer: "I congratulate you. Look, he has won the second medal among fifty-four schoolmates. He has merited it in composition, in arithmetic, in everything. He is a child full of intelligence and good will, a brave lad who has gained the esteem and affection of all. You may be proud of him, I assure you."

The blacksmith, who had been listening with his mouth wide open, looked straight at the superintendent and at the principal, then looked at his son, who stood before him trembling and with his eyes cast down. The father looked as if he remembered and understood then — for the first time — all he had caused the little fellow to suffer, and all the kindness, all the heroic constancy with which he had borne it. A certain stupid admiration shone in his face, then a saddened remorse, and finally a sorrowful and impetuous tenderness, and with a rough gesture, he clasped the child in his arms and pressed him against his breast.

We passed before Precossi and invited him to come with Garrone and Crossi to visit us on Thursday; the others saluted him, some bestowed a caress upon him, others touched his medal, and all spoke a kind word to him. And the father looked at us stupefied, all the time holding the head of his son on his breast, while the boy softly sobbed.

GOOD RESOLUTIONS

Sunday the 5th.

The medal bestowed upon Precossi has caused me a remorse. I have not yet earned one! Because sometimes I do not study, and I am dissatisfied with myself and the teacher; my father and mother are also dissatisfied. I no longer experience the pleasure I once felt in amusing myself, when I work unwillingly and then dart from my desk and run to play, as if I had not played for a month. I do not even sit at the table with my friends with the same content that I once felt. I always hear that internal voice, like a shadow in my soul, which constantly tells me: "That is not right, that is not right."

I see, in the evening, going through the square, so many boys who are coming back from work, in the midst of groups of workmen, tired but merry, and who hasten their steps, impatient to get home to supper. They speak lightly, laughing and clapping their dark hands, soiled with coal or white with plaster, slapping one another on the shoulder. I think that they have worked from sunrise up to that hour. I see many others like them, who have worked all day on the top of roofs, or in front of furnaces, or among machines, or in the water, or even under the ground, eating nothing but a little bread, and I feel almost ashamed, I, who during that time have been doing nothing but scribbling unwillingly four little pages. Ah, I am discontented, indeed! I well know that my father is displeased with me, and he would like to tell me so, but he feels sorry and waits a little longer—that dear father of mine who works so hard. Everything is yours, everything I see around the house, all that I touch, all that I wear, and all that I eat, all that teaches and amuses me; all this is the fruit of your work, and I do not work. All these have cost you many thoughts, privations and fatigues, and I do not toil. Ah, no; it is too unjust, and makes me feel ashamed. I want to begin from to-day; I want to put myself to study like Stardi, with his fists clasped on his temples and with closed teeth, to set myself to work with all the strength of my will and my heart. I want to conquer my drowsiness in the evening, get up early in the morning, exercise my brain without rest, pitilessly cast off laziness. I will toil, I will suffer, till I am ill, if need be. From now on I will put a stop to this lazy and worthless life which lowers me and saddens the others. Up, to work! To work, with all my soul and with all my power! To work, that it may render my rest sweet, my recreations more pleasant, my meals more merry. To work again! and that will restore to me the pleasant smile of my teacher and the blessed kiss of my father.

THE LITTLE RAILWAY TRAIN

Friday the 10th

Precossi and Garrone came to visit me yesterday. I think if they had been two sons of princes. they would not have been received with more delight. Garrone came for the first time.

He is rather shy, and besides he feels awkward to be seen, as he is so tall and still belongs to the third class. We all went to open the door when the bell rang. Crossi did not come, because his father has at last arrived from America, after an absence of six years. My mother kissed Precossi. My father introduced him, saying, "Behold, this is not only a good boy, but he is also a man of honor and a gentleman." And the boy bowed his large, shaggy head, smiling in a consoling way to me. Precossi wore his medal, and was so happy because his father had gone back to work. It is five days since his father has taken any liquor. He wants to have Precossi all the time in his workshop to keep him company, and acts altogether like another man.

We began to play; I brought out all my toys. Precossi stood in amazement before a railway train with an engine which runs by winding it up. He had never seen one before, and he devoured with his eyes those little yellow and red cars. I wound them up for him to play with, and he kneeled down to play, and did not raise his head any more. I have never seen him so interested and pleased.

He said, "Excuse me, excuse me," to everything, motioning to us with his hands not to stop the engine, and he lifted and put down the cars with great care, as if they were made of glass. He was afraid of tarnishing them with his breath, and he polished them up again, examining them top and bottom, and smiling to himself. We all stood and looked at him. We were looking at that slender neck and those poor little ears, that I had seen bleeding one day, and that large jacket, which he wore with the sleeves turned over, and those two little sickly arms, which had been raised so many times to save his face from a beating. Oh, at that moment I would have thrown at his feet all my toys and all my books; I would have taken the last piece of bread from my mouth and given it to him; I would have undressed myself to clothe him; I would have fallen upon my knees to kiss him.

"I will at least give him my little railroad train," I thought; but it was necessary to ask my father's permission. At that moment I felt a bit of paper thrust into my hand. I looked at it. It was written in pencil by my father, and read. *"Precossi has no toys. Does anything suggest itself to thy heart?"*

Instantly I seized the engine and the cars with both hands, and placed them in the arms of Precossi, saying:

"Take it; it is yours." He looked at it, but did not understand.

"It is yours," I said. "I make you a present of it."

Then he looked at my father and my mother, still more amazed, and asked, "But why so?"

My father said, "Enrico gives it to you because he is your friend, because he likes you, and in order to celebrate your medal."

Precossi timidly asked, "May I take it home with me?"

"Certainly," we all answered.

He was already near the door, but still did not dare to go. He was so happy! He was begging our pardon with trembling lips that smiled and laughed. Garrone helped him to wrap up the train in his handkerchief, and bending down, he made the things which he had in his pocket rattle.

"Some day," said Precossi to me, "you will come to the workshop to see my father at work. I will give you some nails."

My mother put a little posy in the buttonhole of Garrone's jacket for him to take to his mother in her name. Garrone told her, with his big voice, "Thanks," without lifting his chin from his breast. But his noble and good soul shone from his eyes.

PRIDE

Saturday the 11th.

Carlo Nobis cleans the sleeve of his coat affectedly when Precossi touches him when passing by! He is vanity incarnate, because his father is rich, but the father of Derossi is also rich! He would like to have a desk all by himself, he is afraid that every one who comes near will soil him, he looks down upon everybody, and always has a contemptuous smile upon his lips. Woe to him who stumbles over his feet when we go marching out two by two! For a mere trifle he flings an insulting word in your face, he threatens to send for his father to come to the school, and yet we know that his father gave him a severe lesson when he called the son of the charcoal man a ragged wretch! I have never seen so much pride. No one speaks to him, no one says good bye when he goes out. There is no one who will prompt him when he does not know his lesson. He likes nobody and feigns to despise Derossi above all because he is the brightest boy, and Garrone because he is the most beloved. But Derossi pays no attention to him, no more than if he were not there, and when the boys tell him that Nobis has abused him, he answers:

"He is so full of such stupid pride that he does not even deserve my blows."

One day, when he was smiling disdainfully at Coretti's cat-skin cap, the latter remarked:

"Go to Derossi and learn how to be a gentleman!"

Yesterday, he complained to the teacher because the Calabrian boy touched his leg with his foot. The teacher asked the Calabrian boy if he had done this purposely.

"No, sir," he answered frankly, and the teacher said:

"You are too fastidious, Nobis." And Nobis replied with that vain air of his:

"I shall tell my father."

Then the teacher grew angry: "Your father will tell you that you are wrong, as he has at other times, and that there is no one but the teacher who can judge and punish in the school." Then he added, pleasantly, "Come, Nobis, change your ways; be good and courteous toward your companions. You see the are sons of workmen and of gentlemen; sons of the rich and the poor. They are all fond of one another and treat one another like brothers, as they are. Why don't you act as the others do? It would cost you very little to be esteemed by all, and you would be so much better satisfied with yourself.

"Well, have you nothing to answer?" Nobis, who had been listening with that disdainful smile, answered coldly:

"No, sir."

"Sit down;" said the teacher, "I pity you. You are a boy without heart."

Everything seemed ended, when the "Little Mason," who sits on the first bench, turned his round face towards Nobis, who sits on the last bench, and made a hare face, so fine and funny, that the whole class burst into a shout of laughter. The teacher reprimanded him, but he was forced to put his hand over his mouth to conceal a smile, and Nobis also smiled but not pleasantly.

THE WOUNDS OF WORK

Monday the 13th.

Nobis can be matched with Franti. Neither of them were moved by the terrible sight which passed under our eyes this morning. Coming out of school with my father, I was looking at some big boys of the second class who had thrown themselves on their knees to wipe off the ice with their cloaks and caps in order to slide swiftly, when we saw coming down the street a crowd of people, walking rapidly, all looking serious and frightened, and speaking in low voices. Among them were three policemen, and following these, two men were carrying a litter. The boys approached from every side. The crowd advanced toward us. Upon the litter was stretched a man as white as a corpse, with his head hanging over upon one shoulder and his hair stained with blood; and blood was also flowing from his mouth and ears. Alongside the litter walked a woman with a babe in her arms, who acted like a lunatic and cried from time to time:

"He is dead! He is dead! He is dead!"

Behind the woman came a boy who had a satchel under his arm and was sobbing.

"What has happened?" asked my father.

A man near him answered: "It is a mason who has fallen from the fourth story while he was at work."

The men who carried the litter stopped a moment. Many turned their faces away in horror. I saw the little school mistress with the red feather supporting the mistress of the upper first who had almost fainted. In the meantime, somebody pushed me with his elbow, it was the "Little Mason," pale and trembling like a leaf. He was surely thinking of his father. I also thought of that. When I am in school my mind is at ease; I know that my father is at home, sitting at his desk, far from danger; yet, how many of my companions are thinking that their fathers are working on a very high scaffold or near the wheels of a machine; and that a motion, a false step may cause their death! They are like so many soldiers' children, whose fathers are in daily peril.

The "Little Mason" looked steadfastly and trembled more and more violently.

My father noticed it and said:

"Go home, boy, go and see your father, and you will find him well and happy; go!"

The "Little Mason" went, turning his head at every step. In the meantime, the crowd began to move again and the woman was screaming in a heart-rending way: "He is dead! He is dead! He is dead!"

"No, no, he is not dead," they were telling her on every side. But she paid no attention and tore her hair in despair. I heard an indignant voice saying: "You laugh!" and saw a whiskered man looking in the face of Franti, who was indeed smiling. Then the man knocked the boy's cap off, saying: "Uncover your head, you wicked boy, when a man who has been hurt through labor passes!" The crowd had already vanished and there was a long streak of blood in the middle of the street.

THE PRISONER

Friday the 17th.

Ah! this is indeed the strangest case of the whole year. Yesterday my father took me to the Moncalieri suburbs to examine a villa to let for the coming summer (because this year we will not go to Chieri), and we found that the man who had the keys is a teacher as well as the secretary of the landlord. He showed us the house and then he took us to his room, where he offered us something to drink. Upon the little table, between the glasses, was a wooden inkstand, conical in shape and carved in a peculiar way.

Observing that my father was looking at it, the teacher said: "That inkstand is very precious to me. Would you like to know the history of it, sir?" and he told it to us.

Years ago he was a teacher in Turin, and went every day during the winter to teach the prisoners in the district jail. He taught in the chapel of the jail, which is a round building. All around the high and bare walls are many little square windows with cross-bars of iron, each belonging to a little cell inside.

He was teaching the lesson, walking up and down in the cold dark chapel, and his pupils were peeping through those holes with their copy-books against the iron bars, their faces only showing in the shadow—frightful, frowning countenances, with grey and rough beards and staring eyes, the faces of thieves and murderers.

There was one among them, in cell No. 78, who was more attentive than the others and studied diligently. He looked at the teacher with eyes full of respect and gratitude. He was a young man with a black beard, and more unfortunate than wicked; a cabinet-maker, who, in a fit of rage at his master (who had wronged him many times) had thrown a plane at his master's head, mortally wounding him, and on that account had been condemned to several years of seclusion. In three months he had learned to read and write, and he read continually. The more he learned, it seemed, the better he became, and the more he repented of his crime.

One day, at the end of his lesson, he made the teacher a sign to come to the little window, announcing that the next morning he would leave Turin to go and expiate his crime in the prisons of Venice; while saying good-bye he begged him with a humble and moved voice to allow him to touch his hand. The teacher offered him his hand, which he kissed and said "Thanks! Thanks!" and disappeared. The teacher drew back his hand, it was wet with tears. Since that time he had never seen him.

Six years passed. "I was thinking of anything else rather than that unfortunate fellow," said the teacher, "when, the day before yesterday, an unknown man came to the house. He had a long black beard and was poorly clad. He asked me: 'Are you the signor master so and so?' Who are you? I asked of him. 'I am the prisoner of No. 78,' he answered. 'You taught me to read and write six years ago, do you remember? At the last lesson, you shook hands with me. Now, I have expiated my crime, and I am here begging you to kindly accept a remembrance of me, a little thing which I have worked at in prison; will you take it in memory of me, signor master?'

"I stood speechless. He thought that I would not accept it, and looked at me as if saying: 'Six years of suffering, are they not enough to cleanse my hands?' and he looked at me with an expression of such deep sorrow that I instantly stretched out my hand and took the object. Here it is."

We looked attentively at the ink-stand. It seemed as though it had been carved with the point of a nail by dint of assiduous patience. There was carved upon it a pen across a writing book, and written around it, "To my teacher.—Remembrance of number 78.—Six years!" And below this writing, "Study and hope."——The teacher said nothing more, and we left.

All the way home, from Moncalieri to Turin, I could not chase from my mind that prisoner, leaning on the little window, that farewell to the master, and that poor ink-stand carved in jail, which told such a tale. I dreamed of it all night, and was still thinking of it this morning.——But I was far from guessing the surprise which awaited me at school! Hardly had I gone to my new bench next to Derossi, and had written the problem in arithmetic for the monthly examination, when I told my companion all the history of the prisoner and about the ink-stand and how it was made with the pen across the copy-book and that inscription around it: "Six years!" Derossi sprang up at those words and began to look first at me and then at Crossi, the son of the vegetable woman, who sat in the front bench with his back turned toward us, all absorbed in his problem.

"Hush!" he said, then, softly taking me by the arm, "Don't you know it? Crossi told me the day before yesterday of his having caught a glimpse of such a wooden ink-stand in the hands of his father, who had returned from America. Instead, he was in prison. Crossi was so small at the time of the crime that he does not remember, and his mother deceived him. He knows nothing of it. Let not a syllable of this escape you!"

I stood there speechless, with my eyes staring at Crossi. Then Derossi solved his problem and passed it under the bench to Crossi and gave him a piece of paper, taking from his hand the monthly story, *Papa's Nurse*, which the teacher had given him to copy, in order to do the work for Crossi. He gave him some pens, patted his shoulder, and had me promise upon my honor that I would not say anything to anybody else, and when he left school he told me hurriedly :

"Yesterday his father came to take him home, he may be there to-day ; do as I do."

We came to the street ; Crossi's father was there, standing a little aside, a man with a black beard which was sprinkled with white, badly clad, with a pensive and discolored face. Derossi shook Crossi's hand in a way that all could see him, and said in a loud voice : " Till we meet again, Crossi," and passed his hand under his chin ; I did the same, but in doing it we both crimsoned, and the father of Crossi looked at us attentively with a benevolent look, but through it there shone an expression of uneasiness and suspicion which caused our hearts to grow cold.

PAPA'S NURSE

(MONTHLY STORY)

In the morning of a rainy day in March, a boy, dressed as a peasant all saturated with rain and mud, with a bundle under his arm, presented himself to the gate-keeper of the Pellegrini hospital in Naples, and handing him a letter of introduction, asked for his father. He had a beautiful oval face, dark and pallid, two pensive eyes, and two full lips, half open, showing his beautiful white teeth. He came from a village in the vicinity of Naples. His father, having left home the previous year to go and seek work in France, had returned to Naples, landing there a few days before this ; when, having suddenly been taken ill, he had hardly had time to write a line to his family, telling them that he would enter the hospital. His wife, in despair on account of the news, and not being able to leave the house because of her sick baby, had sent her oldest child, a lad, to Naples, with a few soldi to assist his *babbo*, as they say there. The boy had walked ten miles to reach the hospital.

The gate-keeper glanced at the letter, called a nurse, and told him to take the boy to his father.

"Whose father?" asked the nurse.

The boy, trembling for fear of sad news, gave his name.

The nurse could not remember any such name.

"An old workman coming from abroad?" he asked.

"Yes," said the boy, growing more anxious, "not so very old. Yes, yes, he came from abroad."

"And when did he enter the hospital?" asked the nurse.

The boy looked at the letter and said: "About five days ago, I think."

The nurse stood for a moment in thought; then suddenly remembering: "Ah," said he, "in the fourth ward, in the farthest bed."

"Is he very sick? How is he?" anxiously asked the lad.

The nurse looked at him for a moment without answering, then he said: "Come with me."

They ascended two stairways, walked to the end of the large corridor and came to the open door of a large ward with a row of beds on each side. "Come," repeated the nurse, entering. The boy took courage and followed him, glancing right and left with a frightened look over the white and emaciated faces of the sick, some of whom had their eyes closed and looked as though they were dead, while others seemed to be staring into the air as though frightened. A great many were moaning like children. The ward was dark and the air impregnated with the sharp odor of medicines. Two sisters of charity were walking around with phials in their hands.

Having arrived at the end of the ward, the nurse stopped at the head of the bed, drew the curtains aside and exclaimed: "Here is your father."

The boy burst into tears, and letting his bundle drop on the floor, put his head upon the shoulder of the sick man, grasping with his hand the arm which lay stretched outside the cover; but the sick man did not stir. The boy arose and looked at his father, and burst into tears again. Then the sick man turned his eyes upon him for a few moments and seemed to recognize him. But his lips did not move. "Poor *babbo*, how he has changed!" The child would not have recognized him. His hair had grown white, his beard was much longer, his face swollen and of a dark red color, his skin was stretched and shining, the eyes had grown smaller, the lips were swollen; he had not one familiar feature except the forehead and the arch of the eyebrows. He was breathing with difficulty.

"*Babbo!* Oh my *babbo!*" said the boy. "It is I. Do you not recognize me? I am Cicillo, your Cicillo, who came from home, sent by mamma. Look at me; do you not recognize me? Speak just one word."

But the sick man, after having looked at him attentively, closed his eyes.

"*Babbo! Babbo!* What is the matter? I am your son, your Cicillo!"

The sick man did not move and continued to breathe with difficulty.

Then the boy, weeping, took a chair and sat down, and remained waiting, without raising his eyes from his father's face. "The physician will soon pass on his visit," he thought. "He will tell me what is the matter." And he became buried in sad thoughts, recalling so many nice things about his good father: the day of his departure, when he had given his last farewell to the ship, the hopes which the family had founded on that trip, the desolation of his mother, and the arrival of that letter; and he thought of death; he saw his father dead, his mother dressed in black and the family in want. He remained some time over these thoughts. A light hand was laid on his shoulder. He started, it was a nun.

"What is the matter with my father?" he asked immediately.

"Is he your father?" asked the sister in a sweet and gentle voice.

"Yes, it is my father and I have come here to see him. What is the matter with him?

"Courage, my boy," replied the sister, "the physician will soon be here," and she left him without saying another word.

Half an hour later he heard the stroke of a bell and saw the physician entering at the further end of the ward, accompanied by an assistant, followed by a sister and a nurse. They began the visits, stopping at every bed. The time of waiting seemed an eternity to the lad. Every time the physician stopped, his anxiety grew stronger. At last they arrived at the neighboring bed. The physician was an old man, tall and round-shouldered, with a grave face. Before he left the nearest bed the lad arose, and when he approached him the boy began to weep.

The physician looked at him.

"It is the son of the sick man," said the sister, "he arrived this morning from his village."

The physician laid his hand upon the boy's shoulder, and then bent over the sick man, felt his pulse, touched his forehead and asked some questions of the sister, who answered: "Nothing new." He stood a moment in deep thought, then he said: "Continue the treatment as before."

The lad taking courage, asked in a sobbing voice: "What is the matter with my father?"

"Have courage, my child," answered the physician, replacing his hand on his shoulder. "He has erysipelas on his face. It is a very grave case, but there is still hope. Assist him. Your presence may do him much good."

"But he does not recognize me!" exclaimed the boy in a desolate tone.

"He may recognize you to-morrow, perhaps. Let us hope for the best and have courage."

The boy would have been glad to ask him more, but he dared not. The physician passed along to another patient. And then the lad began the work of nurse. Not being able to do anything else, he would fix the cover of the sick man, would touch his hand from time to time, would chase the flies which came near, would lean over him at every moan, and when the nun brought the father some beverage, the boy would take the glass and spoon from her hand and give it to him in her stead. At times the sick man looked at him but gave no sign of recognition. However, his gaze rested longer upon him than anything else, especially when he laid the handkerchief over his father's eyes. Thus the first day passed. During the night the boy slept upon two chairs in a corner of the ward, and in the morning he again took up his work of mercy. That day it seemed as if the eyes of the sick man revealed a faint trace of consciousness. At the caressing voice of the lad, it seemed as though a vague expression of gratitude shone for a moment in their depths, and once he moved his lips as though he wished to speak. After a short nap he reopened his eyes and seemed to be looking for his little nurse. The doctor, passing twice, thought he noticed a little improvement. Towards evening, reaching the glass to his father's lips, the boy thought he saw a very faint smile glide over his face. He began to take comfort and to hope. With the hope of being understood, at least confusedly, he talked to him for a long time, of mamma, of his two little sisters, of the return home, and exhorted him with warm and loving words, to take courage. Although doubting if he were understood, still he talked on, because it seemed to him that even if his father did not comprehend him, he would hear his voice with a certain pleasure, a tone of affection and sweetness being unusual in such a place. In this way the second day was passed. Then the third and the fourth, with alternating improvement and changes for the worse, and the lad was so absorbed in his cares that he scarcely ate even a bit of the bread and cheese which the sister brought him twice a day. He took little notice of what was happening around him; the nuns coming or going during the night, or the outbursts of despair, and he scarcely saw the sick and dying near him. He lived with his hope among all those scenes of hospital life, which on any other occasion would have amazed and grieved him. The hours, the days passed by, and he was all the time there with his *babbo*, anxious, agitated, watching his every breath and glance; without any rest to relieve his mind of a fear that froze his heart.

Suddenly, on the fifth day, the sick man began to grow worse.

The physician, upon being questioned, shook his head, as if he meant to say, "that is the end," and the lad flung himself on the chair and burst out sobbing. One thing, however, consoled him. In spite of the fact that the father grew worse, it seemed to him that the sick man was slowly regaining a slight consciousness. He looked at the boy more and more intelligently, and with a growing expression of sweetness; he did not want to take any portion of his medicine except from his hand, and renewed oftener his strenuous efforts to pronounce a word, and sometimes he did it so plainly that the child would grasp his arm firmly, as though inspired by a sudden hope. "Courage, courage, babbo, you will recover, and then we will go home to mamma; have a little more courage!"

It was four o'clock in the afternoon, and at that moment, the boy had abandoned himself to one of those outbursts of tenderness and hope, when, through the nearest door of the ward, a sound of steps was heard, and then a strong voice spoke two words only: "Farewell, sister," which made him jump to his feet with a repressed cry bursting from his throat!

In the meantime, a man entered the ward, with a large bundle in his hand, followed by a sister.

The boy uttered a sharp cry and stood there as if nailed to the floor.

The man turned around and looked at him a moment, then cried: "Ciccillo!" and darted towards him.

The lad fell into the arms of his father without being able to utter a word.

The sisters, the nurses, and the assistant physician, all ran toward them filled with astonishment.

The boy could not recover his voice.

"Oh, my Ciccillo!" exclaimed the father, after having cast an attentive look at the sick man, kissing the boy again and again. "Ciccillo, my child, how does it happen that you are here? Have they taken you to the bed of another man, while I was all the time in despair because I did not see you, for your mother wrote me that she had sent you to me. Poor Ciccillo! How many days have you been here, and how did this happen?

I have come out easily; I am well now! How is mamma? Concettella, and the baby, how are they? I am leaving the hospital, come with me. Oh, great God! who would have thought of this!"

The child tried hard to speak a few words, to give the family news. "I am so glad!" he murmured, "so glad. And what days I have passed here!" He did not stop kissing his father.

But still the boy did not move.

"Come along," said the father, "we can get home to-night. Let us go." And he drew the boy towards him.

The boy turned to look at the sick man.

"But — why don't you come?" asked the father, amazed.

The lad cast another glance at the sick man, who, at that moment, opened his eyes and stared at him; then from his soul poured out a flood of words. "No, *babbo*, —— wait —— behold, —— I cannot. There is that old man. I have been here five days. He looks at me all the time. I thought it was you. I loved him. He looks at me incessantly. I give him to drink and he wishes me to be near him. Now he is very low; have some patience. I have not the courage, I don't know why it is, but I cannot leave him; it would be too painful for me. I will return home to-morrow. Let me stay here a little longer; it is not right that I should leave him; look at the way he gazes at me. I do not know who he may be, but he wants me; he would die if left alone. Allow me to stay, dear *babbo!*"

"Good little fellow!" cried the assistant physician.

The father stood there in perplexity, looking first at the boy and then at the sick man. "Who is he?" he asked.

"A peasant, like yourself," answered the assistant, "who came from abroad and entered the hospital the same day you did. They brought him here in an unconscious state and he has not been able to say anything since. Perhaps he has a family, and sons far away. He may think that your boy is one of his sons."

The sick man was still staring at the boy.

The father said to Ciccillo, "Stay!"

"He will not have to stay much longer," whispered the assistant.

"Stay!" repeated the father; "you have a heart. I will go directly home to relieve mamma of her suspense and anxiety. Here is a *scudo* for your expenses. Good-bye, noble child of mine, till we meet again."

He embraced him, looked at him intently, kissed him again on the forehead and went away.

The lad returned to the bed of the patient, who seemed consoled. Ciccillo again commenced to act as nurse, no longer crying, but with the same eagerness and the same patience as before. He again gave the sick man something to drink, fixed his bed clothes, stroked his hand, and spoke to him sweetly, as if to give him courage. He attended him all day, all the next night and stood close to the bed the following day, but the sick man grew worse and worse continually. His face began to get blue, his breath was heavier, and his suffering became more intense. Some inarticulate cries escaped his lips; the inflammation was steadily increasing. In the evening, when the physician came to make his visit, he said that he would not live through the night. Then Ciccillo redoubled his vigilance, and did not take his eyes off from him for a moment. The sick man looked at him and moved his lips from time to time with a great effort as if to speak. An extraordinary expression would now and then gleam from his eyes, which were gradually growing smaller and dimmer. That night the lad watched him until he saw through the windows the first dawn of day, when a sister appeared. She approached the two, cast a glance at the sick man, and left with hurried steps. A few moments after, she returned with the assistant physician and a nurse, who carried a light.

"It is the last moment," said the physician.

The lad grasped the hand of the sick man. The latter opened his eyes, looked at him, and closed them forever.

In that last minute, it seemed to the boy as though he felt a pressure of his hand. "He has pressed my hand!" he exclaimed.

The physician stood for a moment bending over the sick man and then he rose to his feet. The sister took the crucifix from the wall. "He is dead," cried the boy.

"Good child," said the physician. "Your blessed work is over. Go. May fortune smile upon you as you deserve. God will protect you. Farewell!"

The sister, who had gone away for a moment, returned with a bouquet of violets taken from a glass on the window sill, and handed them to the boy, saying: "I have nothing else to give you. Take this in remembrance of the hospital."

"Thanks," said the boy, taking the bouquet with one hand and wiping his eyes with the other, "but I have so far to walk —— I would spoil it." And, unloosening the bouquet, he scattered the violets upon the bed, saying: "I leave them here in remembrance of the poor dead one. Thanks, sister. Thanks, signor doctor," then, turning to the dead: "Good-bye,"——, while he was trying to think of a name to call him, there came from his heart to his lips that sweet name by which he had called him for five days. "Good-bye, poor *babbo*."

Having said this, he put the little bundle of clothes under his arm and with slow and weary steps he went away. The day was just breaking.

THE WORKSHOP

Saturday the 18th.

Precossi called last evening to remind me that I was to go and see his workshop, which is farther down the street. When I went out with my father this morning, I asked to be taken there for a moment. As we approached the shop, Garoffi came running out with a package in his hand, and the cloak under which he conceals his merchandise was flying in the wind. Ah, now I know where he goes to get the iron filings which he trades for old newspapers, that trafficking Garoffi. Peeping in at the door of the shop, we saw Precossi seated on a pile of bricks, studying his lesson on his knees. He got up quickly and bade us enter. It was a large room filled with coal dust. The walls were covered with hammers, pincers, iron bars, and old pieces of iron of every shape. In a corner there was a fire burning in a fire-place, and a boy was blowing it with a pair of bellows. Precossi's father stood near the anvil, and another lad was holding an iron bar in the fire.

"Oh, here he is," said the blacksmith, taking off his cap. "Here is the boy who gives away railroad trains. You have come to see us work a little, have you not? You will be satisfied." As he said this he smiled. He no longer had that contorted face and those bleared eyes which he once had. The lad handed him a long red hot iron bar, which the blacksmith laid upon the anvil. He was making some curved pieces for railings of balconies. He lifted the heavy hammer and began to strike, pushing the red hot end one way and another, from the end of the anvil to the middle, turning it around in different ways. It was wonderful to see how the iron would bend and twist under those rapid and precise blows of the hammer, until by degrees he shaped it into the form of a beautiful leaf or flower, curled as if it might have been some dough which he moulded with his hand. In the meantime his son was looking at us with an air of pride, as if he wished to say, "Do you see how my father can work?"

"Have you seen how that is done, signori?" asked the blacksmith when he had finished, putting in front of us the iron piece which looked like a bishop's crozier. Then he took us to one side and stuck another iron into the fire.

"That is well done, indeed," said my father. "You are at work again now! The good will has come back."

"Yes, it has come back," answered the blacksmith, wiping the perspiration from his brow and blushing a little, "and do you know who caused it to return?" My father feigned not to understand.

"That brave boy," said the blacksmith, pointing at his son with his finger. "That brave boy there. He studied and was honoring his father, while his father was dissipating and treated him like a beast. When I saw that medal—ah! that little fellow of mine, who is scarcely as tall as a penny's worth of cheese! Come here, that I may look you straight in the face!"

The boy ran immediately to him. The smith took him and placed him on the anvil, holding him by the hand, saying: "Do clean the face of this beast of a father."

Precossi covered his father's black face with kisses until his own was also all black.

"That is the way," said the blacksmith, placing him back on the floor.

"That is the way, indeed, Precossi!" exclaimed my father joyfully, and saying good-bye to the blacksmith and his son, he took me away.

When I was going out, Precossi said to me: "Excuse me," and thrust a little package of nails into my pocket. I invited him to come to my house to see the carnival.

When we reached the street, my father said: "You have given him your railway train, but had it been made of gold and filled with pearls, it would have been a small present for that child, who has reformed the heart of his father."

THE LITTLE CLOWN

Monday the 20th.

The whole city is in an uproar over the carnival season, which is about to come to an end. They are putting up booths and mountebank tents in every square. There is a circus tent under our windows, where a small Venetian company gives performances with five horses. The circus is in the middle of the square and in the corner there are three large wagons, in which the mountebanks sleep and where they disguise themselves. Three small houses on wheels, with little windows and a chimney, always smoking, in each one. Some baby clothes are hanging between the small windows. There is a woman who nurses a baby, cooks, and dances on the rope. Poor people! One speaks the word of mountebank as though it were an insulting one; yet, they earn their bread honestly, amusing everybody, and how they work! They run all day between the circus and the wagons in this cold weather, dressed in tights. They eat two or three mouthfuls of bread and run here and there between the performances. Sometimes, when the circus is crowded, a wind rises which tears the canvas, puts out the lights, and the performance must close. Then they are obliged to return the money and work the whole evening putting the tent in shape again. They have two boys who perform tricks, and my father recognized the smallest one as he was crossing the square. He is the son of a circus master, the same one whom we saw play tricks on horseback last year in the piazza Vittorio Emanuele, but he has grown since then. He is barely eight years old, a fine looking lad with the pretty round face of a gamin, with black curls which come out from

under his conical shaped hat. He is dressed like a clown, wears a large bag-shaped suit with sleeves of white, embroidered with black, and linen shoes. He never keeps still. Everybody likes him. He does all sorts of tricks. In the morning, we see him wrapped up in a shawl, carrying milk to their wagon; then he goes to the stable in Bertola street and brings the horses. He holds a little baby in his arms, carries hoops, wooden horses, wooden bars, and ropes. He cleans the wagons, lights the fire, and when he rests he is always near his mother. My father watches him all the time from the window, and talks with him about his own people, who seem to be very good and to love their children.

One evening, we went to the circus. It was cold and there were but few persons in the audience, but the little clown did all he could to keep the small crowd merry. He would turn somersaults, grasp the tails of the horses, stand on his head, and sing, always smiling, with his pretty brown face. His father was dressed in a red coat, white trousers with top boots and a whip in his hand. It was really sad to see him watch his son. My father felt sorry for them and spoke about it the next day to the artist Delis, who came to visit us. "Those poor people kill themselves working so hard and still do so little business!" He liked the little boy so much, what could be done in their behalf! The artist had an idea:

"Write a beautiful article in the 'Gazette,'" he said, "you who write so well, you will tell of the wonderful performances of the little clown and I will draw his portrait for you. Everybody reads the 'Gazette,' and for once, at least, the people will rush to the circus."—So it was done. My father wrote a fine article, full of witticisms, telling all that we see from the window—enough to make the people eager to know and favor the little clown, and the artist sketched a little portrait, a very pretty and good likeness, which appeared in the Saturday evening 'Gazette.' And, behold, at the Sunday performance, a large crowd rushed to the circus. It had been announced "*Benefit performance for the Little Clown"*—"The Little Clown," as the 'Gazette' had called him. My father took me there into one of the first reserved seats. They had posted the 'Gazette' beside the entrance. The circus was crowded. Many of the spectators held the 'Gazette' in their hands and showed it to the little clown, who laughed and ran from one place to another, looking very happy. The master was also delighted. It is easy to imagine that no paper had ever paid him so much honor before, and the cash box was full. My father sat next to me. Among the spectators we saw some acquaintances of ours. Near the entrance where the horses came in, stood the teacher of gymnastics, the one who has been with Garibaldi. In the second row in front of us, the " Little Mason," with his small round face, was seated next to his father. As soon as he saw me he made the hare face. A little further ahead, I saw Garoffi, counting the spectators and figuring upon the point of his fingers how much the company had taken in. Poor Robetti, the one who saved the child from the omnibus, also sat in a reserved seat not very far from us. He was holding his crutches between his knees. At his side sat his father, the artillery captain, who laid a hand on his shoulder. The performance commenced.—The little clown performed some marvelous feats on horseback, on the trapeze, and on the rope, and every time that he jumped down, all clapped their hands, and many patted his curly locks. Then others of the company displayed their skill in various exercises on the rope. There were jugglers and bare-back riders dressed in clothes glittering with silver. But when the lad was not there, it seemed as though the people were bored. During the performance, I saw the teacher of gymnastics whisper in the ear of the circus master, who immediately cast a glance around the audience as though looking for some one; his eyes rested upon us. My father noticed it, understood all, and, in order not to be thanked, went away, saying to me:

"Stay, Enrico, I will wait for you outside."

The little clown, after having exchanged a few words with his father, gave one more performance, standing on the horse while he was galloping. He changed his clothes four times, appearing as a pilgrim, as a sailor, as a soldier and as an acrobat; and every time he passed near me, he looked at me. When he came down he began to make the tour of the circus with his clown hat in his hand, and all threw soldi and candies to him. I had two soldi ready, but when he was in front of me, instead of reaching out his hat, he pulled it back, looked at me, and passed on. I was mortified. Why should he have behaved like that?

The performance came to a close. The circus master thanked the people and every one got up and crowded toward the exit. I thought myself lost in the crowd, and was about to go out when some one touched my hand. I turned around, it was the little clown, with his beautiful round face and his black locks. He smiled at me, standing there with his hands filled with candies. Then I understood all.

"Will you accept these candies from the 'little clown'?" he asked. I took three or four of them, then he added:

"Take also a kiss."

"Give me two," I answered, and put out my face to him. He cleaned his powdered face with his sleeve, put his arms around my neck and pressed two kisses on my cheek, saying: "Take these, one for you and one for your father!"

THE LAST DAY OF CARNIVAL

Tuesday the 21st.

We witnessed a very sad scene to-day in the Corso, during the procession of the masks. Fortunately, it ended well; but a great misfortune might have happened. In the piazza San Carlo, which was all decorated with yellow, red and white festoons, a multitude of people were thronging, masks of every description were passing, gilded and decorated floats in the shape of pavilions, small theatres and boats, filled with harlequins, warriors, cooks, sailors and shepherds. There was such a confusion that one did not know where to look, and such a loud clash of trumpets, cymbals and hurrahs, that it was deafening. The people in masks on the floats were shouting and singing and addressing the people who were in the street and at the windows, and who answered at the top of their voices, and threw out oranges and confections. Above the carriages and above the throng, as far as the eye could reach, one could see little flags floating, helmets gleaming, plumes waving, and all those pasteboard hats moving; gigantic caps, enormously high hats, extravagant weapons, tambourines, castanets, and all sorts of bottles; it seemed as though the people had all gone crazy. When our carriage entered the piazza, a magnificent float was just in front of us. It was drawn by four horses covered with embroidered trappings, and upon the car, wreathed with artificial flowers, there stood fourteen or fifteen gentlemen, all masked as noblemen of the court of France, all shimmering in silk, wearing huge white wigs and plumed hats; each carried a little sword, and wore a tuft of ribbon and lace upon his breast, which made him look very handsome. They were all singing a French song and throwing sweets to the people, who clapped their hands shouting. Suddenly, upon our left, we saw a man lifting a little girl above the heads of the crowd. She was only five or six years old. The poor thing was crying desperately and moving her arms as if taken with convulsions. The man made his way toward the car of the signori; one of the gentlemen bent down, and the man said aloud:

"Take this child, she has lost her mother in the crowd. Hold her in your arms, her mother cannot be far away and she will see her; I do not see any better way."

The gentleman took the child in his arms; they all stopped singing; the child screamed and struggled; the gentleman took off his mask; the car moved slowly. In the meanwhile, as we were told later, at the other end of the square, a poor woman, almost crazed, was breaking her way through the throng with her elbows and shouting:

"Maria! Maria! Maria! I have lost my daughter! She has been stolen from me! They have suffocated my child!" She raved in this way for a quarter of an hour, going here and there, crushed by the crowd which prevented her from quickening her step. In the meantime, the gentleman on the car held the child pressed against the ribbons and lace on his breast, looking over the piazza and trying to quiet the poor creature, who, not knowing where she was, sobbed as though her heart would break. The gentleman was affected; it was evident that those cries reached his soul. All the others offered the child oranges and candies, but she refused everything, all the time becoming more and more frightened and convulsive.

"Look for the mother!" cried the gentleman to the crowd. "Try to find the mother!"

People turned to the right and left, but the mother was not to be found.

Finally, a few steps from the place where the via Roma enters the piazza, a woman was seen rushing towards the car. Ah!—I will never forget that sight!—She scarcely looked like a woman, her hair was disheveled, her face distorted, her garments torn; she rushed along with a rattle in her throat, and one could not tell whether it was of joy or of anguish, or even of rage, and she threw out her hands like two clasps to grasp her child. The car stopped:

"Here she is," said the gentleman, and having kissed her, he put her into the arms of her mother, who kissed her impetuously, but one of those little hands remained for a second between the hands of the gentleman, who pulled a gold ring with a large diamond setting from his finger, and with a rapid movement slipped it on the finger of the little girl:

"Take it," he said, "this will be your marriage dowry."

The mother stood there as if enchanted. The crowd loudly applauded. The gentleman put on his mask again, his companions began to sing, and the car started off slowly in the midst of a tumult of hand-clappings and hurrahs.

THE BLIND BOYS

Thursday the 24th.

Our teacher is very ill, and in his stead the principal sent the master of the fourth class, who was once a teacher in an institution for the blind. He is the oldest of all the teachers, and his hair is so white that it looks as though he wore a cotton wig. He talks in a peculiar manner, as if singing a melancholy song, but he is good and very intelligent. As soon as he entered the school, he noticed a boy who had one eye bandaged; he approached his bench and asked him what was the matter.

"Take good care of your eye, boy," he said, and then Derossi asked him:

"Is it true, signor master, that you have been a teacher of the blind?"

"Yes, for many years," he answered, and Derossi said softly:

"Please tell us something about it."

The teacher went to his desk and sat down.

Coretti said aloud:

"The institution for the blind is in the Via Nizza."

"You say blind,—blind," said the master, "as you would say sick or poor people, or I know not what. But do you thoroughly understand the meaning of that word? Think of it a moment. Blind! Never to see, never! Never to distinguish the day from the night, never to see the sky, nor the sun, nor even your own parents, nothing of all that surrounds us, nothing that we touch; to be sunk into perpetual darkness, like being buried in the bowels of the earth. Try to close your eyes for a few moments and think what it is to be obliged to remain thus forever. You will immediately be overwhelmed with agony and terror. It would seem to you impossible for one to endure it: that you would grieve, that you would go crazy, that you would die. Still —— poor boys ; when one enters an institute for the blind during the recreation hours for the first time, one would not think that they are so unfortunate as they really are; one will hear them playing the violin and flute, talking in a loud voice, laughing, going up and down the stairs with quick steps, and moving freely through the corridors and dormitories. One must observe them well. There are youths of sixteen and eighteen, robust and merry, who bear their blindness with a certain ease; but one understands, from a certain proud and resentful expression of the countenance, how much they must have suffered, before they became resigned to their misfortune. There are others with sweet and pallid faces, in which one can perceive so much resignation, but so sad that it is evident that they still mourn at times.—Ah! my children. Think that some of them have lost their eyesight in a few days, others have lost it after years of martyrdom, during which they endured many terrible surgical operations, and many are born into a night that never had any dawn for them; they entered the world as they would enter an immense tomb, and do not know how a human face looks. Imagine how much they must have suffered and how much they must still suffer when they think confusedly of the tremendous difference between themselves and those who can see, and they ask themselves,—'Why such a difference if we are not to blame?'

"I spent many years among them, and when I remember that class of unfortunates, all those eyes sealed forever, all those pupils without expression and without light, and then look at you boys—it seems impossible that you are not all happy. Think of it! There are about twenty-six thousand blind persons in Italy! Twenty-six thousand persons who do not see the light! Do you understand? An army so large that it would take hours for it to pass under our windows."

The teacher was silent. Not a breath was heard in the school. Derossi finally asked if it were true that the blind have a finer sense of feeling than we.

The teacher replied: "It is true. All the other senses are more acute in them; because having to replace the sense of sight by the use of the other faculties, they are better exercised in the blind than in those who can see. In the dormitories in the morning, one asks of the others: 'Is the sun out?' And the one who can dress the quickest runs into the court and waves his hands in the air to see if he can feel any perceptible warmth of the sun and then runs back to carry the news: 'Yes, the sun is out!' From the sound of the voice of a person they form an idea of his stature. We judge the soul of a man by the eye, they by the voice; they remember the intonations and accents of a voice for years. They can tell whether there are one or more persons in a room, even if only one talks and the others remain perfectly quiet. By their touch, whether a spoon is clean or not. The girls can distinguish whether the woolens are dyed or natural color. They go two by two through the streets. They can tell the different shops by the smell, even those from which we perceive no odor. They spin the top, and, by listening to its humming, they go straight to it and pick it up without any hesitation. They trundle the hoop, they play nine-pins, jump the rope, build small houses with stones, and pick violets as though able to see; they make mats and baskets, weaving together the straws of different colors quickly and correctly,— to such a degree is their sense of touch trained. The sense of feeling is their eye-sight. To guess the shape of things by feeling them is one of their greatest pleasures. It is affecting to see them when they are taken to the Industrial Museum, where they are allowed to touch anything they wish. They seize with eagerness upon the geometrical bodies, the models of houses, and the instruments. With what joy they rub, and feel, and turn over all those things in their hands, *to see* how they are made. They call that *seeing*."

Garoffi interrupted the teacher to ask him if it were true that the blind boys learn to reckon faster than others.

The teacher replied: "It is true. They learn to figure and to read. They have books made on purpose for them with raised characters. They pass their fingers over them, recognize the letters, and speak the word, and read rapidly. You ought to see how the poor fellows blush when they make a mistake. They also write without ink. They write upon a thick, hard paper with a metal point which makes a great many little hollows, grouped according to a special alphabet. These little punctures stand out in relief on the other side of the paper, so that by turning the sheet over and drawing their fingers across it, they are able to read what they have written as well as what other persons write, and thus they prepare compositions and write letters to one another. They write numbers in the same way and make calculations. They calculate mentally with incredible facility, not being diverted by the sight of things around them as we are. You ought to see how passionately fond they are of hearing some one read, how attentive they are, how well they remember everything, how they discuss subjects, the little ones as well, talking about history and language. Four or five of them sit together on the same bench, and, without turning around, the first converses with the third and the second with the fourth, aloud and all at the same time, without losing a single word, so acute and accurate is the ear! They attach a great deal more importance to the examinations than you, I assure you, and they love their teacher more than you do. They recognize the teacher by his odor as well as by his step. They can tell whether he is in good or bad humor; if he is well or not; simply by the sound of a single word. They want the teacher to touch them when he encourages and praises them, and they feel his hands and arms to express their gratitude. They like each other and are good companions. In times of recreation, they always separate into certain cliques. In the girls' school, for instance, they form groups according to the instrument which they play; the violinists, the pianists, and the flute players, and they will never separate. They seldom lose their affection for persons after having once become attached to them. They find great comfort in friendship. They judge correctly among themselves. They have a clear and profound conception of good and evil. No one becomes so enthusiastic as they when hearing of a generous deed or of a grand act."

Votini asked if they played well.

"They are passionately fond of music," answered the teacher. "The love of music is the joy of their life. Some blind children, when they first enter the institute, are apt to stand for three hours perfectly motionless, listening to the music. They learn music readily and play with a great deal of expression. When the teacher tells one of them that he has no talent for music, he is very sorrowful and begins to study desperately. Ah! If you could but hear the music there! If you could only see them when they play, with their heads thrown back, a smile on their lips, their faces aglow and quivering with emotion, listening in ecstasy to that harmony which pervades the obscurity that envelops them, you would then feel what a divine consolation there is in music! When the teacher tells one of them: You will become an artist, his face brightens and he is overjoyed. The one who is first in music, who succeeds better than the rest at the violin or the piano, is like a king among them; they love him; they venerate him. If there is a quarrel between two of them, they go to him. If two friends become estranged, he reconciles them. The little ones whom he teaches to play, regard him as a father. Before going to sleep they all go and bid him good night. They talk of music continually during the day and at night when they are in bed, almost all of them tired out with study and work and half asleep, still they discuss, in a low voice, operas, composers, instruments, and orchestras. Being deprived of the reading of the music lesson is a great punishment for them. They suffer so much from it, that we hardly ever had the courage to punish them in that way. What light is to our eyes, music is to their hearts."

Derossi asked if one could go and see them.

"Yes, any one can go," replied the master, "but you boys must not go there yet. You may go later when you are in a condition to understand the extent of their misfortune and are able to feel all the compassion which it merits. It is a sad sight, my boys! Sometimes, you see a boy there sitting against an open window, enjoying the fresh air with an immovable countenance, who seems to look at the green plain and the beautiful azure mountains which you see —— and to think that he sees nothing, that he will never see any of that grand beauty! At that moment, your soul is oppressed as though you had become blind.—There are those who are born blind, who, having never seen the world, do not regret anything because they have the image of nothing and these are less to be pitied. But there are boys who have been blind only a few months, who recall everything which they have lost, and, in addition to this, they suffer the grief of feeling their minds obscured, the loving image growing fainter and fainter until the image of the persons to whom they were attached the most dies out from their memory. One of these boys told me one day, with inexpressible sadness: 'I would like to recover my eye-sight again just for a moment, that I might see again my mother's face. I do not remember it any longer!' And when their mothers come to see them, they put their hands upon their faces, they touch them upon the foreheads and ears, to feel how they are made, and they can hardly persuade themselves that they cannot see them. They call them by name time after time, as if to beg of them to give them the power to see their mothers just for once. How many people leave that place crying, even hard-hearted men! When one goes there, it seems as though it were an exception that you are able to see, a privilege scarcely deserved, to see the people, the houses, the sky! There is not one of you, I am certain, who, coming out from that place, would not be disposed to deprive himself of a little of his own eye-sight, if by so doing he might bestow a gleam to those poor children, for whom the sun has no longer light nor the mother a face!"

THE SICK MASTER

Saturday the 25th.

When I came from school last night, I went to visit my master. He made himself sick by working too hard. Five hours of lessons during the day, then an hour of gymnastics, then two more hours of evening school; which means to sleep little, to eat by snatches, and to work breathlessly from morning till night. In this way he has ruined his health, so my mother says. My mother waited for me below at the big door and I went up alone. On the stairs I met Coatti, the teacher with the bushy black beard, who always frightens the boys but never punishes them. He looked at me with his large eyes, and spoke with a voice like a lion's, just for fun, but he did not laugh. I was still laughing when I rang the bell at my teacher's door on the fourth floor, but stopped instantly when the servant bade me enter a poor room, dimly lighted, where my teacher was lying. He lay upon a little iron bedstead. His beard was long. He placed his hand on his brow in order to see me better, and said in an affectionate voice:

"Oh! Enrico."

I approached the bed and he laid his hand on my shoulder and said:

"Good boy, you have done well to come and see your poor master. I am reduced to a bad state, as you see, my dear Enrico. And how is school getting on? What are your schoolmates doing? Everything goes well, does it not? And even without me? You can do without me very well; isn't that so? Without your old teacher?"

I was trying to say no, but he interrupted me.

"Come, come, I know that you do not dislike me," and he heaved a sigh.

I looked at some photographs that were hanging on the wall. "Do you see," he said, "those are boys, who through the last twenty years have given me their photographs. They were good boys. Those are my souvenirs. When I die, my last glance will be given to them; my last thought will be of those boys among whom I have passed my life. Will you not also give me your picture when you are through the elementary course?" Then he took an orange from his stand and put it into my hand.

"I have nothing else to give you," he said, "it is the present of a sick man."

I looked at him, and my whole heart felt sad.

"You must take care," continued the teacher, "I expect to get out of this, but if I never should—— try to become stronger in arithmetic; it is your weak point; make an effort; as sometimes it is not the lack of aptitude but merely the absence of a fixed purpose, of stability, as one might call it."

While he was saying this, he breathed with difficulty, and I saw that he suffered. "I have an ugly fever," he sighed, "I am about gone. I beseech you then, apply yourself to the arithmetical problems. If one does not succeed the first time, he must rest awhile and then try it again; and then, if he does not succeed, after a little rest, he must try once more. Go ahead quietly, without tiring yourself, and without getting excited. Go. Give my regards to your mother, and do not mount these stairs again, we will meet in the school room soon. If we should not meet, think sometimes of your teacher of the third class, who has loved you so much."

I felt like crying when I heard those words.

"Bend your head down to me," he said.

I bent my head over his pillow and he kissed me on my hair. Then he said "Go," and turned his face to the wall.

I flew down stairs in a hurry, as I was anxious to embrace my mother.

THE STREET

Saturday the 25th.

I was watching thee from the window this evening when thou wert returning home from thy visit to thy teacher, and I saw thee push a woman. Pay a little more attention and see how thou dost walk in the street; there are duties to be fulfilled even there. If thou measurest thy steps and gestures in a private house, why shouldst thou not do the same in the street which is the abode of every one. Remember, Enrico, if thou shouldst at any time meet a feeble old woman, a poor woman with a babe in her arms, a cripple with his crutches, a man bending beneath a load, a family dressed in mourning, make way for them respectfully. We must respect old age, misery, maternal love, infirmity, fatigue, and death. Whenever thou seest a person about to be run over by a carriage; if a child, pull him away; if it is a man, make him aware of his danger. Always ask what is the matter with the child who is alone and weeping. Pick up the cane of an old man who accidentally drops it. If two boys fight, separate them; if it is two men, move away; do not look at a performance of brutal violence which offends and hardens the heart. When thou seest a man hand-cuffed between two policemen, do not add thy curiosity to the cruel one of the crowd; he may be innocent. When thou meetest a hospital litter, stop smiling and talking to thy companion; perhaps it may be carrying a dying man; perhaps it may be a funeral procession, one as might come out from thine own house on the morrow. Look with respect at all those boys who come from the different asylums, walking two by two; to the deaf and dumb, to those afflicted with the rickets, to the orphans, to the foundlings. Think that it is a human misfortune and an object of pity passing.

Always pretend not to see a person who has a strange or repulsive deformity. Extinguish the lighted match that thou wilt find at thy feet, which might cause some one to lose his life. Always answer with kindness the stranger who asks thee to point out the way. Never laugh in any one's face, never run without necessity, and do not shout. Respect the street. The degree of education of a person is judged more by the way he behaves in the street than by anything else. A person who will offend in the street will offend in the home. Study the streets. Study the city where thou livest; and, if to-morrow thou wert carried far away, thou wouldst be glad to have it present in thy memory, to be able to rehearse it in thy thoughts; thy city; thy little home, that which has been for so many years thy little world, where thou hast taken thy first steps beside thy mother, experienced thy first emotions, opened thy mind to the first ideas, and where thou hast found thy first friends. It has been a mother to thee. It has educated thee. It has inspired thee with noble sentiments, and protected thee. Study its streets, its inhabitants, and love it; and, if thou shouldst hear it insulted, defend it.

Thy Father.

MARCH

THE EVENING SCHOOLS

Thursday the 2nd.

Last night my father took me to visit the evening school in our Baretti school-house, which was all lighted up, and the workingmen were entering when we arrived. We found the principal and the teachers very angry because a short time before, a pane of glass had been broken out of a window with a stone. The janitor, rushing out, had caught a boy who was passing, but Stardi, who lives opposite the school, had appeared and said:

"It is not he. I saw who did it with my own eyes; it was Franti who threw the stone; and he said to me: 'be careful not to tell on me!' but I am not afraid."

The principal said that Franti would be expelled forever. In the meantime, I was watching the workmen who were entering two or three together. More than two hundred had already entered. I had never seen how beautiful the evening school is. There were boys from twelve years old up, and whiskered men who came back from work carrying books; there were carpenters, firemen with black faces, masons with their hands white with lime, bakers with their hair all powdered, you could smell varnish, hides, beeswax, oil, and odors from all kinds of trades. A squad of artillerymen entered, in their uniforms and led by a corporal. They went quietly to their benches, removed the board underneath upon which we put our feet, bent their heads and commenced work immediately.

Some of them went to the teacher and asked explanations concerning the lesson. I saw the young, well-dressed teacher, "The Little Lawyer," surrounded by three or four workmen at the desk, making some corrections with his pen. I saw a lame boy who lives with a dyer. He had a book all stained with red and blue dyes. My teacher has recovered and he was there, too. Tomorrow, he will return to school. The doors of the class rooms were all open. When they commenced the lessons, I was surprised to see how attentive they all were, with their eyes fixed on their books. The principal said that the greater number, in order not to be late, had not even stopped at home to eat a mouthful of supper and were hungry. After a half hour of school, some of the younger ones could scarcely keep awake; some of them would fall asleep with their heads on the desk, and the teacher would waken them by tickling their ears with a pen holder. The older ones kept awake and sat with their mouths wide open, listening to the lessons without even winking. It seemed strange to see all those bearded men in our benches. We went to the upper floor, and I ran to the door of my class room and saw at my place a man with a large mustache who had his hand bandaged; perhaps he had hurt himself in working around some machinery, and still he tried to write.

What pleased me most was to see in the place of the Little Mason, right on the same bench and in the very same corner, his father as big as a giant, who sat there all curled up in such a narrow space, with his chin on his fist and his eyes on the book, so intent upon his lesson that he hardly breathed, and he was not there by chance. The first night he came to school he said to the principal:

"Signor principal, do me the favor of putting me in the same place that my 'hare face' has." He always speaks of his son in that way.

My father kept me there until the close, and when we came out, we saw on the street many women with babes in their arms waiting for their husbands, and they would take the books from the men and the men carried the children, and all went home in that way. For a moment the street was filled with people and noise, then all was silent, and we saw only the tall and weary figure of the principal who was going home.

THE FIGHT

Sunday the 5th.

It was what might have been expected. Franti, having been expelled from the school by the principal, wanted to avenge himself, and he waited for Stardi at the corner of the street after school was over. When he was going by with his sister—for whom he calls every day at an institute in via Dora Grossa—Franti challenged him. My sister Silvia, coming from her school, saw it all, and came home thoroughly frightened. This was what happened: Franti, with his cap of wax-cloth drawn over his ears, ran on tip-toe behind Stardi and pulled his sister's braid of hair, giving it such a strong pull that he almost threw her on the ground. The little girl uttered a cry and Stardi turned around. Franti, who is very much taller and stronger than Stardi, thought:

"He will not utter a word; or, if he does, I will break his bones."

But Stardi did not stop to reflect, and, small and thick-set as he is, he jumped upon that big fellow and began to beat him with his fists. However, he could not hold his own and was receiving more than he gave. There was no one but girls in the street, and they could not separate them. Franti threw him on the ground, but he got up instantly, and then down he went again on his back, and Franti pounded away as though he were striking a door; in a moment he tore off half of his ear, bruised one eye and made his nose bleed. But Stardi was tenacious and roared:

"You may kill me, but I will make you pay dear for it!" And Franti was down again, kicking and cuffing, and Stardi from under was butting him with his head and striking him with his heels. A woman cried from the window: "Bravo, little fellow!" Others were saying: "It is a brother who defends his sister." "Courage!" "Beat him hard!" And they all shouted to Franti: "You coward; you overbearing brute!" But Franti was growing more and more ferocious, and holding out his leg he caused Stardi to fall and was on top of him again.

"Surrender!" "No!" "Surrender!" "No!" In a flash Stardi was on his feet; he grabbed Franti by the vest and with a furious blow hurled him upon the pavement and fell with his knee upon his chest. "Ah! the infamous fellow! he has a knife!" cried a man, running to disarm Franti. But Stardi was beside himself with rage and grasped Franti's arm with both hands, biting his fist so hard that Franti dropped the knife. His hand was bleeding. Several more people had come up by this time, who separated them and put them on their feet again. Franti ran away in a sorry plight, and Stardi stood there with his face all scratched, with a black eye, but the victor.

His sister was still crying and some of the girls were picking up the books and copy-books which were scattered in the street. They were saying all around: "Bravo! little fellow, "who has defended his sister." But Stardi was thinking more of his satchel than of his victory, and immediately began to examine the books one by one to see if there was anything missing or spoiled. He cleaned the books with his sleeve, looked at the pen, put everything back in its place, and then as quiet and serious as ever, said to his sister: "Let us go, as I have a composition to write and four problems to solve."

THE BOYS' RELATIVES

Monday the 6th.

This morning Stardi's father, a big, tall fellow, was waiting for his son, fearing that he might meet Franti again; but they say Franti will not trouble us any more, as they are going to put him in the reform school. Many of the parents were there this morning. Among them was the wood-huckster, the father of Coretti, whose son is a perfect image of him—quick, jolly, with a tiny mustache brought to a point, and two colors of ribbon in the buttonhole of his jacket. I know the relatives of nearly all the boys from seeing them when they call for them. There is a grandmother, bowed down, who wears a white cap, and no matter if it rains or snows, she calls four times a day to take to and from school her little grandson who belongs to the upper primary. She takes off his coat, fixes his necktie, brushes him, polishes him up, and looks at his copy-books; one can see that she has no other thought, that she sees nothing in this world that is nicer than he. The artillery captain comes often, the father of Robetti, the boy who walks on crutches and who saved the child from under the omnibus, and as all the companions of his son as they pass salute him, he returns the compliment to every one, and never forgets any one. He bends down over each boy, and no matter if they are poor and badly dressed, he only seems the more pleased and is always ready to thank them.

At times we see some very sad things. One gentleman did not come for a whole month, as his son had died, and he sent a maid-servant for the other. Returning yesterday and seeing the classmates of his little dead son, he went into a corner and broke down sobbing, putting his hands over his face. The principal took him by the arm and led him into his office.

There are fathers and mothers who know by name all the companions of their children. There are some girls of the neighboring schools, and some High School pupils who call for their younger brothers. There is an old gentleman, who was a colonel, who, when he sees a boy drop a pen or a book in the middle of the street, picks it up for him. One can also see nicely dressed ladies who talk about school matters with other women who wear handkerchiefs on their heads and carry baskets on their arms and who say:

"It was a very difficult problem this time!" "That grammar lesson will never come to an end this morning!"

If any of the boys in the class are sick, they all know it; when he gets better, they all rejoice. This morning, there were eight or ten gentlemen, ladies, and working women around Crossi's mother, the vegetable vender, to inquire about the poor boy of my brother's class who lives in her court, and who is very low. It seems that a school makes everybody friends and equals.

NUMBER 78.

Wednesday the 8th.

Last evening, I witnessed a very touching scene. For some time, whenever the vegetable woman passed by Derossi she would look at him with an expression of great affection; as Derossi, after having found out about the ink-stand and the prisoner of number 78, has fallen very much in love with her son Crossi, the little fellow with the red hair and the withered arm, and helps him to do his work at school, prompts his answers, gives him paper, pens, and pencils; in short, treats him like a brother, as though to compensate him for his father's misfortune, which he understands perfectly well.

The vegetable vender had been gazing at Derossi for several days and seemed loth to take her eyes from him. She is a good woman and lives only for her boy, and Derossi, who assists him to recite his lessons well, Derossi, who is a little gentleman and the first of the school, seems to her like a king or a saint. For several days she has gazed at him all the time and acted as though she wished to tell him something but felt ashamed. Yesterday morning, she at last took courage and stopped him in front of the big door, saying:

"Please excuse me, little master, you who are so good and who like my son so well, do me the kindness to accept this little souvenir from a poor woman," and she pulled from her vegetable basket a white and gold pasteboard box.

Derossi blushed to the roots of his hair and refused it, saying resolutely: "Give it to your son, I will not accept anything."

The woman looked mortified and begged his pardon, stammering: "I did not mean to offend you. They are nothing but caramels."

But Derossi said "No" again, shaking his head.

Then the woman drew from her basket a little bunch of

radishes and said timidly: "At least accept these, they are fresh; you may take them to your mother."

Derossi smiled and said: "No, thanks, I do not wish anything. I shall always do all I can for Crossi. I cannot accept anything, but I thank you just the same."

"But you are not offended?" anxiously asked the woman.

Derossi said no twice, smiling, and left her; while she exclaimed with delight:

"Oh, what a good boy! I have never before seen such a nice boy as he is!"

That appeared to be the end of it; but, behold, at four o'clock in the forenoon, instead of the mother of Crossi, his father appears, with his white and melancholy face. He stopped Derossi and from the way he looked at him, I immediately surmised that he suspected Derossi knew his secret.

He looked him straight in the eye and said, in a sad and touching voice:

"You like my son. Why do you like him so well?"

Derossi's face grew as red as fire. He would have liked to answer: "I love him because he has been so afflicted, also because you, his father, have been more unfortunate than guilty, and have nobly expiated your crime, and are a man of heart."

But he lacked the courage to say it; because, at the bottom

of his heart he still felt fear and almost loathing in the presence of this man who had spilled the blood of another and who had spent six years in a prison.

The man guessed everything, and, lowering his voice, he said in Derossi's ear, while trembling:

"If you love my child, you do not dislike me.—You do not despise the father, do you?"

"No! no! on the contrary," exclaimed Derossi with a soulful impulse.

Then the man made an impetuous movement as though he wished to put his arm around Derossi's neck, but he dared not, and instead he took one of his golden curls and smoothed it between two of his fingers. Releasing it, he placed his hand upon his mouth and kissed the palm of it, looking at Derossi with wet eyes as if to make him understand that the kiss was meant for him. He then took his son by the hand and went away with hurried steps.

THE LITTLE DEAD BOY

Monday the 13th.

The classmate of my brother, who belongs to the upper first, and who lives in the court-yard of the vegetable vender, is dead. Mistress Delcati, all sorrowful, came, Saturday afternoon, to inform the master of his death; Garrone and Coretti immediately offered their services to carry the coffin. The dead child was a nice little boy. He earned the medal last week. He loved my brother and had given him a broken money box. My mother always patted him when she met him. He wore a cap with two bands of red ribbon on it. His father is porter at a railway station.

Last evening, which was Sunday, we called at the house to go with the body from there to the church. We remained on the ground floor. The court-yard was filled with boys of the upper-first, with their mothers, and they were holding candles. Five or six teachers and some of the neighbors were also there. The teacher who wears the red feather and Mistress Delcati had gone into the house, and we could see through a window that they were crying, and we could hear the mother of the child sobbing very loud. Two ladies, both mothers of two schoolmates of the dead boy, had brought two wreaths of flowers.

We started out at five o'clock sharp. A boy carrying a cross was at the head of the procession, then a priest; after the priest, the coffin—a very small one, poor child—covered with black cloth upon which were laid the two wreaths of flowers presented by the ladies. The medal and the honorary mention, which the boy had earned during the year, were fastened to the black cloth on the side of the coffin. Garrone and Coretti with two other boys of the court were carrying the bier. Behind the coffin, first of all, came Mistress Delcati, who wept as though the little boy had been her own child; behind her, the other teachers; and behind the teachers the boys, some of the smallest of whom were carrying bouquets of violets in one hand, looking at the bier as if stupefied, their other hand clinging to their mothers, who carried the candles for them. I heard one of them ask: "And will he never go to school again?"

When the coffin was carried out of the court, a heart-rending cry was heard from the window. It was the mother of the child, but they soon persuaded her to go back to her rooms. When we reached the street, we met the pupils of a boarding school, passing in a double row, and, seeing the bier with the medal and the school mistresses, they all took off their caps. Poor fellow! He went to sleep forever with his medal. We shall never again see him with his red cap. He was in his usual health, and yet in a few days he died. The last day, he made an effort to sit up and work at his lesson in word-lists, and wished to have his medal on the bed, fearing some one might take it from him. No one will ever take it from you, poor child. Farewell! Farewell! We shall always remember you at the Baretti school. Sleep in peace, little boy.

THE DAY BEFORE THE 14TH OF MARCH

This day has been a merrier one than yesterday. It is the thirteenth of March! The eve of the distribution of the prizes to take place at the theatre Vittorio Emanuele, the grand and beautiful feast of every year. This time the boys who have to go on the stand and distribute the prizes as they are presented, are not picked up at haphazard. The principal came into the school room this morning, after the class was over, and said:

"I have good news for you, boys." Then he called "Coraci!" the Calabrian boy.

The Calabrian boy stood up. "Will you be one of those who carry the prize certificates to the authorities in the theatre to-morrow?"

"Yes," the Calabrian boy replied.

"Very well," said the principal, "then there will also be a representative of Calabria, and it will be a fine thing. The municipality has wished this year that the ten or twelve boys who hand the prizes should be boys from all parts of Italy, chosen from the different public schools. We have twenty public schools and five annexes, seven thousand pupils in all. Among such a large number, it was not difficult to find boys belonging to the different regions of Italy. Two representatives of the Islands, a Sardinian and a Sicilian, were found in the Torquato Tasso school house. The Boncompagni school furnishes a little Florentine, the son of a wood carver. There is a Roman born in Rome from the Tommaseo school. There are Venetians, Lombards, natives of Romagna, a Neapolitan from the Monviso school, the son of an army officer. Our school furnishes a Calabrian, you, Coraci, and a Genoese, and including the

Piedmontese, that will make twelve. It will be very nice, don't you think so? Your brothers from all parts of Italy will be there. When the twelve appear together on the stage, you must receive them with a roar of applause. They are only boys, but they represent the country as if they were men. A small tri-colored flag is as much an emblem of Italy as a large banner, is it not true? Applaud them very warmly; show that your little hearts are all aglow and that the soul of a ten year old boy grows enthusiastic in the presence of the holy image of your country." Having said that, he left.

The teacher, smiling, said: "Well, Coraci, you are the deputy of Calabria," and we all clapped our hands and laughed.

When we reached the street, they surrounded Coraci; some of them took him by his legs, lifted him up, and carried him in triumph, shouting: "Hurrah for the deputy of Calabria!" in order to make a noise, of course, not to make fun of him, but rather to honor him with all our hearts, as he is a boy whom everybody likes; and he smiled. They carried him thus to the corner of the street, where they ran across a gentleman with a black beard, who began to laugh. The Calabrian boy said: "That is my father." And then the boys placed his son in his arms and scampered away in all directions.

THE DISTRIBUTION OF PRIZES

March the 14th.

At two o'clock in the afternoon, the theatre was crowded, jammed full, with thousands of boys, ladies, teachers, workmen, women of the people, and little children. There was a flutter of feathers, a moving of hats, ribbons, and curls. A loud and merry murmur was heard from every side. The theatre was decorated with festoons of red, white, and green cloth. They had built two little staircases from the stage down to the parquet: one on the right, for those who ascended upon it; the other one to the left, by which they were to come down after they had received the prizes. A row of red arm chairs were placed on the front of the platform, and on the back of one of the chairs hung a laurel wreath. At the back of the platform was a trophy of flags, and on one side a green table, upon which lay all the prize certificates, tied up in tri-colored ribbons. The band stood in the parquet under the stage. The teachers and the mistresses filled one-half of the first gallery, which had been reserved for them. The seats and aisles of the pit, were crammed with boys who were to sing, and they were holding their music in their hands. In the background and all around, one could see teachers and mistresses placing in due order those who were to receive prizes; and their parents were giving a last touch to their hair and a last pull to their neckties.

As soon as I entered a side box with my parents, I noticed in the box in front of us the teacher who wears a red feather, who laughed, showing the beautiful dimples in her cheeks, and in her company was my brother's teacher, and also the "Little Nun," all dressed in black; also with them was my good teacher of the first upper, who looked so pale, poor woman, coughing so hard that she could be heard from one side of the theatre to the other. In the pit, I immediately saw that dear big face of Garrone and the little blonde head of Nelli, who was clinging close to his shoulder. A little further ahead, I saw Garoffi, with his nose like an owl's beak, who was making a great effort to collect the printed lists of those who had won the prizes; he had already gathered a large pile which he put to some use in bartering—as we will find out to-morrow. Next to the door was the wood huckster with his wife, both in their Sunday clothes, with their boy who was to receive the third prize of the second class. I was astonished to see him without the cat-skin cap and the chocolate colored jacket; this time he was dressed like a little gentleman. I saw for a moment, in one of the galleries, Votini with a large lace collar, and then he disappeared. In a proscenium-box, jammed with people, there was the artillery captain, the father of Robetti, the boy who walks on crutches and who saved the child from under the omnibus.

At the stroke of two, the band began to play and at that moment the mayor, the prefect, the judge, the state-attorney, and many other gentlemen, all dressed in black, ascended the stairway on the left and seated themselves in large arm-chairs on the front of the platform. The band stopped playing, the director of the singing school came to the front with a baton in his hand. At a signal from him all the boys in the pit arose, and, obeying another signal, they commenced to sing. There were seven hundred who sang a most beautiful song! Seven hundred voices of boys who sang together — how beautiful it was! The people were all silent, listening to that sweet song, a limpid and gentle melody like a church chant. When the song was ended, they all applauded, and then the organ was silent again. The distribution of prizes was about to commence. The little teacher of the second class, with his red head and bright eyes, had already come to the front of the stage, as he had to read the names of those who were to receive prices. He awaited the entrance of the twelve boys who were to hand over the certificates. The newspapers had already announced that there would be boys from all the provinces of Italy. They all knew it, and expected them, looking eagerly toward the side from which they would enter. The mayor, the other gentlemen on the stage, the whole theatre was silent. Suddenly, the twelve came running upon the stage and stood in line, smiling. The whole audience — three thousand persons — sprang to their feet at once, breaking into an uproar which seemed like a roar of thunder. The boys were for a moment dumfounded.

"Behold Italy!" said a voice from a box. I recognized Coraci, the Calabrian boy, dressed in black as he usually is. A gentleman of the municipality was with us who knew them all and was pointing them out to my mother: " The little blonde is a representative of Venice. The Roman boy is that tall lad with the curly hair." There were two or three dressed like the sons of well-to-do people; the others were sons of workmen; but all were of good appearance and clean. The Florentine boy, who was the smallest of all, had a blue sash around his waist. They all filed in line in front of the mayor, who kissed them on the forehead one after another, while the gentleman nearest to him was telling him the names of the cities which each one represented: " Florence, Naples, Bologna, Palermo——" And as every one passed, the audience would clap their hands. They all moved toward the green table to take up the certificates, and the teacher began to read the list, calling out the different schools, the classes and names, and those who received the prizes began to go up, passing in line.

Hardly had the first one ascended, when from behind the scenes a very soft music of violins was heard, which continued during all the time they were passing; a gentle air, which resembled the murmur of many soft voices; the voices of all the mothers, of all the teachers and mistresses, as if they were giving advice, begging, or administering loving reproofs all together. In the meantime, those who received the prizes were passing one after another in front of those gentlemen sitting there, who handed them the certificates, whispering to each one a sweet word or bestowing a kind caress. The boys from the pit and from the galleries applauded every time that a very small lad passed, or one dressed like a poor boy, or those who had an abundance of blonde curls and who wore red and white garments. Some of the boys from the upper first would get confused in passing and did not know which way to turn, and the whole house laughed. One passed by, who was not more than two spans high, with a large bow of red silk ribbon on his back; he could hardly walk and stumbled upon the carpet and fell; the prefect put him on his feet again, and they all laughed and clapped their hands. Another lad stumbled in going down the stairway into the pit. Some people shouted, but he was not hurt. All sorts of boys passed; some with roguish faces, some with faces as red as cherries, some very small and cunning ones, who laughed in the face of everybody and as soon as they came down into the pit, were taken away by their fathers and mothers. When it came the turn of our school, I was very much amused. Many passed by that I knew; Coretti, newly dressed from head to foot, with that beautiful merry smile of his showing all his white teeth. Who knows how many myriagrams of wood he had carried that morning? When the mayor handed him his certificate, he asked him the meaning of the red mark which he had on his forehead, and in doing so laid one hand on his shoulder. I looked around in the pit and noticed his father and mother. They were laughing, covering their mouths with their hands. Then Derossi passed by, all dressed in blue with shining buttons, with his golden curls, holding his head high, so handsome, so sympathetic, that I wished to throw him a kiss, while all those gentlemen wanted to speak and shake hands with him. The teacher cried out: "Giulio Robetti!" And the son of the artillery captain was seen coming on his crutches. Hundreds of boys knew of the occurrence and the news was scattered around in a moment; a tempest of applause broke out which made the theatre tremble; the men rose to their feet, the ladies began to wave their handkerchiefs, and the poor boy halted in the middle of the stage, astounded and trembling. The mayor drew him to his side, gave him the prize and kissed him, and taking the laurel wreath from the large chair, he placed it on the bar of one of his crutches. Then he escorted him as far as the proscenium-box, where his father was seated, and the latter lifted him bodily and placed him inside, in the midst of an indescribable shouting of "Bravo! Hurrah!" During all this time, the soft, gentle music of the violins continued to fill the ear, and the boys were still passing; those of the Consolata, almost all sons of workmen; those of the Boncompagni, of whom many were farmers' boys; those of the Rayneri school, who were the last of all to pass.

As soon as it was over, the seven hundred boys in the pit sang another most beautiful song. Then the mayor spoke, and after him the judge, who terminated his speech by saying to the boys:

"But do not leave this place without giving a salute to those who toil hard for you and who have consecrated to you all their power, all their intelligence, all their heart, who live and die for you. There they are!" and he pointed to the gallery where the teachers were; and from the galleries, from the boxes, from the pit, all the boys arose and extended their arms toward the teachers and mistresses, who answered by waving their hands, hats and handkerchiefs, all standing, with a feeling of deepest emotion in their hearts. After this, the band played again and the audience sent a last noisy salute to the twelve boys from all the provinces of Italy, who presented themselves at the proscenium in line with their hands interlaced and under a shower of bouquets!

A QUARREL

Monday the 20th.

It was not on account of envy because he had won the first prize and not myself, that I quarreled with Coretti this morning. No, it was not on account of envy; still I was in the wrong. The teacher had placed him next to me; I was writing upon my copy-book and he pushed me with his elbow and caused me to make a blot and spoil the monthly story, "*Blood of Romagna,*" which I had to copy for the "Little Mason" who is sick. I got angry and said a rude word to him.

He smilingly answered: "I did not do it purposely."

I ought to have believed him, for I know him; but he vexed me because he smiled, and I thought: "Oh, now that he has had the first prize, he has grown proud." And, soon after, to avenge myself, I gave him a push which spoiled a whole page.

He reddened with anger and said to me: "You did that purposely," and lifted up his hand.

The teacher saw him and he put it down again, but he added: "I will wait for you outside!"

I felt ill at ease; my anger cooled off and I repented. No, Coretti could not have done it purposely; he is good, I thought. I remember when I saw him at his home, how he worked and how he assisted his sick mother, and then how warmly I had welcomed him at my home, and how well my father had liked him. How much I would have given if I had not said that rude word, if I had not insulted him! The advice which my father had given me came to my mind.

"Are you in the wrong?" "Yes." "Then ask his pardon."

But this I did not dare to do. I was afraid to humiliate myself. I looked at him from the corner of my eye; I saw his coat was ripped on the shoulder, perhaps because he had carried too much wood. I felt that I liked him, and I said to myself: "Courage!" but the words, "I beg your pardon," stuck in my throat.

He looked at me askance from time to time and seemed to be more worried than angry. But then I also looked at him disdainfully, to show him that I was not afraid.

He repeated: "We will meet outside!" and I, "We will meet outside!" But I was thinking of what my father had told me once: "If thou art wrong, defend thyself, but do not strike!"

And I said to myself: " I will defend myself, but I will not strike."

However, I felt discontented and sad. I could no longer listen to the teacher.

At last the school closed. When I was in the street alone,

I saw that Coretti was following me. I halted and stood still, awaiting him with my ruler in my hand.

He approached me, I raised the ruler. No, Enrico," said he, with his kind smile, putting aside the ruler with his hand, "let us be friends again as before."

I was stupified for a moment, then I felt as though a hand had pushed my shoulder, and I found myself in his arms.

He kissed me and said: "No more quarrels between us!"

"No, never! Never! Never!" I answered. We separated satisfied. But when I ran home and told all to my father, thinking to please him, he frowned and said:

"You ought to have been the first one to extend your hand because you were wrong!" Then he added: "You ought not to have raised the ruler upon a schoolmate better than yourself; upon the son of a soldier!" And snatching the ruler from my hand, he broke it in pieces and threw it against the wall.

MY SISTER

Friday the 24th.

Why is it, Enrico, that, after our father had reproved you for having behaved so badly with Coretti, you have still been so unkind to me? You cannot imagine the grief I have felt. Do you know that when you were a baby, I would stand hours and hours beside your cradle instead of going to amuse myself with my companions; and when you were sick, I would leave my bed in the middle of the night to see if your forehead was hot? Do you not know that if a terrible mishap should strike us, I would act as a mother to you, I would love you? Do you not know that when our father and mother will not be any longer here below, I will be your best friend? The only one with whom you may be able to speak of our bereaved dead, and of your childhood! And that if it were necessary, I would work for you, Enrico, in order to earn bread and to allow you to study, and that I will always love you when you are a man, and that I will follow you with my thoughts when you go far away, because we have grown up together and we have the same blood in our veins! Oh, Enrico, be sure that when you are a man, if a misfortune should befall you, if you should be alone, be sure that you will look for me; that you will come to me and cry: "Silvia, my sister, allow me to stay with you! Let us speak of the times when we were happy, do you remember? Let us speak of our mother, of our home, of the thousand-beautiful days, so far

away!" Oh, Enrico, you will always find your sister with her arms open to you. Yes, dear Enrico, forgive me also for the reproof that I have bestowed upon you. Now, I shall never remember any wrong on your part; and, even if you should cause me other sorrows, what do I care? You will always be my brother just the same. I shall only recollect my having held you in my arms when you were a baby; of having loved father and mother with you; of having seen you grow up, and of having been for many years your trusted companion! But do write me a good word upon this very writing-book, and I will get it and read it before evening. In the meantime, to show you that I am not angry with you, seeing that you were tired, I have copied the monthly story, "Blood of Romagna," which you had to do for the "Little Mason," who is sick. Look in the drawer at the left of your desk. I wrote it last night while you were asleep. I beg of you, Enrico, write a good word to me.

Your Sister Silvia.

Dear Sister:
I am not worthy to kiss your hand.

Enrico.

BLOOD OF ROMAGNA

(MONTHLY STORY)

The house of Ferruccio was quieter than usual that evening. The father, who kept a little dry-goods store, had gone to Forli to make some purchases and his wife had accompanied him, taking with them the little girl, Luigina, to see a doctor who was to perform an operation upon one of her eyes which had become diseased; and they would not return before the next morning. It was nearly midnight. The woman who came to work by the day had gone at sunset. There was no one in the house but the grandmother, whose lower limbs were paralyzed, and Ferruccio, a boy of thirteen. It was a small house with only a ground floor. It was situated upon the highway, within gunshot of the village, a little distance from Forli, a city in Romagna. Next to this dwelling there was an empty house, which had been partly burned two months before, and upon which one could still see the sign of an inn. There was a small vegetable garden behind the little house, and it was surrounded by a hedge through which opened a small rustic gate. The door of the shop served as house-door also and opened upon the highway. A deserted country extended on every side, vast cultivated fields planted with mulberry trees.

It was nearly midnight. Rain fell and the wind blew. Ferruccio and the grandmother were still up and were sitting in the dining-room, between which and the garden was a little room encumbered with old pieces of furniture. Ferruccio did not come home until eleven that night, after an absence of several hours, and the grandmother had expected him with open eyes, full of anxiety. She was sitting in a large arm-chair, where she was accustomed to pass the whole day, and, at times, even the whole night, as an oppression of breath would not allow her to lie down.

The wind dashed the rain against the window panes; the night was very dark. Ferruccio had come home tired and muddy, with his coat all torn, and with the mark of a stone on his forehead. He had been fighting with his companions, using stones as weapons; as usual, they had come to blows. Not satisfied with that, he had gam-  bled and lost all his soldi, and had left his cap in a ditch.

Although the room was lighted only by a small oil lamp placed on the corner of the table next to the big arm-chair, still the grandmother had noticed in what a miserable plight her grandson was, and she had partly guessed and partly made him confess his misdeeds.

She loved the boy with all her soul. When she knew everything, she began to weep.

"No, no," she said after a long silence, "You have no heart for your poor grandmother. You have no heart if you will take advantage of the absence of your father and mother in that way and cause me grief. You have left me alone the whole day long. You have not had the least bit of pity for me. Beware, Ferruccio! You put yourself in a bad way which may lead to a sad end. I have seen others commence in the same way and become very bad. One commences by running away from home, by quarreling with the other boys, by gambling one's soldi, and, little by little, from stone fights the boy passes to stabbing with knives, and from gambling to other vices, and from vices——to thieving!"

Ferruccio stood about three paces from her leaning on a cupboard and listening with his chin dropped on his breast. He was frowning, still excited from the heat of the fight; a lock of his luxuriant auburn hair hung across his forehead, and his beautiful blue eyes were as transfixed.

"From gambling to thieving," repeated the grandmother, continuing to weep. "Think, Ferruccio, think of that scourge of this section of the country, of that Vito Mozzoni, who is now in the city, a ragged vagabond, who, at the age of twenty-four, has already been twice in prison, and caused his poor mother, whom I knew well, to die of a broken heart, and his father to flee to Switzerland in despair. Think of that perverse character, whose greeting your father is ashamed to answer. He is always around with men who are more wicked than himself, and he will continue to grow worse until he comes to the gallows. Listen, I knew him as a lad, I knew him when he was like you. Think that you may lead your father and mother to the same end that he has led his parents!"

Ferruccio was silent. He was not perverse at heart; on the contrary, his escapades arose rather from his superabundance of spirits and from boldness than from wickedness; and his father had trained him badly in this respect, holding him capable of the finest sentiments, and, when put to the proof, of noble and generous actions; so he left the bridle upon his neck, expecting that he would become wise without any suggestions. Ferruccio was good rather than perverse, but obstinate, and it was very difficult, even when his heart was oppressed with repentance, for him to allow himself to say those good words which gain forgiveness for us:

"Yes, I am wrong; I shall not do it again, I promise you; forgive me!'

His soul was full of tenderness at times, but his pride prevented it from coming out.

"Ah, Ferruccio!" continued the grandmother, seeing that he remained silent. "You do not say a single word of repentance to me! Do you not see to what a state I am reduced, that I am about ready to be buried. You ought not to have the heart to make me suffer, to make the mother of your mother weep; as old as I am and so near to my last day of life—your poor grandmother, who has loved you so much, who rocked you night after night when you were a baby but a few months old, and who would not eat that she might play with you, do you know that? I always used to say: 'This boy will be my consolation!' But now you will kill me! I would gladly give the little that remains of my life to see you be good again, obedient as you were in those days when I led you to the Sanctuary. Do you remember that, Ferruccio? When you filled my pockets with little stones and grass? When I carried you home in my arms fast asleep? At that time you loved your poor grandmother. Now I am a paralytic. I need your affection as I need the air which I breathe, because I have no one else in this world, poor woman, half dead as I am. Oh, Lord!——"

Ferruccio was about to throw himself at the feet of his grandmother, moved by emotion, when he seemed to hear a sly noise, a sort of creaking in the next room, the one which opened on the garden. But he could not make out whether it was the shutters shaken by the wind or something else.

He stood listening.

The noise was repeated. His grandmother also heard it.

"What is the matter?" she asked after a moment, somewhat troubled.

"The rain," murmured the boy.

"Then, Ferruccio." said the old woman, wiping her eyes, "you will promise me to be good; that you will nevermore make your poor grandmother weep——" A new noise interrupted her.

"It does not seem to be the rain!" exclaimed she, growing pale, "go and see!"

But she added immediately: "No, stay here!" and grasped Ferruccio by the hand.

They both stood with suspended breath — they only heard the noise of the rain coming down.

All at once they both shivered.

It had seemed to them that they heard a noise of feet in the little room.

"Who's there?" asked the boy, gathering up his courage.

No one answered.

"Who is there?" cried the boy again, frightened nearly to death.

Scarcely had he pronounced these words, when they both uttered a shriek of terror. Two men sprang into the room; one grasped the boy and put his hand over his mouth; the other one grabbed the old woman by the throat; the first one said:

"Silence, if you don't want to die!"

The second:

"Hush!" and he raised a knife.

Each had a black handkerchief upon his face, with two small holes for the eyes.

Nothing but the gasping breath of the four was heard for a moment, and then the dropping of the rain; the old woman's throat rattled and her eyes were starting from their sockets.

The man who held the boy whispered in his ear: "Where does your father keep his money?"

The boy answered with a faint voice, while his teeth chattered: "Over there in the cupboard."

"Come with me," said the man.

He dragged him into the small room, holding him securely by the throat. There was a dark lantern upon the floor.

"Where is the cupboard?" he asked. The boy, gasping, pointed out the cupboard.

Then, in order to be sure of the boy, the man threw him on his knees in front of the cupboard, clasping his neck between his legs in such a way that he could strangle him if he attempted to cry, and holding the knife in his teeth and the lantern in his hand, he pulled from his pocket, with his other hand, a sharp iron point, stuck it into the lock, broke the door and opened it on both sides, upset everything in a hurry, closed the doors again, and re-opened them to make another search; after this he grasped the boy once more by the throat and pushed him into the other room where the other fellow was holding the old woman, who was in convulsions, with her head turned back and her mouth open.

He asked him in a low voice: "Have you found it?" and his companion answered: "I have found it." And he added: "Look at the door."

And the one who had been holding the woman ran to the door of the garden to see if there was any one there, and he said from the little room, with a voice which sounded like a whistle, "Come!"

The one who had remained alone, and who was still holding Ferruccio, showed a knife to the boy and to the old woman, who was re-opening her eyes, and said: "Not a word, not a sound, or I will come back and cut your throat.'

And he looked sharply at both for a minute.

At that moment, the sound of many voices was heard at a distance on the highway.

The thief turned his head quickly toward the door, and in doing so the handkerchief fell from his face.

The old woman gave vent to a shriek: "Mozzoni!"

"Curse you, woman!" roared the recognized thief. "You must die!"

He rushed upon her with his knife lifted, and the old woman fainted.

The murderer dealt the blow.

With a quick movement, and giving a desperate shout, Ferruccio had thrown himself upon his grandmother and had shielded her with his body. The murderer ran away, knocking against the table and upsetting the lamp which went out.

The boy slid down softly from over his grandmother's body, and fell on his knees, remaining in that attitude, with his arms around her waist and his head upon her breast.

A few moments passed; it was very dark; the song of the "contadini" was slowly dying out in the distance. The old woman recovered her consciousness.

"Ferruccio!" she called, with a scarcely audible voice, while her teeth were chattering.

"Grandmother," answered the boy

The old woman made an effort to speak, but the fright had paralyzed her tongue.

She remained silent for a moment, trembling violently. Finally she succeeded in asking:

"Are they no longer here?"

"No."

"Have they not killed me?" gasped the old woman in a choked voice.

"No——you are safe," said Ferruccio in a faint voice. "You are safe, dear grandmother. They have taken the money away. But papa had almost everything with him."

His grandmother sighed.

"Grandmother," said Ferruccio, still on his knees and clasping her around the waist, "dear grandmother — you love me, do you not?"

"Oh, Ferruccio! My poor child!" answered tne woman, placing her hand on his head. "How frightened you must have been! Oh, Lord of Mercy! Light the lamp—we are now in darkness; I am still afraid."

"Grandmother," said the boy, "I have always caused you sorrow."

"No, Ferruccio, do not speak in that way; I don't think of it any more; I have forgotten, I love you so much!"

"I have always caused you sorrow," continued Ferruccio, speaking with difficulty and in a trembling voice. "But I have always cared for you. Will you forgive me? Do forgive me, grandmother."

"Yes, my child, I forgive you, I forgive you with all my heart. Just think, if I should not forgive you! Rise up from your knees, my child. I will never scold you again. Be good, you are so kind, Ferruccio! Let us light the lamp. Let us take a little courage. Rise to your feet, Ferruccio."

"Thanks, grandmother," said the boy, speaking each time in a fainter voice. "Now——I am satisfied. You will remember me, grandmother——will you not? You will remember me always——your Ferruccio."

"Oh, my Ferruccio!" exclaimed the grandmother, astounded and uneasy, placing her hands upon his shoulders and leaning her head so as to look in his face.

"Remember me," again murmured the child, in a voice as faint as a breath. "Give a kiss to mother——to father, to Luigina——Farewell, grandmother——"

"In the name of heaven, what is the matter with you?" cried the woman, anxiously feeling the head of the boy who had fallen across her knees; and then, with all the voice she had in her throat, she shouted, in desperation: "Ferruccio! Ferruccio! Ferruccio! My child! My love! Angels of Paradise, help me!"

But Ferruccio did not answer. The little hero, the savior

of the mother of his mother, stabbed in the back from the knife thrust of the robber, had surrendered his noble soul to God!

THE LITTLE MASON SERIOUSLY ILL

Tuesday the 17th.

The Little Mason is dangerously ill. The teacher told us to call and see him; and Garrone, Derossi, and myself agreed to go together. Stardi might have come, but the teacher gave us for a lesson the description of the *Cavour Monument*, and he said that he must go and see the monument in order to write a more accurate description. We also invited the vain boy, Nobis, just for fun, but he answered us, in a dry manner, "No." Votini also excused himself, perhaps because he was afraid of soiling his clothes with plaster. We went after school was over. It was raining. On the way Garrone stopped and said, with his mouth full of bread:

"What are we going to buy?" and he jingled two soldi in his pocket.

We gave two soldi each and bought three large oranges.

We went up to the garret. In front of the door, Derossi took off his medal and put it in his pocket. I asked him why.

"I don't know," he replied. "I do not wish to put on any airs—it seems to me more delicate to enter without a medal."

We knocked at the door, and the father opened it for us— that tall man who looks like a giant. He had a sorrowful face and looked worn out by grief.

"Who are you?" he asked. Garrone answered:

"We are schoolmates of Antonio, and we are bringing him three oranges."

"Ah, poor Tonino!" exclaimed the mason, shaking his head. "I am afraid he will never be able to eat your oranges!" and he wiped his eyes with the back of his hand.

He bade us come in. We entered a room under the roof. The Little Mason was lying on a little iron bedstead; his mother was leaning on the bed with her face in her hands, and scarcely turned around to look at us. Some brushes, a trowel, and a plaster sieve hung on the wall of the room, and over the feet of the sick boy was laid the jacket of the mason, all white with plaster. The poor boy was very emaciated, and scarcely able to breathe. Oh dear Tonino, so good and so merry, my little companion, how it pained me, how much I would have given to see him make the hare face, poor Little Mason! Garrone put an orange on the pillow next to his face. The odor wakened him; he took it resolutely, but let it go, and looked at Garrone fixedly.

"It is I, Garrone," said the latter, "do you not recognize me?"

He smiled, but it was scarcely perceptible, and with difficulty he raised his hand from the bed and reached it to Garrone, who took it between his and laid his cheek upon it, saying:

"Courage, courage, Little Mason! You will soon recover; you will soon return to school, and the teacher will put you near me. Are you satisfied?"

But the Little Mason did not answer. The mother burst out sobbing:

"Oh, my little Tonino! My poor Tonino! So brave and so good, and to think that God wishes to take him away!"

"Hold your tongue!" cried the mason, in despair. "Be silent, for the love of God, or you will make me lose my head!" Then he said, anxiously:

"Go, go, boys; thanks; go home; what can you do here? Go."

The sick boy had closed his eyes again, and looked as though he were dead.

"Do you need anything" asked Garrone.

"No, my good child, thanks," replied the mason. "Go

home." And as he said this, he pushed us out on the landing and closed the door.

We were hardly half way down the stairs, when we heard him call:

"Garrone! Garrone!" We went up again in a hurry, all three of us.

"Garrone!" cried the mason with a changed voice, "he has called you by name. It has been two days since he has spoken; he has called you twice; he wants you, come at once. Ah, great God! If this were only a good sign!"

"Good-bye," Garrone said to us; "I will stay!" And he rushed into the room with the father. Derossi's eyes were filled with tears. I asked him:

"Do you weep for the Little Mason? He has spoken, he will get well."

"I believe it," replied Derossi. "But I was not thinking of him—I was thinking of that kind and noble soul, Garrone!"

THE COUNT CAVOUR

Wednesday the 29th.

"*Is it not the description of Count Cavour that thou must write? Well, thou canst do it. But who the Count Cavour was, thou canst not yet understand. For the present, learn only this: that he was for many years the prime minister of Piedmont; that it was he who sent the Piedmontese army into the Crimea to resuscitate, with the victory of Cernaia, our military glory which had fallen with the defeat at Novara. It was he who caused one hundred and fifty thousand Frenchmen to descend from the Alps and chase the Austrians from Lombardy. It was he who governed Italy in the most solemn period of our revolution, who gave, during those years, the most powerful impulse to the holy undertaking of the unification of the country. He, with his shining talent, his invincible constancy, his more than human activity. Many generals passed terrible hours upon the field of battle, but he passed more terrible ones still in his study, while that enormous undertaking of his might have crumbled down at any moment, like a frail edifice at the shock of an earthquake; hours, nights of toil and of anguish, from which he came out with shattered reason and with death in his heart. It was this gigantic and fearful undertaking, while consumed with fever, that shortened his life by twenty years. He still struggled desperately against the disease in order to do something more for his country. " It is strange," he would say, painfully, upon his death-bed, " I no longer know how to read; I can read no more." While they were bleeding him and the fever was increasing, he was thinking of his country, and said imperiously: " Cure my clouding mind; I need all my faculties to deal with grave matters." In his last moments, when the whole city was agitated and the king stood by his bedside, he was saying anxiously: " I have many things to tell you, Sire, many things to show you, but I am sick; I cannot do it." And he was inconsolable! His feverish thoughts continually hovered over his country, the new Italian provinces which had been united to us, and he was troubled about the many things which remained to be done, when the delirium overtook him. " Educate Childhood!" he exclaimed between his gasps for breath. " Educate Childhood and Youth—govern with freedom!" The delirium increased, death was upon him, and he invoked with ardent words General Garibaldi, with whom he had had some disagreements, and Venice and Rome, which were not yet liberated. He had visions of the future of Italy and of Europe; dreamed of foreign invasions; asked where the army corps and the generals were—he still trembled for his people. His great sorrow—dost thou understand?—was not to feel his life ebbing out; it was to see himself flee from his country, which still needed him and for which he had, in a few years, worn out the immeasurable power of his wonderful organism. He died with the cry of battle in his throat—his death was as great as his life. Now reflect a little, Enrico, what sort of a thing our work is which seems t* weigh so much upon us, what are our griefs, what is death itself compared to those toils, those formidable anxieties, the tremendous agonies of those men upon whom a world and its vital interest rests! Think of these, my child, and when thou passeth in front of that marble image cry: "Glory!" in thy heart.

Thy Father.

APRIL

SPRING

Saturday the 1st.

The first of April! Only three more months! This has been one of the finest mornings of the year. I was so happy at school because Coretti asked me to go with him to-morrow to witness the arrival of the king. His father, *who knows* the king, will accompany us. And also because my mother has promised to take me that same day to visit the Infant Asylum in Corso Valdocco. I was also content because the "little mason" is better, and because last night when the teacher was passing he said to my father: "He is better, he is better."

Then, too, it was a beautiful spring morning. From the windows of the school-room we could see the blue sky. The trees in the garden are all sprouting. The windows of the houses were wide open and there were flower-vases and boxes filled with blooming plants on the sills. The master did not laugh, because he never does, but he was in good humor, so much so that the straight wrinkle on his forehead was scarcely visible, and while he was explaining a problem upon the black-board, he jested, and you could see that he felt a pleasure in breathing the air which came from the garden through the open windows, with that good, fresh fragrance of the earth and of the trees, which makes one think of the walks in the country.

While he was explaining, we could hear a blacksmith in a street near by, who was beating something upon the anvil; and in the house opposite, a woman sang her babe to sleep. In the barracks of Cernaia, far away, the trumpets were sounding. The boys all seemed happy, even Stardi. Suddenly, the blacksmith began to hammer and the woman to sing in a higher key. The teacher stopped to listen. Then he said softly, looking out of the window:

"A sky which smiles, a mother who sings, an honest workman who labors, and some boys who study—that is really a fine thing."

When we left the class room I noticed that all the others were merry. They all walked in file, stamping their feet and singing in a playful way, as though it were the eve of a four days' vacation. The school-teachers were jesting; the one with the red feather tripped behind the boys like a school girl; the parents of the boys were talking to one another, laughing, and the mother of Crossi, the vegetable vender, had many bouquets of violets in her basket, and they filled the hall with perfume. I never experienced so much happiness as on this morning when I saw my mother waiting for me in the street, and I told her so when I met her.

"I am happy, and what is it that makes me so happy this morning?"

My mother smiled and answered that it was the fine season and a good conscience.

KING UMBERTO

Monday the 3rd.

At ten o'clock sharp, my father saw Coretti, the woodhuckster, and his son, who were waiting for me in the square, and he said to me: "Here they are, Enrico, go and see thy king."

I went down quickly. The father and son were more alert

than usual, and it occurred to me that they resembled each other very much this morning. The father wore the medal of valor upon his jacket between two commemorative medals, and his little mustache was curled up and pointed like two pins.

We started at once toward the railway station, where the king was to arrive at half past ten. Coretti's father smoked his pipe and rubbed his hands. "Do you know," he would say, "that I have not seen him since the war of sixty-six? A trifle of fifteen years and six months! First, I spent three years in France, then I went to Mondovi, and I have never before happened to be in the city when he came. It is all a matter of luck!"

He spoke of King Umberto as he would speak of a comrade. "Umberto commanded the sixteenth division; Umberto was twenty-two years and as many days old; Umberto rode on horseback," and so on.

"Fifteen years," he said in a loud voice, and quickened his step. "I have a great desire to see him again; I left him a prince; I shall see him a king. I have also changed much; I have passed from a soldier to a wood-huckster," and he laughed.

His son asked: "If he sees you, do you think he would recognize you?"

He began to laugh.

"Are you crazy?" he replied. "It would be too hard for him. There was only one like him, while we were as thick as flies, and he did not stop to look at us one by one."

We reached the Corso Vittorio Emanuele; there were many people hurrying toward the station. A company of Alpine soldiers with their trumpets were passing; two mounted carabineers went galloping by. The sky was brilliant and serene.

"Yes!" exclaimed Coretti's father, growing excited. "I am so pleased to see him again, the general of my division. Ah, how fast I have grown old! It seems to me but a day since I had a knapsack on my shoulder and a gun in my hands,

In the midst of that turmoil on the morning of June twenty-fourth, when we were about to come into battle. Umberto was going and coming with his officers, while the cannons thundered from a distance. All looked at him and said: 'Let us hope that there may not be a bullet for him!' I was a thousand miles away in my thoughts, never dreaming that in a few moments I should be so near him, in front of the lances of the Austrian Uhlans, only four steps from each other, boys! It was a beautiful day; the sky was like a looking-glass, but it was very warm! — Let us see if we can enter."

We had reached the station. There was a large crowd; carriages, guards, carabineers, societies with their banners, and the band of a regiment was playing. Coretti's father tried to get under the portico, but he found it impossible. Then he thought he would put himself in the first line of the crowd which was making an opening at the exit. By forcing his way with his elbows, he succeeded in pushing himself ahead of us. The crowd was wavering and pushing us here and there. The wood-huckster had spied the first pillar on the portico where the guards allowed no one to stand. "Come with me," he said, and, taking us by the hand, he crossed the empty space with two leaps and placed himself there with his shoulder against the wall.

A police officer ran to him and said: "You cannot stay here."

"I belonged to the Fourth battalion of the forty-ninth!" answered Coretti, touching his medals.

The policeman looked at him and said: "Stay."

"Didn't I tell you so!" exclaimed Coretti triumphantly. "It is a magic word that *Fourth of the forty-ninth!* Have I not a right to see him, my general, with comfort; I, who was in his command! I saw him near then; it is right that I should see him near now, and that I call him my general! He was my commander in battle for a long half hour, as in those moments it was he who commanded the battalion, while he was in the midst of it, and not Major Ubrich, by thunder!"

In the meanwhile, we could see in the hall where the trains arrived, and outside, a gathering of gentlemen and officers, and in front of the door carriages stood in line with the coachmen and grooms dressed in red.

Coretti asked his father if King Umberto had his sword in his hand when he was inside the square.

"He might have had his sword in his hand," he answered, "to ward off the blow of a lance, which might have struck him as well as any one else. Ah, those unchained demons! They came upon us like the wrath of God. They swept around the groups, the squares, the cannons, and they seemed like a wild wind in a hurricane, breaking through everything. There was such a confusion of Allessandria cavalrymen, of Foggia lancers, of infantry, of Uhlans, of Bersaglieri—such a pandemonium that we could not see around us. I heard some one crying: 'Your Highness! Your Highness!' and saw the lowered lances coming. We discharged our guns; a cloud of smoke hid everything——Then the cloud vanished——The earth was covered with horses of the Uhlans, with wounded and with dead. I turned around and saw in our midst Umberto on horseback, looking around quietly, as if he were about to ask: 'Is there any one who has been scratched, my boys!' And we shouted 'Hurrah!' right in his face, and acted like crazy men. Great God! What a moment that was!——See, the train is coming."

The band played, the officers took their places, the crowd stood on tip-toe.

"He will not come out right away," said a guard. "They are delivering a speech to him."

Coretti's father was beside himself. "Ah, when I think of it," he said, "I always see him there. He does his duty among people afflicted with cholera, among those whose homes are destroyed by earthquakes—and anywhere else I know of. And brave he was in battle, too; I have him constantly in my mind as I saw him then, in the midst of us, with that tranquil face; and I am sure that he also remembers the fourth battalion of the forty-ninth, though he is now a king, and he would like to see us for once at his table all together, those whom he saw once around him in such a moment. Now he has generals and lords and high officers; at that time he had nothing but poor soldiers. If I could only exchange a few words with him alone, our general of twenty-two; our prince, who was then entrusted to our bayonets—— It is fifteen years since I saw him, our Umberto. Ah! this music excites my blood, upon my honor!"

A crash of applause interrupted him. Thousands of hats were lifted in the air, four gentlemen dressed in black entered the first carriage.

"It is he!" cried Coretti, remaining there as if dumbfounded.

Then he said: "By our Lady, how grey he has grown!"

We all three took off our hats; the carriage was coming along slowly, in the midst of the throng, shouting and waving their hats. I looked at Coretti's father. He seemed like another man, he looked as if he had grown taller, stern and pallid, standing close against the pillar. The carriage came in front of us not more than a step from the pillar. "Hurrah" cried many voices.

"Hurrah!" cried Coretti after the others.

The king looked in his face and glanced for a moment at his three medals.

Then Coretti lost his head and shouted: "The fourth battalion of the forty-ninth!"

The king who had already turned to the other side, turned again towards us, and, gazing into Coretti's eyes, held his hand out of the carriage.

Coretti bounded forward and shook it. The carriage moved on. The crowd broke in and separated us from each other and we lost sight of Coretti's father, but it was only for a moment. We soon found him again, panting, with his eyes wet, and he was calling his son's name and holding his hand lifted in the air. The son hastened to him, and he cried: "Here, little fellow, while my hand is still warm," and he laid his hand over his face, saying: "This is a caress from the king."

And he stood there as if in a dream, with his eyes fixed upon the distant carriage, smiling, with his pipe in his hand, in the midst of a group of curious people, who were looking at him. "It is one of the forty-ninth," they were saying. "It is a soldier who knows the king." "And the king has recognized him." "It is he who reached out his hand." "He has handed the king a petition," said one louder than the others.

"No," cried Coretti, turning around brusquely; "I have handed him no petition. There is something else which I would give him."

They all looked at him.

He smiled and said: "My life!"

THE INFANT ASYLUM

Tuesday the 4th.

Yesterday, after breakfast, my mother took me to the Infant Asylum of Corso Valdocco, as she promised. She went to recommend the little sister of Precossi to the directress. I had never seen an asylum. How amused I was! There were two hundred little boys and girls, and they were so small that a pupil of our first lower class might be taken for a man as compared to them. We arrived just as they were filing into the refectory, where there were two long tables with many round holes and in each hole a black soup plate, filled with rice and beans, and a tin spoon lay beside it. Coming in, some of the children fell down and lay on the floor until one of the teachers ran to pick them up. Some of them would stop in front of a soup plate, thinking it was their place, and hurriedly swallow a spoonful, when one of the teachers would come up and say:

'Go ahead!" and he would go three or four steps and swallow another spoonful of soup, and then go ahead again until he arrived at his own place, having lawlessly taken half a portion of soup. At last, after much pushing and crying "Hurry up! Hurry up!" they were all placed in order and began to say their prayer. All those in the inside rows, who, in order to pray, had to turn their back to the soup plate, would twist their heads back to keep an eye on the soup lest some one should fish in it; and they prayed in such a funny way, with their hands together and their eyes turned toward the ceiling, but with their hearts on their soup. Then they began to eat, oh, what a sight that was! One would eat with two spoons, another filled his mouth with his hands; some would pick out the beans one by one and put them in their pockets; others would wrap them up in their little aprons and crush them together to make paste. There were some who did not eat because they were so interested in watching the flies. Some, coughing, sprinkled a shower of rice all around. It looked like a poultry yard. However, it was a pretty sight; those two rows of little girls with their hair done up in a knot with red, blue or green ribbons. One of the teachers asked a line of eight little girls: "Where does the rice grow?"

All of them opened their mouths, filled with soup, and answered together, singing: "It-is-born-in-the-water." Then the teacher gave the order: "Raise your hands!" It was so nice to see those little arms fly up from children who a few months ago were in their swaddling clothes. All those little waving hands looked like butterflies, white and rosy.

Then they went to the recreation room, but first they took from the wall their little baskets containing their breakfasts. As they came out into the garden, they scattered themselves around and began to take out their provisions—bread, stewed prunes, a small piece of cheese, a hard-boiled egg, some small apples, a handful of boiled vetch-peas or a chicken wing. In a moment the whole garden was covered with crumbs, as if they had spread food for a flock of birds there. They were eating in the strangest positions; like rabbits, mice and cats; nibbling, licking and sucking. One child had fastened some rice on his breast and was smearing it around with a medlar as though he were polishing a sword. Some little girls were crushing pieces of soft cheese in their hands, and it trickled through their fingers like milk and ran inside their sleeves without their noticing it. They were running around, following each other with apples and rolls in their teeth like dogs. I saw three who were excavating the inside of a hard egg with a little stick, thinking to find a treasure in there, and were scattering it around on the ground, then picking it up crumb by crumb with a great deal of patience, as if it were pearls. There was something singular about some of them. There were eight or ten bending their heads to look inside of a basket, as one would have looked at the moon inside of a cistern. There must have been about twenty standing around a midget about a span high, who held in his hand a little sugar bag, and they were all making bows to him in order to be allowed to dip their hand into it. He gave it to some, and to others, after being well begged, he only granted his finger to suck.

By this time, my mother had come into the garden and was kissing first one and then another. Many of them would go to meet her or cling to her dress and ask her for a kiss with their upturned faces, opening and closing their mouths, like little birds asking for food. One offered her a quarter of an orange which had already been bitten; another a crust of bread; one little girl gave her a leaf, and another, in great earnestness, showed her the point of her index finger, and, looking closely, one could see a microscopical swelling which she had gotten the day before by touching a lighted candle. They would place under her eyes some very small insects, so small that it was a mystery to me how they could see to pick them up. Some showed her half corks of bottles; some, shirt-buttons; some, little flowers picked from the vases. A child with a bandaged head, wishing to be heard at any cost, stammered out a story, I could not comprehend what, about a tumble he had taken, but not a word could be understood. A girl wished my mother to bend down, and she whispered in her ear: "My father makes brushes." In the meantime, many accidents were happening, which forced the teachers to run here and there. Some of the girls cried because they could not undo the knot in their handkerchiefs; others disputed, with their nails and shouts, over two apple-seeds; a little boy who had fallen upon an upturned stool sobbed without being able to rise.

When we were about to leave, my mother took three or four of them by the arm, and then others ran from all directions to be taken up also, with their faces all smeared with the yolk of egg or with orange juice. Some grasped her hands, others got hold of her fingers to see her ring; one pulled her watch-chain, and another tried to pull her hair.

"Look out," said one of the teachers, "they will ruin your dress!"

But my mother cared little for her dress and continued to kiss them, and they crowded around her more and more. The nearest ones had their arms stretched out as if they were trying to climb, and those more distant were trying to make their way through the crowd, and all were crying;

"Good-bye!" "Good-bye!" "Good-bye!"

At last she succeeded in running away from them and went into the garden. Then they all ran and put their heads between the iron bars of the railing to see her go by, throwing their arms out to salute her. They offered her pieces of bread, small pieces of fruit, and cheese rind, and all cried together:

"Good-bye! Good-bye! Good-bye! Come back to-morrow. Come again."

My mother in passing along put her hand upon those hundred little heads, as upon a garland of fresh roses.

She finally reached the street safely, all covered with crumbs and spots, mussed up and disheveled; her hands filled with flowers and her eyes filled with tears, as happy as though she had come from a feast. We could still hear the voices inside, like a great twittering of birds, crying:

"Good-bye! Good-bye! Come again, *lady.*"

AT THE GYMNASIUM

Wednesday the 5th.

The weather continuing fine, they made us go from the indoor gymnasium to the other in the garden, which is fitted up with apparatuses.

Yesterday, Garrone was in the principal's room when the mother of Nelli came — the blonde lady dressed in black — to have her boy excused from the exercises. She spoke with her hand upon Nelli's head, and every word cost her an effort. "He cannot do it," she said to the principal. Nelli appeared to be very much grieved at being excused from the gymnasium; at having to suffer this humiliation.

"You will see, mother, that I can do like the others," he said.

His mother looked at him in silence, with an air of pity and affection. Then she said with hesitation: "I fear that his companions"—— She meant to say that they might ridicule him.

But Nelli answered: "It doesn't matter, and then Garrone is there. I am satisfied if he is the only one who does not laugh."

And then they allowed him to join us. The teacher, the one who has a scar on his neck and who has been with Garibaldi, led us immediately to the vertical poles which are very high, and it was our task to climb to the top and stand upright on the transverse beam. Derossi and Corretti went up like two monkeys. Precossi also mounted quickly, although embarrassed in that large jacket which reaches to his knees, and, in order to make him laugh while he was going up, they all repeated his interjection: "Excuse me, excuse me." Stardi puffed up, growing red like a turkey, and closing his teeth so that he looked like a mad dog; but, even at the risk of bursting, he would have gone to the top, and he got there. When Nobis got to the top, he assumed the air of a conquering emperor. Votini slid down twice in spite of his beautiful new suit with blue stripes, made expressly for gymnastics.

In order to go up more easily they had all daubed their hands with colophony rosin, as it is called, which the trafficking Garoffi had sold to them for a soldo a bag, thereby making a profit.

It was Garrone's turn next and he went up, eating bread, with great ease; and I believe that he would have been able to carry one of us on his shoulder, he is so thick-set and strong, like a little ox. After Garrone, came Nelli. As soon as they saw him grasping the bar with his long thin hands many began to laugh and ridicule him, but Garrone crossed his arms on his breast and darted such an expressive glance at the boys that they well understood that he would immediately deal them blows, even in the presence of the teacher, and they all stopped laughing at once.

Nelli commenced to climb with difficulty, poor thing. His face was scarlet, he was breathing hard, and the perspiration ran from his forehead. The teacher said: "Come down." But he answered, "No," making an effort and growing obstinate, while I was expecting every moment to see him tumble to the ground half dead. Poor Nelli! I was thinking if I had been like that, and my mother had seen me how she would have suffered, my poor mother; and thinking of this, I grew very fond of Nelli, and I would have given a great deal to have seen him succeed in ascending the bar, and to be able to push him from below without being seen. In the meanwhile, Garrone, Derossi, and Coretti were saying: "Up! Up! Nelli! Courage! Another effort! Up!" and Nelli made another violent effort, placing his elbow, and finding himself only two spans from the top.

"Bravo!" cried the others. "Courage! Another push!" and behold Nelli grasped the transverse bar. All clapped their hands.

"Bravo!" said the teacher, "but that is enough; come down now." But Nelli wanted to go up on top like all the others, and after a little hesitation succeeded in placing his elbows upon the bar, then his knees, then his feet, until he sat up panting and smiling, and looked at us.

We again clapped our hands. Then he looked in the street. I looked that way, and through the plants which covered the iron railings of the garden I saw his mother walking on the sidewalk, not daring to look up. Nelli came down and the boys all made much of him. He was excited and rosy, and his eyes were sparkling; he did not look like the same boy. His mother came to meet him when we came out, and embracing him, she asked a little uneasily:

"Well, my dear child, how did it go?' All his companions answered:

"He has done very well! He went up like the others!" "He is strong, do you know it?" "He is quick!" "He does just as well as the others."

It was a pleasure to see the joy of that woman! She tried to thank us, but she was not able. She shook hands with three or four of us, caressed Garrone, and then took her boy away.

We watched her for a few moments as she walked along hurriedly, talking and gesticulating with Nelli, **both more contented than any one had ever seen them.**

MY FATHER'S TEACHER

Tuesday the 11th.

What a beautiful excursion I had yesterday with my father! This is how it happened. The day before yesterday, while we were at dinner, reading over a newspaper, my father gave vent to an exclamation of surprise. Then he said: "And I thought him dead for the last twenty years! Do you know, he is still alive, my first teacher of the elementary school, Vincenzo Crosetti, who is now eighty-four years old? I see here that the ministry have bestowed upon him the medal of merit for having taught for the last sixty years. *Sixty years*, do you understand? And it is only two years since he stopped teaching. Poor Crosetti! He lives only an hour's ride from here by the railway, at Condovi, the place of our old garden woman of the villa of Chieri." And he added: "Enrico, we will go and see him."

Through the whole evening, he spoke of no one else but him. The name of his elementary teacher called to his mind a thousand things that happened when he was a boy. It reminded him of his first companions and of his dead mother. "Crosetti!" he exclaimed, "was forty years old when I was with him. It seems to me that I can see him now; a little round-shouldered man, with clear eyes, and his face was always clean shaven. Rather severe, but with good manners, and he always loved us as a father, and never forgave us any escapades. By dint of study and privations, he rose from being a farmer. He was an honest man. My father was pleased with him and treated him like a friend. Why he has gone from Turin to live at Condovi is more than I can guess! He surely will not recognize me. It matters not, I will recognize him. Forty-four years have passed! Forty-four years, Enrico, and to-morrow we will go and see him."

Yesterday morning at nine o'clock we were at the railway

station of Susa. I wanted to have Garrone go with us, but he could not on account of his mother being ill. It was a fine spring morning. The train ran through green meadows and blooming hedges, and the air was full of fragrance. My father was happy; and every once in awhile he put his arm around my neck, speaking to me as to a friend and looking out at the country.

"Poor Crosetti!" he would say, "he is the first man who liked me and who did me some good after my father. I have never forgotten some of his good advice, as well as some dry reproaches which sent me home with a lump in my throat. His hands were short and thick. I can still see him as he entered the school, placing his cane in the corner and hanging his cloak on the hat-rack, always with the same gesture. He had an even temper, was always conscientious and full of good wishes, and so attentive that it seemed as though he were teaching every day for the first time. I remember as well as though I heard him now, when he looked at me and said: 'Bottini, eh! Bottini! hold the index and the middle finger upon thy pen!' He must have changed much in forty-four years."

As soon as we reached Condovi, we went to look for our old garden woman of Chieri, who keeps a small shop in an alley. We found her with her boys and she gave us a hearty welcome, telling us the news of her husband who is about to return from Greece, where he has been working for the last three years. She also told us about her oldest daughter, who is now in the Deaf and Dumb Asylum at Turin. Then she showed us the way to go to find the teacher, who is known by every one.

We left the place and went through a steep lane, flanked by blooming hedges.

My father no longer talked; he seemed absorbed in his memories, and once in awhile he would smile and shake his ad.

Suddenly he stopped and said: "Here he comes. I am willing to wager that it is he."

A little old man with a white beard was coming toward us. He wore a broad-brimmed hat, was walking with a stick, dragging his feet, and his hands were trembling.

"It is he!" repeated my father, hastening his step.

When we came near him, we halted. The old man also stopped and looked at my father. He still had a fresh face, and his eyes were clear and had a lively expression.

"Is it you?" asked my father, taking off his hat. "The teacher, Vincenzo Crosetti?" The old man also took off his hat and said: "It is I," with a tremulous but full voice.

"Well," said my father, taking him by the hand, "allow an old pupil of yours to shake your hand and ask you how you are. I have come from Turin to see you."

The old man looked at him in amazement, and then said: "You honor me too much——I do not know——When were you my pupil? If you please. Tell me your name, I beg."

My father gave him his name, Alberto Bottini, and told him the year that he had been in his school and where, adding: "You probably do not remember me, and it is quite natural, but I remember you very well!"

The teacher bent his head and looked down, thinking, and he murmured two or three times the name of my father, who in the meanwhile gazed at him smiling.

All of a sudden, the old man raised his face, with his eyes wide open and said slowly: "Alberto Bottini, the son of the engineer Bottini? The one who lived on Consolato square?"

"The same," answered my father, holding his hand.

"Then," said the old man, "allow me, dear sir, allow me," and coming forward he embraced my father, his head scarcely reaching his shoulder. My father laid his cheek upon his forehead.

"Have the kindness to come with me," said the teacher.

Without saying anything more, he turned and retraced his steps toward his house. In a few minutes, we entered the yard in front of a small house with two doors, one of which opened through a little white wall.

The teacher opened the second door and bade us enter. The room was white-washed; in one corner stood a cot-bed with a cover of white and blue squares; in another, a little table with a small bouquet upon it; there was an old geographical map nailed to the wall, and the room also contained four chairs; and an odor of apples was perceptible.

We all three sat down. My father and the teacher silently looked at each other for a few moments.

"Bottini!" exclaimed the teacher, his eyes upon the brick floor, where the sun revealed a checker board. "Oh, I remember well. Your mother was such a kind lady! During the first year, you sat for a time on the first bench at the left near the window. See how well I remember? I still see your curly hair." Then he paused a moment to think. "You were a pretty lively boy, eh? The second year, you were taken ill with the croup. I remember when they brought you back to school wrapped up in a shawl, and you were so emaciated. Forty years have passed since then, is it not so? You are so kind to remember your poor teacher! Others have come, too, in the past years to see me here; some of my old pupils: a colonel, some priests, and several gentlemen." He asked my father what profession he followed. Then he said: "I congratulate you, I congratulate you with all my heart. Thanks. It has been a long time since I had seen any of my old pupils and I fear that you may be the last one to visit me, dear sir."

"Do not talk so," said my father. "You are well and still strong. You must not say such things."

"No, no," replied the teacher. "Do you see this trembling!" and he showed his hands. "This is a very bad sign. It came upon me three years ago while I was still teaching. At first, I paid no attention to it, thinking it would pass away. But instead it remained, or rather it kept on increasing. The day came when I was no longer able to write. Oh! that day, the first time I made a blot upon the copy-book of one of my pupils, it was a blow to my heart, my dear sir. I went ahead for a little time, but I finally had to give up. After sixty years, I was obliged to say good bye to the school, to the pupils, to the work. And it was a hard thing, do you know, it was a hard thing. The last time I gave a lesson, they all escorted me home and made much of me, but I was sad, I felt that life had come to an end for me. The year previous I had lost my wife and my only child. Now I live upon a few hundred lire of pension. I work no more. My only occupation, as you see, is to look over my old school books, some collections of educational journals, some books which my pupils have given me. There they are," he said, pointing to a little bookcase. "There are the souvenirs of my past——It is all I have left in this world."

Then in a changed and jolly tone: "I want to surprise you, dear Signor Bottini."

He got up and approached a table, opened a long narrow drawer containing several little bundles, all bound together with a paste-board back, upon which was written a date in four figures. After searching for a moment, he opened one of them, turned over several papers and pulled out a sheet, grown yellow with age, and handed it to my father. It was his lesson of forty years ago! He read on the top of it: "Alberto Bottini, Dictation, April 3, 1838." My father recognized at once his large hand writing when a boy and began to read, smiling; all of a sudden, tears came to his eyes. I got up and asked him what was the matter.

He passed an arm around my waist, and pressing me to his side, he said: "Look at this sheet of paper. Do you see? These are the corrections of my poor mother. She would always strengthen the l's and the t's. And the last lines are hers. She had learned to imitate my hand writing, and when I was tired or sleepy she would finish the work for me. My dear, sainted mother!"

And he kissed that page.

"Here they are," said the teacher, showing other bundles, "here are my souvenirs. Every year, I put aside a piece of work of each of my pupils, and they are all put in their order by number. At times, I look them over and read a line here and there, and a thousand things come back to my mind, and it seems to me that I live in the past. How many have passed away, my dear sir? If I close my eyes, I see faces over faces, class after class, and hundreds and hundreds of boys. Who knows how many of them are already dead. I remember some of them very well. I remember well the best and the worst, those who have given me much satisfaction, and those who caused me some sad moments, and I have had some who were serpents, do you know? And a large number of them! But now, you understand me, it seems as though I already belonged to the other world, and I love them all alike."

"And do you remember any roguish trick of mine?" asked my father, smiling.

"You, sir?" replied the old man, also smiling, "not at this moment. But I do not mean to say that you never did anything wrong. Still, you were a boy who had judgment; you were serious for your age. I remember the great affection you had for your mother——And you have been good and kind to come and see me! How could you leave your business to come and see a poor old teacher?"

"Listen, Signor Crosetti," replied my father quickly, "I recall the first time my poor mother accompanied me to school. It was the first time that she had ever been separated from me for two hours, or had left me outside of the house in any other hands than those of my father—in the hands of an unknown person. For that good creature, my entering school was like an entrance into the world, the first of a long series of necessary and painful separations. It was society which for the first time, was tearing from her her son who would never be to her quite the same as before. She was moved and so was I. She recommended me to you with a trembling voice, and when she went away, she saluted me from the door with her eyes filled with tears. At that moment, you made a gesture with your hand, placing the other one upon your breast as if to tell her: 'Madam, trust in me.' From that look and from that gesture, I perceived that you had understood all the thoughts, all the sentiments of my mother. That look which meant 'Courage!' that gesture which was a solemn promise of protection, of affection, of indulgence—I have never forgotten it—It has ever since remained engraved upon my heart, and that remembrance is what caused me to leave Turin this morning, and here I am after forty years, to tell you: Thank you, dear teacher!"

The teacher did not answer, he was caressing my hair with his trembling hand which glided from my hair upon my forehead, and from my forehead upon my shoulder.

During this time, my father looked at these bare walls, at that poor bed, at the piece of bread and the phial of oil upon the window, and it seemed as though he wished to say: "Poor teacher, after sixty years of work, is this all your recompense?"

The old man was contented, and again commenced to speak with vivacity of our family, of the other teachers, of those years, of my father's school-mates, some of whom he remembered, and others whom he did not, and each gave the other news of them. At last, my father interrupted the conversation by begging the teacher to come down to the village and have luncheon with us. He ceremoniously replied: "Thank you, thank you." But he seemed to be uncertain about it. My father took both his hands and begged him again. "How can I eat," said the teacher, "with these poor hands which tremble so; it would be a punishment to the others!" "We will help you," said my father. Then he accepted, shaking his head and smiling.

"It is a fine morning," he said closing the outside-door, "it is a fine morning, dear Signor Bottini! I assure you that I shall keep it in mind as long as I live."

My father took the teacher by the arm, the old man took my hand, and we descended the lane. We met two little bare-footed girls leading some cows, and a boy passed us running with a large load of straw on his shoulders. The teacher told us that they were pupils of the second class, who during the morning would lead the cattle to pasture or work in the fields, bare-footed, and in the evening would put on their shoes and go to school. It was almost noon and we met no one else. We reached the hotel in a few minutes. We seated ourselves at a table, putting the teacher between us, and immediately ordered our luncheon. The hotel was as quiet as a convent. The teacher was very jolly, and as his excitement increased, he trembled so that he could hardly eat; but my father cut his meat, broke his bread and put salt upon his plate. In order to drink he was obliged to hold the glass with both hands, and even then he shook so that the glass would click against his teeth. He talked constantly, with warmth, about the reading books when he was a youth, about the schools of those years, about the praises which his superior had bestowed upon him, and about the regulations of the last years; all the time with that serene face a little redder than before, in that gay voice, and he laughed almost like a young man. My father looked and looked at him, with the same expression with which, at times, I surprised him looking at me at home, when he thinks and smiles to himself with his face leaning to one side. The teacher let some wine trickle upon his breast; my father got up and cleaned it off with a napkin. "No, no, I will not allow you," he said, and laughed. He would speak some words in Latin. Finally, raising his glass, which danced in his hands, he said very seriously: "To your health, my dear engineer, to your children, and to the memory of your good mother!" "To your health, my good teacher!" answered my father, pressing his hand. The landlord and some others who were at the other end of the room looked at us and smiled as though they were pleased with the celebration which was granted to the teacher of their place.

The teacher wished to accompany us to the station when we left, at two o'clock. My father again gave him his arm and he took me by the hand, while I carried his cane. The people all stopped to look at us as we passed; all knew him, and some saluted him. At one place on the road, we heard from a window several boys' voices reading together and spelling aloud. The teacher stopped and seemed to grow sad.

"That—dear Signor Bottini," he said, "that is what pains me: to hear the voices of the boys at school, and to think that I can no longer be among them, while some one else is there. I have heard this music for the last sixty years, and I have grown to love it——Now I am without a family, I no longer have children."

"No, teacher," said my father, resuming the way, "you still have many children scattered all over the world, who remember you as I do."

"No, no," replied the teacher, sadly, "I no longer have any children, and without children I cannot live much longer. My hour will soon strike."

"Do not say so, teacher; do not think it," said my father. "At any rate, you have done much good! You have lived your life nobly."

For a moment the old teacher inclined his head towards my father and shook my hand.

We had just entered the station, the train was about to leave.

"Good-bye, teacher," said my father, kissing him on both cheeks.

"Good-bye, thanks, good-bye," answered the teacher, taking one of my father's hands in his and pressing it upon his heart.

I kissed him also and felt that his face was wet. My father pushed me inside the car. Then taking, with a quick movement, the rough cane from the teacher's hand and putting in its stead his own beautiful one with a silver handle which had his initials upon it, he exclaimed: "Do keep it in remembrance of me!" The old teacher tried to return it to him and take back his own, but my father entered the car and closed the door.

"Good-bye, my good teacher."

"Good-bye, my child," answered the teacher, while the train was moving, "and may the Lord bless you for the consolation which you have brought to a poor old man."

"Until we meet again," cried my father, his voice filled with emotion.

But the teacher shook his head, as if saying: "We shall never meet again."

"Yes, yes," repeated my father, "until we meet again."

The old man raised his trembling hand toward the skies and answered: "There above!"

CONVALESCENCE

Thursday the 20th.

Who would have thought when I was returning so merry and happy from that lovely excursion with my father that for ten days I would see neither the country nor the sky! I have

THE HEART OF A BOY

been dangerously ill. I have heard my mother sobbing; I have seen my father very, very pale, gazing at me fixedly; and my sister Silvia and my brother talking softly. The doctor, with his eye-glasses, was there every moment, saying things which I could not understand. I have, indeed, been on the point of saying good-bye to all. Ah, my poor mother! There are at least two or three days of which I remember scarcely anything, and it seems as though I had a dark and perplexing dream. It seemed that I had seen next to my bed my good teacher of the first superior, who was trying to stifle her cough with her handkerchief, in order not to disturb me. I have a confused remembrance of my teacher bending down to kiss me and he prickled my face a little with his beard. And I saw, as through a mist, the red head of Crossi and the blonde curls of Derossi, the Calabrian boy dressed in black, and Garrone, who brought me a mandarin

orange with the leaves on the stem, and ran away immediately because his mother was ill. Then I woke up, feeling as though I had been having a long dream. I knew that I was better because my mother smiled and I could hear Silvia singing softly. Oh, what a sad dream I had! After that, I improved every day. The Little Mason came and made me laugh for the first time since my illness by making his hare face, and how well he does it now that his face is a little elongated, owing to his sickness, poor boy! Coretti came to see me; also Garoffi, who presented me with two tickets to the new raffle for a pen-knife with five blades which he bought from a second-hand dealer in via Bartola. Yesterday, while I was sleeping, Precossi came and placed his cheek upon my hand without waking me, and, as he came from his father's workshop with his face covered with charcoal dust, he left a black mark upon my sleeve. I found pleasure in seeing it when I awoke. How green the trees have become in a few days! and how I envy the boys whom I see running to school with their books, when my father takes me to the window. In a short time, I shall also return to school; I am so impatient to see all the boys again, and my desk, the garden, the streets, and to know all that has happened in this time; I wish once more to occupy myself with my books and copy-books, which it seems to me a year since I have seen. Poor mother! how pale she has grown. My poor father, how tired he looks. And when my schoolmates come to see me, they walk on tiptoe and kiss me on the forehead. It makes me feel bad to think that some day we shall separate. Perhaps, I shall continue to study with Derossi and some of the other boys, but how is it about the balance of them? When I get through the fourth elementary, it will be a good-bye to all; we shall not see each other again. They will no longer come to my bedside when I am ill. Garrone, Precossi, Coretti—so many fine boys! Such good and kind companions! Never again!

THE FRIEND OF THE WORKMAN

Tuesday the 20th.

Why "never again," Enrico? That will depend upon thyself. When thou art through the fourth elementary, thou wilt go to the high school and those companions will go to work; but thou will remain in the same city perhaps for many years to come. Why then wilt thou not see one another again? When thou wilt be at the university or at college, thou wilt seek them in their shops and in their stores, and it will be a great pleasure to thee to find once more the companions of thy childhood who have become men at work. I should be displeased to know that thou didst no longer go to see Coretti and Precossi, no matter where they were. Thou wilt go and spend hours in their company; and thou wilt see, while studying human life and the world, how many things thou wilt be able to learn from them that no one else will be able to teach thee about their own trades, their families, as well as much about thy country. Be careful, if thou dost not keep those friendships, it will be hard for thee; if thou shouldst not acquaint thyself with similar persons in the future—I mean other friendships outside the class to which thou belongest, and only live among a separate class. The man who acquaints himself with but a single social class is like the student who reads a single book. Do purpose from this time on to keep these good friends even after separating, and cultivate their friendship in preference to that of others, because they are sons of workmen. The men of the upper class are the officers and the workmen are the soldiers of work. Thus in society as well as in the army, the soldier is not less noble than the officer, as nobility lies in the merit and not in the profit; it depends upon the valor and not upon the rank. But, if there is a superiority of merit, it belongs to the soldier, to the workman, who draws from his own work a mine of profit. Love and respect those among thy companions who are the sons of the soldiers of labor. Honor in them the struggles and sacrifices of their parents. Despise the difference of fortune and of rank, upon which only the base regulate their sentiments and courtesies. Reflect that the blessed blood which redeemed thy country came almost entirely from the working class; from the shops and from the fields. Love Garrone, love Precossi, love Coretti, love the Little Mason; for in their small breasts are shrined the hearts of princes; and swear to thyself that no change of fortune will ever alienate thee from those blessed juvenile friendships of thy soul. Promise thyself that, if in forty years from now, thou shouldst pass through a railway station and shouldst recognize in the garments of a railway engineer with a black face thy old friend Garrone —— Ah, it is not necessary that thou shouldst promise it; I am certain that thou wouldst jump on the engine and throw thy arms around his neck, even if thou wert a Senator of the Kingdom.

Thy Father.

GARRONE'S MOTHER

Saturday the 29th.

The first thing I heard when I returned to school was sad news. Garrone did not come to school for many days because his mother was seriously ill. She died last Saturday. Yesterday morning, as soon as we entered the school, the teacher said to us:

"A great misfortune has happened to poor Garrone—the greatest misfortune that can befall a child; his mother is dead. He will come back to the class to-morrow. I beg you all to respect the terrible sorrow which wrings his soul. When he comes in, greet him with affection, but in a grave manner. Let no one jest; let no one laugh at him, I beg of you."

Garrone came in this morning a little later than the others. My heart sank when I saw him. He looked haggard; his eyes were red, and he could hardly stand. It seemed as though he had been ill. He was all dressed in black, and one could scarcely recognize him; it was a pitiful sight. All looked at him breathlessly. As soon as he entered the room and saw the place where his mother had waited for him nearly every day, and that bench where she had so often bent down on the days of examination to give him the last word of encouragement, and where he had so many times thought of her, while impatient to get out and run to meet her, he could not restrain himself from weeping. The teacher drew the boy to him and pressed him to his breast, saying:

"Weep, poor boy, but have courage. Your mother is no longer here below, but she sees you; she still loves you; she still lives beside you, and some day you will see her again, because you are good and honest like her. Have courage!"

Having said this, he escorted him to his bench near me. I did not dare to look at him. He pulled out his books, which he had not opened for several days, opening his reader where there was an engraving representing a mother holding her child by the hand. He burst into tears again and laid his head upon his arm. The teacher made us a sign to let him alone, and commenced the lesson. I wished to give him something, but did not know what. I put my hand on his arm and whispered in his ear:

"Do not weep, Garrone."

He made no reply, but without raising his head from the desk, he put his hand in mine and held it there for some time. Coming out, no one spoke to him; they all passed him by with respect and in silence. I saw my mother waiting for me, and ran to embrace her, but, looking at Garrone, she rebuked me. I did not immediately understand the reason, but I noticed that Garrone, who was standing a little to one side, was looking at me, gazing with a look of inexpressible sadness, as if he meant to say:

"You embrace your mother, and I cannot embrace mine any more. You still have your mother; mine is dead."

Then I understood why my mother had rebuked me, and I walked beside her without putting my hand in hers.

GIUSEPPE MAZZINI

Saturday the 29th.

Garrone, pale and with eyes swollen from weeping, came to school again this morning. He scarcely glanced at the small presents which we had put upon his desk to console him. The teacher had brought a page of a book to read to him to give him courage. First, he notified us that at one o'clock to-morrow we should go to the City Hall to witness the awarding of a medal of civic valor to a boy who had saved a little child from the river Po, and Monday he would dictate the description of the celebration in the place of the monthly story. Then, turning to Garrone, who kept his head down, he said to him:

"Garrone, make an effort and write what I am about to dictate." We all took our pens and the teacher commenced the dictation.

"Giuseppe Mazzini, who was born in Genoa in 1805, and died in Pisa in 1872, was a great patriotic soul. He had the mind and inspiration of a great writer. He was the first apostle of the Italian Revolution. For the love of his country, he lived for forty

years in poverty; an exile, persecuted; a fugitive, heroically steadfast in his purpose and in his resolutions. Giuseppe Mazzini, who adored his mother, and who had derived from her all that which in her strong and kind soul was noblest and purest, wrote in this way to a faithful friend to console him upon the greatest of misfortunes. These are his words: 'My friend, you will never behold your mother again upon this earth. This is a tremendous truth. I do not come to see you because your sorrow is one of those holy and solemn sorrows that one must suffer and conquer alone. Do you understand what I mean by these words, '*You must conquer your sorrow?*' Conquer that which is least holy in the sorrow, least purifying, annihilate that which, instead of bettering the soul, weakens it?

But the other side of sorrow, the most noble side, the one which absorbs and elevates the soul, that one must remain with you and never leave you.' Nothing takes the place of a good mother here below. In sorrows, in consolations, that life will still crown you; you will never forget her. You must remember her, love her, mourn her death in a manner worthy of her. Oh, friend, listen to me. Death does not exist; it is nothing. One cannot even understand it. Life is life, and follows the laws of life: it is progress. Yesterday, you had a mother upon earth; to-day, you have an angel somewhere else. All that is good survives, increasing in power through our earthly life. It is so with the love of your mother. She loves you now more than ever. And you are more responsible for your actions now in her eyes than you were before. It depends upon your deeds whether you meet her again, whether you see her in another existence. For the love and reverence due your mother, you must become better and cause her joy. Because of this, you must from now henceforth, at every act, say to yourself: Would my mother approve of it? Her transformation has placed near you a guardian angel to whom you must refer everything that you do. Be strong and good. Fight this unhealthy and desperate sorrow. Have the tranquility of great souls in great sufferings: that is what she wishes."

"Garrone," added the teacher, "*be strong and peaceful, that is what your mother wishes.* Do you understand?" Garrone made a sign of assent with his head, while flowing tears fell upon his hands, upon his book, and upon his desk.

CIVIC VALOR

(MONTHLY STORY)

At one o'clock, we found ourselves with our teacher in front of the City Hall to witness the awarding of the medal of civic valor to the boy who has rescued his companion from the River Po.

Upon the balcony on the facade of the building was a large tricolored flag. We entered the court-yard of the palace.

It was already crowded with people. We could see at the end a table with a red cover and some papers laying upon it. Behind this there was a row of large gilded chairs for the mayor and the council. The ushers of the municipality, with blue waistcoats and white stockings, were there. A detachment of civic guards, wearing many medals on their breasts, were standing on the right side of the court-yard; next to them, a detachment of customhouse officers; and on the other side, the firemen, in full dress uniform; and there were many soldiers scattered around, who had come to look on: cavalry soldiers, bersaglieri, and artillery men. Among these, some gentlemen, some working men, some army officers, women and boys, who were crowding around. We were pressed into a corner, where there had already gathered many pupils of the other schools with their teachers, and near us there was a group of country boys, between ten and eighteen years of age, who were laughing and talking in a loud manner, and we understood that they all belonged to the Borgo Po, class-mates or acquaintances of the one who was to receive the medal. The employees of the City Hall could be seen leaning out of the windows, and the loggia of the library was also crowded with people, pressing against the iron railings. In the one on the opposite side, which is over the entrance door, stood a number of girls of the public schools, many *Daughters of Soldiers*, with their pretty blue veils. It seemed as though we were in a theatre. They all talked, merely looking from time to time toward the red table to see if any one was appearing. The band was playing at the end of the portico. The sun shone upon the walls. It was a beautiful sight.

Suddenly they all began to clap their hands in the court-yard, in the loggia, and the windows.

I stood on tip-toe to see.

The throng which was behind the red table had made an opening and a man and woman had come through. The man held a boy by the hand. It was the one who had rescued his companion.

The man was his father, a mason, in Sunday clothes; the woman his mother, a little blonde wearing a black dress. The boy was small and also blonde, and he wore a grey jacket. Seeing all those people, and hearing all that thunder of applause, all three stood there not daring to look or move. An usher of the municipality pushed them next to the table into the light.

All were silent for a moment. Then the applause broke forth again from every side. The boy looked at the windows and then at the loggia where the *Daughters of the Soldiers* stood—holding his cap in his hands, looking as though he did not know where he was. It seemed to me that he looked a little like Coretti, although his face was somewhat redder. His father and mother kept their eyes fixed upon the table.

In the meantime, the boys of Borgo Po, who had come near us, were pushing themselves ahead and making gestures toward their companion, in order to be noticed by him, and calling him in a low voice: "Pin! Pin! Pinot!" By persevering in calling him, they attracted his attention. The boy looked at them and hid a smile behind his cap.

Finally all the guards placed themselves in the position of "attention."

The mayor entered, accompanied by many gentlemen.

He had a white beard and wore a large tricolored sash around his waist. He went to the table and stood there, and the others placed themselves on the side and behind him. The band ceased to play, the mayor made a gesture and all were silent.

He began to speak. I could not understand the first words very well, but I knew that he was telling about the deed of the boy. Then his voice began to grow louder and sounded clear and sonorous through the whole court, so that I could not miss a word. "——When, from the shore, he saw his companion struggling in the river, already overtaken by the terror of death, he tore his clothes from his back and ran without hesitating for a moment. They cried to him: 'You will drown yourself!' He did not answer. They grasped him, but he freed himself; they called him, but he was already in the water. The river was swollen and the risk very great even for a man. But he flung himself against death with all the power of his little body and his great heart. He overtook and got hold of the unfortunate boy just in time; he was already under the water, but he drew him to the surface and fought furiously with the waves which were about to overwhelm him with his companion, who was clinging to him; he disappeared many times but came up again with a desperate effort, obstinate, invincible in his noble purpose. Not like a boy who wishes to save another boy, but like a man, like a father who fights to save his son who is his hope and his life. God did not allow such a generous deed to be fruitless. The swimming child wrested his friend from the giant river and brought him safely to land, and with the others gave him the first comforts. After that, he returned home alone quietly, to tell ingenuously of his deed.

"Gentlemen, the heroism of man is beautiful and worthy of veneration; but that of a child, in whom no aim of ambition or other interests may be possible, in a child who must have the more hardihood in proportion to his strength; in a child, from whom we ask nothing, who is considered nothing, who seems to be so noble and amiable, not only when he accomplishes what he undertakes but also when he recognizes the sacrifices of others. Heroism in a child is divine! I will say nothing more, gentlemen. I do not wish to cover such simple grandeur with superfluous praises. Behold before you the noble and valorous rescuer. Soldiers, salute him like a brother;

mothers, bless him as a son; children, remember his name, impress upon your mind his face, that he may never be erased from your memory and from your heart. Approach, boy. In the name of the King of Italy, I bestow upon you the medal of civic valor.''

A rousing hurrah, in a chorus of many voices, echoed through the palace. The mayor took the medal from the table and fastened it on the breast of the boy. Then he embraced and kissed him.

His mother placed a hand over her eyes and his father hung his head before such honor.

The mayor shook hands with both of them and taking the decree of decoration, bound with a ribbon, he gave it to the woman.

Then he turned to the boy and said: "May the remembrance of this day, so glorious for you, so joyful for your father and mother, maintain you through all your life on the road of virtue and honor. Good bye!"

The mayor went out. The band commenced to play, and everything seemed to be over, when a squad of firemen made their way in, and a child of eight or ten years, pushed ahead by a woman, ran toward the boy wearing the medal and fell into his arms.

Another crash of applause and hurrahs rang through the court-yard. All immediately understood that he was the boy who had been rescued from the Po, and had come to thank his rescuer. After having kissed him, he took his arm to escort him out. They were at the head of the line; next came the father and mother. It was difficult for them to make their way through the crowd, which, forming a line composed of guards, soldiers, boys and women, all mingled together. They all pushed ahead, standing on tip-toe to see the boy. Thousands who stood in his way touched his hand. When he passed in front of the school boys, they all waved their caps in the air. The boys of Borgo Po made a big uproar, pulling him by his arms and by his jacket and exclaiming: "*Pin! Hurrah for Pin! Bravo, Pinot!*"

He passed very near me; his face was all aflame. He was very happy, with his medal hanging on a red, white and green ribbon. His mother was weeping and laughing, and his father was twisting his moustache with his hand. He trembled as if he had a fever. They were still applauding from the windows, from the balconies, and from the loggia.

As they were about to pass under the portico, the *Daughters of the Soldiers* suddenly threw down a shower of pansies, violets and daisies, which fell upon the head of the boy, of the father, of the mother, and were scattered on the ground. Some of the crowd began to pick them up hurriedly, in order to present them to the mother. In the meanwhile the band at the end of the court was playing a very soft and beautiful tune which seemed like a song of many silvery voices fading away along the banks of a river.

MAY

THE CHILDREN WITH THE RICKETS

Thursday the 5th.

I took a vacation to-day, because I was not feeling well, and my mother permitted me to go with her to the asylum for children afflicted with the rickets, where she went to recommend a child of our janitor, but she did not allow me to enter the school.

Dost thou not understand, Enrico, why I did not allow thee to enter? I did not wish to place in front of these unfortunates, there in the middle of the school, almost as a show, a healthy and robust boy. They have too many occasions to make sorrowful comparisons. What a sad thing! Tears came from my heart when

I entered that room. I saw about sixty boys and girls ——— Poor tortured bones! Poor hands! Poor little shriveled and distorted feet! Poor deformed bodies! I immediately observed some pretty faces, some eyes full of intelligence and affection; there was a little girl having a face with a pointed nose and chin, who looked like a little old woman, but she had a sweet and celestial smile. Some of them looked quite pretty in their faces and without defects, but when they turned around, how different! A weight fell upon one's soul. The physician was there visiting them. He stood them upon the benches and lifted their little dresses, touching the swollen stomachs and the enlarged joints, but they did not seem at all bashful, poor creatures! One could see that they were accustomed to be undressed, examined and turned around to be seen from every side; and to think that they are now in the best stage of their disease and they do not suffer much any more! What must they not have suffered when their bodies began to be deformed, when, with the growing of their deformity, they saw the affection of their companions diminishing toward them! Poor children! Left alone for hours in the corner of a room, or in the court-yard, badly fed, and at times even scoffed at. Some of them tormented for months with bandages and orthopedic apparatuses! Now, however, thanks to care and good food and gymnastics, many improve. The teacher made them go through some gymnastic exercises. It was a pitiful sight, at certain commands, to see them stretch from under the benches all those bandaged limbs squeezed between splints, knotty and deformed — those limbs that should have been covered with kisses! Several of them were not able to rise from the bench and sat there with their heads bent down upon their arms, caressing their crutches with their hands, others making a thrust with their arms would lose their breath and fall down upon the bench and sit there pale but smiling in order to conceal their sorrow. Ah, Enrico! You other boys do not appreciate health, thinking it is so small a thing to be well! I was thinking of the beautiful, strong and thriving boys that their mothers carry around in triumph, proud of their beauty, and I felt as if I wanted to take all those poor little heads and press them upon my heart in despair; and say: "Were I alone in the world, I would never move from here, I would consecrate my life to you, wait upon you, act as a mother to you until my last day"——*They sang with such thin, sweet and mournful voices that the music touched my soul, and when the teacher praised them, they appeared to be so glad. While she was passing between the benches, they would kiss her hands and arms as though they felt much gratitude to those who labored for their benefit. They are very affectionate. Some also have talent—those little angels—and the teacher told me that they study well.. This young teacher had a kind face, but with a certain expression of sadness like the reflection of the misfortunes which she consoles and caresses. Dear girl! Among all the creatures who earn their living by toil, there is not one who earns it in a more holy way than you, sainted creature!*

Thy Mother.

SACRIFICE

Tuesday the 9th.

My mother is good and my sister Silvia is exactly like her, she has the same kind and gentle heart. Last night I was copying a part of the monthly story, "*From the Appennines to the Andes*," of which the teacher has given us each a portion to copy, because it is so very long, when my sister Silvia entered on tip-toe and told me softly, speaking in an anxious tone: "Come with me to mamma. I heard some one talking this morning. Some of papa's business has turned out bad. He was sad and mamma was trying to encourage him. We are in stringent circumstances, do you understand? There is no more money. Papa said it would be necessary to make some sacrifices in order to meet our loss. Now it is essential that we two also make some sacrifices, do you not think so? Are you not ready? Well then, when I speak to mamma, you must nod assent and promise upon your honor, that you will do all that I am about to tell her."

After saying this, she took me by the hand and led me to our mother, who was sewing, all wrapped up in her thoughts. I sat down on one side of the sofa and Silvia on the other, and she immediately said:

"Mamma, listen, I wish to speak to you. We both wish to speak to you." Mother looked at us in astonishment.

Silvia then began: "Is it not true that papa is without money?"

"What do you mean?" asked my mother, blushing. "No, it is not true. What do you know about it? Who has told you this?"

"I know it," said Silvia resolutely. "Listen, mamma, we must make some sacrifices too. You had promised me a fan for the end of May, and Ernico was expecting his paint box. We no longer want them; we do not want any *soldi* to be wasted; we shall be just as well satisfied without. Do you understand?" Mother tried to speak, but Silvia continued: "No, it must be so. We have come to this conclusion. As long as papa does not have money, we do not want any dessert or other fine things, we will be satisfied with soup alone; and we will only eat bread for breakfast in the morning. This will reduce the expense for the table, as we spend more than is necessary now. Besides we promise you that you shall see us just as contented as before. Is it not so, Enrico?"

I answered, yes. "Always as contented as before," repeated Silvia, closing mamma's mouth with her hand, "and if there are any other sacrifices to make, either in dress or anything else, we shall be glad to do so. We are ready to sell our presents; I would give everything I have, I will wait upon you like a maid, we shall not have anything ordered out of the house, and I will work with you the whole day, I will do everything you wish, I am disposed to do everything! To do everything!" she exclaimed, throwing her arms around mother's neck, "provided that papa and mamma may never experience any sorrow, in order that I may see you both calm and in good spirits as you were before, with your Silvia and your Enrico, who love you so much, and who would give their lives for you!"

I had never seen my mother so happy as when she heard those words. She never kissed us on the brow in that way before, weeping and laughing and unable to speak. After awhile, she assured Silvia that she had misunderstood the situation, that we were not in such reduced circumstances as she thought; luckily for us, we were not destitute. She thanked us hundreds of times, and was cheerful all the evening, and when my father came home she told him everything. He did not open his mouth, my poor father! But this morning, when I was taking my seat at the table, I experienced a great pleasure mingled with some sadness. I found my box of paints under my napkin, and Silvia found her fan.

THE FIRE *

Thursday the 11th.

I had just finished copying my portion of the story, "*From the Appennines to the Andes*," this morning, and was trying to find a theme for my individual composition, which our teacher asked us to write, when I heard an unusual sound of voices on the stairs and soon after two firemen entered our apartment,

---

* This happened the night of January 27th, 1880.

who asked my father's permission to inspect the stoves and the chimneys, as a smoke-pipe was on fire upon the roof, and they did not know which one it was. My father told them to go ahead, and, although we had no fire lighted anywhere in our apartment, they went around from room to room, laying their ear against the walls to hear if a fire was roaring inside of the flues which run from the other stories of the house.

While they were going through the other rooms, my father said to me: " Enrico, here is a theme for your composition, 'The Firemen.' Listen to me and write it down. I saw them at work one evening two years ago, when I came out of the Balbo theatre late at night. Going through the via Roma, I saw an unusual light and a crowd of people were running; a house was on fire. Tongues of flame and clouds of smoke were bursting from the windows and from the roof. Men and women appeared on the window sills and disappeared, uttering despairing cries. There was a great noise in front of the door of the house, and the crowd shouted: " They are burning alive! Help! Help! The firemen!" At that moment a wagon arrived and four firemen sprang out of it. They were the first ones to arrive and they rushed inside the house. Hardly had they entered when a horrible sight was witnessed. A woman peeped from a third story window, shouting and clutching at the railing, climbed over it and remained suspended in that way, almost in space, with her back turned, bending under the smoke and flames which were creeping from room to room and leaped almost to her head. The crowd uttered a cry of horror. The firemen, who had by mistake been stopped at the second floor by the horrified lodgers, had already made an opening through the wall, and rushed into room, when a hundred cries from below told them:

" ' Up to the third story!' "

" They flew to the third story. A terrible destruction was going on there; wooden beams were falling; the corridors were filled with flames and a stifling smoke. The only way that remained by which to reach these lodgers was to pass over the roof. They rushed up immediately, and a minute after, a man was seen like a black phantom going over the tile roof in the midst of fire and smoke; it was the corporal of the firemen, who was the first to reach the side of the roof which corresponded to the suite of rooms cut off by the fire.

"In order to reach this point, it was necessary to go over an extremely narrow place between the dormer window and the eaves. All the remainder of the house was in flames and that little space was covered with snow and ice and there was not a projection one could grasp with the hand.

"'It is impossible for him to go through there!' said the crowd below.

"The corporal came out on the edge of the roof; every one shuddered and stood looking, with suspended breath; he passed over; an immense hurrah arose to the sky. The corporal pushed further ahead, and having reached the threatened point, began with furious blows of his hatchet to split the beams, shingles and tiles in order to make an opening by which he could enter the room below. All this time the woman remained suspended outside the window; the fire was raging above her head; one moment more and she would have fallen into the street.

"The opening was made, the corporal was seen taking off his shoulder belt and sliding down; the other firemen having arrived followed him. At the same moment, a very tall patent ladder, which had just been brought, was placed on the entablature of the house in front of the windows from which the flames and maddening cries were issuing. But every one thought it was too late.

'"No one can be saved!' they were crying. 'The firemen will be burned to death!' 'It is all over!' "They are dead!' Suddenly the black figure of the corporal, illuminated by the flames overhead, appeared at the window over the balcony. The woman clasped her arms around his neck;

he caught her by the waist with both arms and pulled her up
and laid her inside the room. The crowd gave vent to a shout
of a thousand voices which deafened the uproar of the fire.

" ' But how about the others? How can they get down.'
The ladder was leaning on the roof in front of another window,
but a wide space intervened between them.

" ' How will they be able to reach it?'

"While the crowd were saying this, one of the firemen came
out of the window, thrust his right foot upon the window sill
and the left upon the ladder, and standing thus in the air, he
grasped the lodgers one by one as the other firemen reached
them out to him from the window, handed them over to his
companion who had come up on the ladder, and who, after
securing them on the ladder, one after the other, and with the
assistance of the firemen below, helped them to descend to the
street. The woman who had clung to the balcony was the first
to come out, then a little girl, another woman and an old man
followed. All were saved. After the old man, the firemen
came down; and the corporal, who had been the first to run up,
was the last one to descend.

"The crowd received them all with an outburst of applause
but when the last one appeared, the van-guard of the rescuers,
the one who had faced the abyss before the others, the one who
would have died if it had been necessary for any one to lose his
life, the crowd saluted him like a triumphing conqueror, shouting and stretching their arms with a loving impulse of admiration and gratitude, and in a few moments his obscure name,
Giuseppe Robbino, resounded from thousands of lips. Do you
understand? This is true courage! The courage of the heart
which does not stop to reason, which does not waver, which
goes blindly like a flash of lightning wherever he hears the cries
of the dying. Some day, I will take you to see the firemen
manœuvering and will point out to you Corporal Robbino,
as I am sure that you would be very glad to meet him, would
you not?"

I answered that I should.

"Here he is," said my father.

I turned around startled. The two firemen, having finished their inspection, were crossing the room to go out.

My father pointed to the smaller of the two, who had stripes of braid on his sleeves, and said to me: "Shake the hand of Corporal Robbino."

The corporal, smiling, reached his hand to me; I shook it; he saluted me and left.

"Remember it well," said my father, "among thousands of hands that you will shake in your life, there may not be ten that are worth this one."

FROM THE APENNINES TO THE ANDES

Many years ago a Genoese lad of about thirteen, son of a workman, went from Genoa to America, all alone, to search for his mother.

Two years before she had gone to Buenos Ayres, the capital of the Argentine Republic, to enter the service of some rich family, in order to earn in a short time enough to put the family in better circumstances; for, owing to various mishaps, they had fallen into poverty and debt. There are thousands of women who would take such a long journey with that object. The people who went into service there, on account of the large salaries which they received, would return home in a few years with several thousands of lire.

The poor mother had wept bitter tears at being separated from her children—the oldest was eighteen and the youngest eleven—but she departed full of courage and hope. She had quite a pleasant voyage, and as soon as she landed, through the influence of a Genoese cousin of her husband, who had been established in business there for a long time, she found work with a good Argentine family, who paid her high wages and treated her kindly. For a short time she kept up a regular correspondence with her family. As they had agreed, the husband would direct letters to the cousin, who transmitted them to the woman, and the latter remitted the answers to him and he would send them to Genoa, adding some lines of his own. Earning eighty lire a month and not spending anything for herself, she was sending home a nice little sum of money every three months, with which the husband, who was an upright man, was gradually paying his most urgent debts, and by degrees regaining his good reputation. In the meantime he was working and satisfied with his own affairs, always cherishing the hope that the mother would return soon, as the home seemed empty without her. The younger child especially, who loved his mother so much, was depressed and unable to reconcile himself to his mother's absence.

A year had passed since they had parted, and after receiving a brief letter in which the woman said she was not feeling well, they received no more news. They wrote to the cousin twice, but he did not reply. They wrote to the Argentine family by whom she had been employed, but probably the letter did not reach its destination, as they had misspelled the name in the address, and they never received an answer.

Fearing some mishap had occurred, the husband wrote to the Italian consul at Buenos Ayres to make some inquiries. After three months the consul wrote back that, in spite of the advertisements in the papers, no one had even appeared to give any information concerning such a person. It must have been that the woman had not given the Argentine family her true name, thinking to spare the reputation of her family, whom she thought might be disgraced by her being a servant. A few months more passed without any news. Father and sons were in consternation, and the smaller of the boys was oppressed by a sadness which he could not conquer. What could be done? To whom should they have recourse? The first thought of the father had been to go and look for his wife in America. But how about his work. Who would support his sons? The oldest son could not go away, as he was just beginning to earn something, and he was necessary to the family. So they lived on in constant anxiety, asking each other, day after day, the same painful questions, and looking silently at each other.

Finally, one evening, Marco, the younger of the two boys, said resolutely: "I will go to America to look for my mother."

His father shrugged his shoulders sadly but did not answer. It was a loving thought but an impossibility to undertake a trip to America alone at the age of thirteen, when it took a month to get there! But the boy patiently persisted. He spoke of it that day and the day after, and every day with great calmness, reasoning with the good sense of a man. "Others have gone there," he would say, "who are smaller than I. When once on the boat, I will reach there the same as any one else. When I arrive, I have only to find the shop of my cousin. There are so many Italians there that some one will show me the way. When I find my cousin, I can easily find my mother. If I do not find him, I will go to the consul, I will look for the Argentine family. No matter what happens, there is work for all there and I will also find work, at least until I can earn enough to return home." Thus little by little he almost persuaded his father to let him go. His father had the greatest esteem for him; he knew that he was judicious and courageous; that he was accustomed to privations and sacrifices; and that all these good traits would acquire double force in the holy undertaking of finding his mother whom he adored. In addition to this, it happened that the captain of a steamer, a friend of an acquaintance of his, having heard something about the matter, pledged himself to provide a third-class ticket for him to America.

After a little further hesitation, the father consented and the trip was decided upon. They filled a bag with clothes, put some "scudi" in his pocket, and gave him the address of his cousin; and on a beautiful morning in the month of May, they saw him on board.

"My child! My Marco!" said his father, pressing the last kiss upon his cheek, with tears in his eyes, as he stood upon the steps of the steamer which was about to leave, "have courage. You leave on a holy undertaking and God will help you."

Poor Marco! He had a strong heart, prepared for all the hardest trials of that voyage, but when he saw his beautiful Genoa disappear, when he found himself upon the high seas on that large steamer thronged with emigrants, alone, unknown to every one, with a little bag which held all his fortune, a sudden discouragement seized him. He remained for two days sitting at the bows like a lost dog, eating scarcely anything, oppressed by a great desire to weep. Every kind of sad presentiment, was passing through his mind, and the saddest, the most terrible was the most persistent in its return, the thought that his mother might be dead. In his painful and broken sleep, he always saw the face of a stranger looking at him with an air of pity, and whispering in his ear: "Your mother is dead." Then he would awake with a suppressed cry on his lips.

Nevertheless, at the first sight of the Atlantic Ocean, after passing the Straits of Gibraltar, he began to have a little courage and hope, but it was of short duration. That immense but never varying sea, the increasing heat, the sadness of all the poor people who surrounded him, the thought of his own solitude returned to depress him. The days which followed, empty and monotonous, were confused in his memory as it happens with a sick person. It seemed to him that he had been at sea for a year. Every morning when he awoke, he felt a new stupor at being there alone, on that immense body of water, on a voyage to America. Beautiful flying fishes fell from time to time upon the boat. He saw those marvelous tropical sunsets, those great blood-red clouds all aflame, those nocturnal phosphorescences, that make the ocean appear like a sea of lighted lava, all of which did not give him the impression of real things but of prodigies seen in dreams.

He experienced some days of bad weather, during which he remained locked in the dormitory, where everything was rolling and cracking, in the midst of a frightful chorus of lamentations and imprecations, and he believed that his last hour had come. He sailed for three days through a yellowish sea, through days of unbearable heat, of infinite annoyance, of hours interminable and sinister, during which the passengers, enervated and stretched motionless upon the berths, looked like dead bodies. It seemed as though this voyage would never come to an end. Sea and sky, sky and sea, to-day like yesterday, and to-morrow like to-day—the same, always the same—eternally.

He would lean over the bulwarks for hours, looking at that boundless sea, dumbfounded; thinking vaguely of his mother until his eyes closed and he was falling down into sleep, and in his dream he would again see that strange face looking at him with pity and whispering in his ear: "Your mother is dead!"

At that voice, he would wake with a start and resume his dreamings with open eyes, looking at the unchangeable horizon.

The voyage lasted twenty-seven days! The last days were the best. The weather was beautiful and the air was fresh. He had formed the acquaintance of an old man, a Lombard, who was going to America to join his son, a farm laborer near the city of Rosario. The boy told him everything about his home, and the old man would repeat to him from time to time, patting him on the back of the neck: "Courage, my boy, you will find your mother in good health and contented." The companionship of the old man comforted him, and his presentiments became more joyful. Sitting at the bow, under that beautiful starry sky, next to the old farmer who was smoking his pipe, in the midst of a group of emigrants, he fancied the scene of his arrival at Buenos Ayres a hundred times. He would see himself in a certain street, finding his cousin, rushing into the shop and asking him: "How is my mother? Where is she? Let us go at once! Let us go at once!" They would run together, ascend the steps, a door would open—— and here his mute soliloquy would stop and his imagination would be lost in the inexplicable sentiment which caused him to look slily at a little medal which he wore on his neck, murmuring his prayers while kissing it.

They arrived at Buenos Ayres the twenty-seventh day after their departure. It was a beautiful rosy morning in the month of May when the steamer dropped anchor in that immense river La Plata. On the shore of the river stretched out the vast city of Buenos Ayres, the capital of the Argentine Republic. The fine weather seemed to him to be a good omen. He was fairly beside himself with joy and impatience. His mother was only a few miles distant from him! In a few hours he would see her! He was in America, in the New World, and he had had the courage to come alone! All that extremely long voyage seemed to him as nothing. It seemed to him that he had dreamed and awoke at that point. He was so happy that he experienced no surprise or distress when he went through his pockets and found that one of the packages into which he had divided his little treasure in order not to lose it all, was gone. Some one had stolen it from him. He had only a few lire left, but what did he care now that he was so near his mother? With his bag in his right hand, he left the steamer with the other Italians and stepped into a little tug boat which carried him near the shore. Then he got into a row-boat, bearing the name of *Andrea Doria,* and came upon the wharf. He bade good-bye to his old Lombard friend and started with long strides toward the city.

As soon as he arrived at the entrance to the first street, he stopped a man who was passing and begged him to tell him which way to go to reach the street of los Artes. It happened that he stopped an Italian workman. The latter looked at him with curiosity and asked him if he knew how to read. The boy made a sign of assent. "Well," said the workman, pointing out the street from which he came, "go up the street reading the names at the corners until you find the one you want." The boy thanked him and began walking up the street before him.

It was a straight and rather narrow road, and seemed endless, flanked on either side by low, white houses, which looked like so many little cottages. It was crowded with people, carriages and large wagons, making a deafening roar. Here and there hung enormous flags of various colors upon which was written in large letters the announcement of the departure of steamers for unknown cities. All the way, turning to the right and left, he saw the streets stretching as far ahead as one could see, all lined with low, white houses and filled with people and wagons. The streets all terminated in the boundless American plain, similar to the horizon on the sea. The town seemed to him infinite. He thought that one could walk for days and days and for weeks, always seeing here and there other streets like those, and that the whole of America was covered with them. He looked attentively at the names of the streets, some of them very strange, which he could only read with great effort. Every new street he reached his heart would throb, hoping it might be the one he wanted. He looked at every woman, thinking that he might meet his mother. He saw one walking in front of him who caused the blood to leap in his veins. He overtook her; looked at her—it was a negress. He kept going and going, hastening his steps. When he reached a certain street and read the name, he stood there as though rooted to the sidewalk; it was the street of los Artes. He turned into it and saw the number 117; the store of his cousin was 175. He hurried his gait, almost running, until he reached the number 171, then he was obliged to stop and take breath, and he said to himself: "Oh, my mother, my mother! Is it really true that I will see you in a few moments?" He ran forward and came to a small dry-goods store. It was the one. He peeped in and saw a woman with eye-glasses.

"What do you want, boy?" she asked him in Spanish.

The boy, speaking with difficulty, said, "Is this not the store of Francesco Merelli?"

"Francesco Merelli is dead," replied the woman in the Italian tongue.

The boy felt as if he had received a blow upon his breast.

"When did he die?"

"A long time ago," replied the woman. "It is several months since he died. He met with failures and fled. It is said that he went to Bahia Blanca, a great distance from here, and that he died as soon as he reached there. This store is my own."

The boy grew pale.

Then he said rapidly: "Merelli knew my mother, who was here in the service of Mequinez. He was the only one who could tell me where to find her. I came to America on purpose to find my mother. Morelli sent her our letters. I must find my mother."

"Poor child," said the woman, "I do not know. I will

ask the boy out in the court-yard; he knew the young man who was running errands for Merelli. It may be that he knows something about it."

She went to the end of the store and called the boy, who came in directly. "Tell me," said the store-keeper, "do you remember that young man whom Merelli sent at times to carry letters to a woman in service in the house of his countryman?" "To Signor Mequinez," the boy replied. "Yes, madam, I remember. He lives at the end of the street los Artes."

"Thanks, madam, thanks!" cried Marco. "Tell me the number. Do you know it? Accompany me at once, I still have a few soldi left."

Marco said this with so much warmth, that without waiting for the order of the woman, the other boy exclaimed: "Let us go," and started out immediately.

Almost running and without saying a word, they went to the end of a very long street, entered the entrance hall of a small white house, stopped in front of a beautiful iron gate from which a court, filled with vases of beautiful flowers, could be seen. Marco pulled the bell vigorously.

A young lady appeared. "Does the family of Mequinez live here?" anxiously inquired the lad.

"They did live here," answered the young lady, pronouncing her Italian with a Spanish accent. "The Zeballos live here now."

"And where have the Mequinez family gone?" asked Marco with a palpitating heart.

"They have gone to Cordova."

"Cordova!" exclaimed Marco, "where is Cordova? And how is it about the woman they had in their service? The woman, my mother! That woman was my mother! Did they take her with them?"

The young lady looked at him and said: "I do not know. My father who knew them before they left may be able to tell you. Wait a moment."

She ran away and came back in a short time with her father, a tall gentleman with a grey beard. He looked for a moment at that sympathetic type of a little Genoese sailor with blonde hair and aquiline nose and said in bad Italian: "Is your mother a Genoese?"

Marco replied' "yes!"

"Well, the Genoese woman went with the family she served. I am certain that she did."

"And where have they gone?"

"To the town of Cordova."

The lad drew a deep sigh and then said with resignation, "Then I must go to Cordova."

"*Ah, nino!*" exclaimed the gentleman looking at him with an air of compassion. "Poor boy! It is hundreds of miles from here to Cordova."

Marco grew as pale as death and leaned upon the iron railing.

The gentleman, moved to pity, opened the door and said: "Let us see—come in a moment. Let us see what can be done." He offered Marco a seat, sat down and had him tell his story, listening to him very attentively. He stood a moment in thought and then said resolutely: "You have no money, have you?"

"I have still—a little," answered Marco.

The gentleman again thought for about five minutes and then seated himself at a desk and wrote a letter, sealed it, and handing it to the boy, said to him: "Listen, Italianito. Take this letter and go to Boca. It is a small town, half Genoese, at about two hours distance from here. Any one can show you the way. Go there and look for the gentleman to whom this letter is addressed, and whom every one knows. Take this letter to him. He will arrange for you to leave to-morrow for Rosario, and he will recommend you to some one out there who will take it upon himself to see that you reach Cordova, where you will find the Mequinez family and your mother. In the meanwhile, take this, and he thrust a few lire into his hand. "Go, and have courage. You will find your countrymen everywhere; you need not be ashamed. Adios."

The boy said: "Thanks." He could find no other words with which to express himself. He went out with his bag, and taking leave of his little guide, he started slowly towards Boca, filled with sadness and amazement, as he marched through those noisy streets.

All that happened to him from that moment until the evening of the next day was always confused and uncertain in his memory, like the vagaries of a person in a fever. He was so tired, disappointed, and despondent. He slept in a small room of a house in Boca the first night, by the side of a porter of the harbor. He passed nearly the whole of the next day sitting upon a pile of planks as if in a trance, gazing at thousands of ships, large boats, and tug boats, and that evening he found himself on the poop of a large sailing vessel, laden with fruit, which was leaving for the city of Rosario, managed by three robust Genoese, bronzed by exposure to the sun, whose voices and beloved dialect furnished him a little comfort.

The voyage lasted for three days and four nights. It was a continued surprise to the little traveler. Three days and four nights on that marvelous river of Parana. In comparison to it, our river Po is nothing but a rivulet, and the length of Italy quadrupled does not equal the length of its course. The boat moved slowly against that immense body of immeasurable water. It passed between long islands which were once the haunts of serpents and tigers, now covered with orange and willow trees, something like floating woods; and now it passed through narrow canals, from which it seemed it would never come out; then it sailed through vast expanses of water looking like large tranquil lakes; then again between islands and through the intricate channels of an archipelago, in the midst of enormous masses of vegetation. A most profound silence reigned. For long distances, the shores, the solitary and vast waters offered the suggestion of an unknown river, upon which that poor sailing vessel was the first one in the world to venture. The farther he advanced, the more that monstrous river dismayed him. He would imagine that his mother could be found at the source of that river and that the voyage would last for years. Twice a day he ate a little bread and salt meat with the boatmen, who, observing that he was sad, did not say a word to him. During the night, he slept upon the deck, and woke once in awhile astounded by the limpid light of the moon, which was glittering over the vast waters and whitening the distant shores, and his head was oppressed. "Cordova!" he repeated that name: "Cordova!" like the name of one of those mysterious cities of which he had heard in some fable. Then he would think: "My mother passed through here, she has seen these islands, these shores," and then those places did not seem so strange and solitary to him, upon which the gaze of his mother had rested. During the night, one of the boatmen sang. That song reminded him of the songs which his mother sang him to sleep when he was a babe. The last night when he heard that song, he sobbed. The boatman stopped, and then he cried out: "Courage! Courage, my child! What is the use? A Genoese does not cry because he is so far away from home! The Genoese go around the world, glorious and triumphant!"

Hearing those words, Marco shook himself, raised himself haughtily, beating the helm with his fist: "Yes," he said to himself "should I have to search through the whole world and travel years and years yet, and walk hundreds of miles, I shall go ahead until I find my mother. Even if I should reach her dying and drop dead at her feet, if I may only see her once again! Courage!"—In this state of mind, on a rosy morning at daybreak, he arrived in front of the city of Rosario, situated on a high bank of the Parana, where the beflagged yards of hundreds of ships from all over the world were mirrored in the water.

After landing, he went up to the city, with his bag in his hand, to look for the Argentine gentleman for whom his protector at Boca had given him a visiting card with a few words of recommendation written upon it. He beheld those interminable streets, traversing in all directions, flanked by low, white houses; and above the roofs there were great bundles of telegraph and telephone wires which looked like enormous spider webs. The streets were filled with swarms of people, horses and wagons. His mind was confused; he thought for a moment that he was entering Buenos Ayres again, and that he would have to look for his cousin once more. He walked around for about an hour, making turn after turn, and it seemed to him all the time as though he were walking over the same street. By constantly inquiring, he found the house of his new protector. He rang the bell. A big, blonde man, with a gruff voice, who looked like a country steward, awkwardly asked him, with a strange pronunciation, "What do you want?"

The boy spoke the name of the master.

The steward replied, "The master left last night with all his family for Buenos Ayres."

The boy was speechless.

Then he stammered, "But I—I know no one here! I am alone!" and he showed the card.

The country steward took it and read it, and said brusquely, "I do not know what to do about it. I will hand it to him when he comes back in a month."

"But I—I am alone. I am in want," said the boy in a beseeching voice.

"Come, come, now," said the man, "are there not enough parasites who come from your country to Rosario to beg? Go back and do your begging in Italy."

And he closed the gate in his face.

The boy stood there as though petrified.

Then he slowly took up his bag again and went out with

his heart full of anguish and his mind in a whirl, at once assailed by a thousand sorrowful thoughts. What was there to be done? Where could he go? From Rosario to Cordova was a day's ride by rail. He had only a few lire. Deducting what he needed for that day, he would scarcely have anything left. How could he find money for his trip? He could work, but how, and of whom should he ask work? Ask for alms! No, no; to be rebuked, humiliated and insulted as before? No, never, never again; he would rather die! With that thought, and seeing in front of him a very long street which lost itself far away in the boundless plain, his courage gave way again. He threw his bag on the sidewalk, and sat with his shoulders against the wall, bending his head upon his hands, without crying, in an attitude of desolation.

The people in passing jostled him with their feet, the wagons filled the air with noise; some boys stopped to look at him. He remained in that position for a long time.

At last he was startled by a voice, half Italian and half Lombard, which called out: "What is the matter, little fellow?"

He raised his head at these words and immediately jumped to his feet, uttering an exclamation of surprise: "You here!" It was the old Lombard farmer with whom he had formed a companionship during his voyage.

The surprise of the farmer was not less than that of the boy, but the latter did not give him time to question him, and he told rapidly all that had happened to him since he left him at the wharf in Buenos Ayres. "Now I am without money. That is my condition. I must work. Find me some work, that I may be able to earn a few lire; I will do anything; I will carry merchandise, sweep the streets, I can run errands, I can work in the country, I will be satisfied to live upon black bread, if only I may be able to leave soon, if only I may find my mother again. Do me this favor; some work; give me some work, for the love of God, as this is more than I can endure!"

"The deuce," said the farmer, looking around and rubbing his chin. "What a tale!—— One can easily say 'some work.' Let us think a little. There may be a way to find thirty lire among so many compatriots!"

The boy was looking at him, comforted by a ray of hope.

"Come with me," said the farmer.

"Where?" asked the boy, picking up his bag.

"Come with me."

The farmer started out and the boy followed him. They went for a long distance in the street without talking. The farmer stopped at the door of an inn, which had a sign in the shape of a star upon which was written: "*La Estrella de Italia.*" He looked in and turning to the boy said playfully: "We have come at a good time."

They entered one of the large halls where there were several tables and a number of men seated, who were drinking and talking loudly. The old Lombard approached the first table, and from the way in which he saluted the six customers who sat around it, one could see that he had been in their company only a short time before.

They were red in the face and were clinking their glasses, shouting and laughing. "Comrades," said the Lombard, standing up and presenting Marco: "Here is a poor boy, a countryman of ours, who came from Genoa to Buenos Ayres searching for his mother. When he reached Buenos Ayres, they told him: 'She is not here, she has gone to Cordova.' He comes to Rosario in a boat, traveling three days and three nights, with two lines of recommendation; he presents the card and they make an ugly face at him. He has not the shadow of a centesimo. He is here alone and in despair. I know him; he is a boy full of heart; let us think a little. Can he not find enough here to pay for his ticket to Cordova and find his mother? Shall we abandon him here like a dog?"

"Never in the world!" "That shall never be said!" they

cried together, striking their fists on the table. "A countryman of ours!" "Come here, little fellow." "We, too, are emigrants here!" "Look what a fine rogue." "Out with your money, comrades!" "Good boy! He came here alone. He has lots of pluck!" "Have a drink, compatriot!" "We will send you to your mother, never fear."

One pinched him in the cheek, another patted him on the shoulder, and a third relieved him of his bag. Some of the other emigrants arose from the neighboring tables and approached. The story of the boy made the rounds of the inn. Three Argentine customers came in from the next room, and in less than ten minutes the Lombard farmer, who was passing the hat, gathered in over nine dollars.

"Do you see," he said, turning toward the boy, "how quickly one does business in America?"

"Drink," cried another, reaching out a glass of wine, "to the health of your mother." They all raised their glasses, and Marco repeated:

"To the health of my——" but a sob of joy choked his utterance, and replacing his glass upon the table, he threw his arms around the old man's neck.

He left for Cordova the next morning before daybreak, bold and smiling, his heart filled with happy presentiments. But there is no joyousness which reigns for a long time surrounded by the sinister aspects of nature. The weather was dark and disagreeable. The train was empty and ran through an immense plain, bereft of every sign of vegetation. He found himself alone in a very long car which resembled those that are used for carrying the wounded. He gazed to the right and left, seeing nothing but a boundless solitude, and here and there were scattered small dwarf trees with distorted trunks and branches, in such shapes as he had never seen before, as though they had been twisted and gnarled by wrath and anguish. Rank and dark vegetation could be seen everywhere, which gave to the prairie the appearance of a boundless cemetery. He would doze for a half hour and then look around him again; always seeing the same spectacle. The railway stations were lonesome like the huts of hermits, and not a voice could be heard. It seemed to him that he was on a lost train, abandoned in the middle of a desert. He fancied that every station he passed by ought to be the last, and from that point he was going to enter into some mysterious and frightful land inhabited by savages. A sharp breeze blew in his face. When sailing from Genoa about the last of April, his friends had not thought that in South America he would find a wintry season and they had clad him in summer clothes. After many hours, he began to suffer from the cold, and in addition to this suffering he felt the lassitude of the previous days, filled with violent emotions, and of harassing and sleepless nights. He fell asleep and slept for a long time; when he awoke, he felt chilled and sick. A vague terror seized him for fear he might be taken ill or die on his way, and be thrown into the midst of that desolate plain, where his body would be torn by dogs and birds of prey, like the bodies of horses and cows which he had seen at different places near the railway track, and from which he would turn away his eyes in disgust. In the midst of the restless agitation of that sad silence of nature, his imagination would become excited and grow very somber. Was he over-confident of finding his mother in Cordova? And if she had not gone there? If that gentleman of the via los Artes should have made a mistake? And if she were dead?

With such oppressing thoughts, he fell asleep again and dreamed he was in Cordova; it was night and he heard from every door and from every window people cry: "She is not here! She is not here!" This roused him with a start, terrified with horror; when he saw at the end of the car three bearded men, wrapped in shawls of various colors, who were talking softly among themselves and looking at him. A suspicion that they were murderers flashed through his mind, and he thought they were planning to kill him, to rob him of his bag. To the cold and the oppression of his heart fear was added; and his perturbed fancy became distorted, while the three men still gazed at him.

One of them got up and moved towards him. Then he lost his self-control, and, running to meet him with his arms outstretched, he cried: "I have nothing! I am a poor boy! I came from Italy to look for my mother! I am alone, do not hurt me!"

The men understood everything and were moved to pity. They caressed and quieted him, saying many words which he could not understand, and, noticing that his teeth were chattering with the cold, they put their shawls around him and had him sit down again. He fell asleep once more when it was growing dark. When they woke him up, he was in Cordova.

Ah, what a breath he drew, and with what impetuosity he rushed out of the car. He asked a railway employe at the station where the engineer Mequinez lived. The latter gave him the name of a church next to which was the Mequinez dwelling. The boy hurried hither. It was night when he entered the city. It seemed to him that he was again entering Rosario, and that he saw those straight streets flanked by small white houses and crossed by straight and endless streets. There were few people out, but under the light of the street lamps far apart he saw some strange faces of an unfamiliar color, something between a black and greenish complexion. Raising his eyes from time to time, he beheld churches of a peculiar architecture, which were outlined black and enormous against the sky. The city was dark and silent; but after having crossed that immense desert, it seemed cheerful to him. He inquired his way of a priest, and soon after found the church and the house. He pulled the bell with a trembling hand, while pressing the other on his breast to suppress the palpitation of his heart, which seemed to be jumping into his throat.

An old woman came to open the door with a lamp in her hand.

At first the boy was unable to speak.

"For whom are you looking?" inquired the woman in Spanish.

"For the engineer Mequinez," said Marco.

The woman crossed her arms on her breast and answered, nodding her head, "You are also one of those who are after the engineer Mequinez! It seems to me that it must be about time for this thing to stop. They have bothered me now for more than three months. Is it not enough that it was published in the newspapers? It will be necessary to have it posted on the corners of the streets that the Senor Mequinez has gone to live in Tucuman!"

The boy made a gesture as though he were in desperation; then, breaking into a wild rage, he said: "It is a curse! I shall have to die on my way without being able to find my mother! I am going crazy; I will kill myself! My God! What did you call that place? Where is it? How far from here?"

"Eh, poor lad," cried the old woman, moved to pity, "It is not a trifle. It must be four or five hundred miles, at the least."

The boy covered his face with both hands, and then asked, sobbing, "And now——what can I do?"

"What can I tell you, poor child?" answered the woman. "I do not know."

Suddenly, however, a thought flashed through her mind, and she hurriedly suggested: "Hear me, now I think of it. Turn to the right and you will find at the third door a courtyard. There is a capataz, a merchant, who leaves to-morrow morning for Tucuman with his carretas and his oxen. Go and see if he feels like taking you along. Offer him your services; probably he will make a place for you on one of his wagons."

The boy thanked the woman, ran away, and two minutes after he was in a vast court-yard, lighted by a lantern, where several men were about to load bags of wheat upon some very large wagons, similar to the movable houses of the mountebanks, with a round roof and very high wheels, while a tall man with a long mustache, wrapped in a sort of mantle of black and white plaid, wearing high top boots, was directing the work. The boy approached the latter, and expressed his wish, saying that he had come from Italy and that he was searching for his mother.

The capataz (the head conductor of that convoy of wagons) cast a glance at him from head to foot, and said drily, "I have no room."

"I have fifteen lire," said the boy in a beseeching manner; 'I will give them all to you. And I am willing to work on the way. I will go and haul water for the oxen; I will do anything. A little bread is enough for me. Do grant me a little place, signore!"

The capataz looked at him again and answered, in a milder tone: "There is no room——and besides——we are not going to Tucuman; we are going to another city, Santiago dell 'Estero. At a certain place we should have to drop you and you would have a long distance to go on foot."

"I am ready to walk double the distance!" exclaimed Marco; "I am ready to walk, do not worry about that; I will go, no matter how: do make a little room for me, signore, for heaven's sake; do not leave me here alone!"

"Think of it; it is a long trip of twenty days."

"It does not matter."

"It is an uncomfortable trip!"

"I will endure it all."

"You will have to travel alone."

"I fear nothing; if only I can find my mother again. Have pity upon me!"

The capataz put a lantern up to his face and scrutinized him; then he said: "Well, you may go!"

The boy kissed his hand.

"For to-night, you may sleep on a wagon," said the capataz, leaving him there. "I will wake you to-morrow morning at four o'clock. *Buenas noches!*"

The next morning at four, while it was still starlight, the long row of wagons started out with a great deal of noise, each wagon being drawn by six oxen, followed by a large number of animals for relays. The boy awoke and they put him inside one of the wagons, and he immediately fell into a profound sleep. When he awoke, the convoy had stopped in a solitary spot. All the men — the *peones* — were sitting in a circle around a quarter of a calf, which was roasting over a large fire in the open air, stuck upon an iron spear planted firmly in the ground. They all ate together, slept awhile and started out again. The journey continued, regulated like a march of soldiers. Every morning they would set out at five and halt at nine; they would leave again at five in the evening, halting again at ten. The *peones* were riding on horseback, stimulating the oxen with long poles. The lad would light the fire for the roast, feed the animals, clean the lanterns, and carry the water for the men to drink. The country passed before him like an indistinct vision. There were vast woods of small dark trees; villages containing but a few houses scattered around, with red facades and battlements. He gazed over extensive spaces, perhaps the ancient beds of rivers or large salt lakes, glimmering with salt as far as the eye could reach; and continually, on every side, a plain, a solitude, a silence.

At rare intervals, they would meet two or three travelers on horseback, followed by a herd of horses, galloping like a whirlwind. The days were all alike as they had been at sea, tiresome and endless. However, the weather was beautiful, but the *peones* were becoming more and more exacting every day,

and they treated the boy as though he were their bounden
servant; some of them even threatened him and abused him
brutally; some forced him to serve them without mercy, making him carry great loads of forage, and sending him long
distances for water; and the poor boy, worn out with fatigue,
could not even sleep at night, constantly shaken by the violent
jolts of the wagon, and disturbed by the deafening noise of
the wheels and wooden axles. In addition to this, the wind
had risen and a thin, reddish, greasy dirt enveloped everything,
penetrating into the wagons and making its way through his
clothes. It filled his eyes and mouth (depriving him of his
eyesight and making it difficult for him to breathe), in a persistent and unbearable manner. Exhausted by fatigue and loss
of sleep, ragged and dirty, reproved and maltreated from morning until night, the poor lad became more and more dejected as
the days passed. He would have lost his wits entirely if the
capataz had not once in awhile spoken a kind word to him.
Oftentimes, when in a corner of the wagon, unseen, he would
cry, hiding his face inside of his bag which now contained only a
few rags. Every morning he got up, more feeble and more discouraged, and looked at the country, always seeing that same
boundless and unchanging plain like an ocean of sand, and he
would say: "Oh, I cannot endure this until night! To-day I
will die on the way!" His fatigue was growing and the maltreatment increased. One morning he was slow in carrying
the water, and in the absence of the capataz one of the men
beat him. After this example, they began to beat him habitually; when they were giving him an order they would give
him a blow, saying: "Take that, vagabond! Take that to
your mother!" His heart was almost broken. He fell sick
and remained for three days upon the wagon, with a cover over
him, shaking with fever and seeing no one but the capataz
who came now and then to offer him a drink and to feel his
pulse. He thought himself lost and was invoking his mother
desperately, calling her by name a hundred times. "Oh, my

mother! Help me! Come and meet me, I am dying! Oh, poor mother, I will never see you again! Poor mother, you will find me dead on the way!' And he folded his hands upon his breast and prayed. Then he began to recover, owing to the care of the capataz. He regained his health; but with the return of his health came the most terrible day of his journey, the day in which he had to be left alone. They had been on the way for more than two weeks, when they came to the place where the road to Tucuman parted from the one which leads to Santiago dell' Estero. The capataz told him they were about to separate. He furnished him with some information concerning the road, tied the bag upon his shoulders in such a way that it would not annoy him in walking, and saying little to him, as if he feared to show emotion, he bade him good bye. The lad had barely time to kiss his hand. The other men who had treated him so harshly also seemed to feel a little pity at seeing him left alone, and made him signs of farewell as they moved away. He returned the salute with his hand and stood looking at the convoy until it was lost in the reddish dust of the country, and then sadly started out on his way.

Something, however, comforted him a little from the beginning. After all those days of travel across the boundless plain having all the time the same aspect, he saw in front of him a chain of very high azure mountains, with white tops, which recalled to his mind the Alps and which made him feel as though he were approaching his own country. It was the Andes, the dorsal spine of the American Continent, that immense chain which extends from Terra del Fuego to the glacial sea of the Arctic Pole, through one hundred and ten degrees of latitude. He was also comforted by feeling that the air was all the time growing warmer, and this happened because he was going to the north and nearing the tropical regions. At great distances from each other, he passed by small groups of houses with a little shop where he would buy something to eat He met men on horseback; from time to time, he saw women and boys sitting motionless on the ground with grave faces, entirely new to him, of an earthen color, with oblique eyes and prominent cheek bones. They looked at him fixedly and followed him with their eyes, turning their heads like automatons. They were Indians.

During the first day, he walked as far as his strength would permit and slept under a tree. The second day, he walked less and with less spirit. Towards evening, he began to be afraid. He had heard in Italy that there were serpents in these countries. He would stop, thinking he heard them crawling, and then he would start on a run and a cold chill would creep over him. A great compassion for himself would overtake him at times, and he cried silently, all the time walking on. Then he thought: "How my mother would suffer if she knew that I am so frightened," and the thought of that would give him courage. In order to distract his thoughts and forget his fear, he would think of many things concerning his mother. He recalled her words when she left Genoa, and the gesture with which she was accustomed to arrange the blankets under his chin when he was in bed. When he was a little child, she would take him in her arms saying: "Stay with me for a moment," and he would stay that way for a long time, with his head leaning upon her, thinking and thinking. He was saying to himself: "Will I ever see you again, dear mother? Will I ever reach the end of my journey, mother?" And he walked on and on amidst unknown trees and vast plantations of sugar-cane, and over immense prairies, with those azure mountains, which pierced the serene sky with their peaks, always before him.

Four days —— five —— then a week passed. His strength was gradually decreasing, his feet were bleeding. Finally, one evening towards sunset, some one told him: "Tucuman is only five miles from here."

He uttered a cry of joy and hastened his step as though he had suddenly regained his lost vigor, but it was a brief respite.

His strength suddenly failed him, and worn out he fell upon the brink of the ditch. However, his heart was beating with happiness. The sky above, thick with shining stars, had never seemed so beautiful to him. He contemplated the firmament while lying on the grass trying to sleep, and thought perhaps his mother was looking at him. He exclaimed: "Oh, my mother, where are you? What are you doing at this moment? Do you think of your child? Do you think of your Marco, who is so near you?"

Poor Marco, if he could have seen in what a state his mother was at that minute, he would have made a superhuman effort to go ahead and reach her at the earliest possible moment. She was sick in bed in a room on the ground floor of a lordly house where lived the Mequinez family, who had grown very fond of her, and who were bestowing upon her every attention. The poor woman was sickly when the engineer Mequinez had suddenly been obliged to leave Buenos Ayres and she had not entirely recovered with the good air of Cordova. In addition to this, the fact of not receiving any answer to her letters either from her husband or from their cousin; the vivid, growing presentiment of a great calamity, and the continual anxiety in which she had lived, not knowing whether to leave or to remain, expecting every day some bad news, had caused her to grow worse. At last, a very grave illness had manifested itself, an internal lesion. She had not left her bed for the last fifteen days. A surgical operation was necessary to save her life. Just at that moment when Marco was invoking her, the master and mistress of the house stood at her beside, trying with much kindness to persuade her to allow the operation to be performed, while she, weeping, persisted in her refusal. A good surgeon from Tucuman had come the previous week, but in vain.

"No, dear masters," she exclaimed, "it is not worth while; I no longer have the strength to endure it; I would die under the knife of the surgeon. It is better that you let me die now. I do not care to live any longer. Everytuing has come to an end with me. It is better that I should die before I know what great misfortune has happened to my family."

But the master was telling her that it must not be so, that she should take courage, that she would soon receive an answer to the last letter which had been sent direct to Genoa if she would only allow the operation to be performed; she ought to do it for the sake of her children!

The suggestion of her children did nothing but aggravate her anguish and the profound discouragement which had prostrated her for a long time. Hearing those words she burst into tears:

"Oh, my poor children! My poor children!" she exclaimed, clasping her hands, "perhaps they are no longer alive! It is better that I should die, too. I thank you, my dear masters, I thank you with all my heart. But it is better that I should die. I know I would not recover even after the operation had been performed; I am certain of it. Thanks for all the cares that you have bestowed upon me, my kind masters. It is useless for the surgeon to come back to-morrow; I wish to die. It is my destiny that I should die here. I have decided."

They still tried to console her, and said: "No, do not say so," and would take her by the hands and beg of her. But she closed her eyes, worn out with exhaustion, and fell into a sort of a trance which made her look as if she were dead. Both the master and mistress remained there a short time, and by the dim light of a small lamp they gazed with great compassion upon that admirable mother, who, in order to save her family, had come to die seven thousand miles from her native country; to die after having suffered so much; poor woman, so honest, so good, but so unhappy.

Early in the morning of the next day, with his bag on his shoulder, bent and limping, but full of spirit, Marco entered the city of Tucuman, one of the youngest and most flourishing cities of the Argentine Republic. It seemed to him that he again beheld Cordova, Rosario and Buenos Ayres. There were the same long, endless, straight streets, with those low, white houses; but on every side there was a young and luxuriant vegetation, a perfumed air, a marvelous light, a limpid and profound sky, such as he had seen in Italy. As he was going through the streets, that feverish agitation, which had overtaken him at Buenos Ayres, again took possession of him; he looked at the windows and the doors of the houses, gazed at the women who were passing, with the anxious hope of meeting his mother. He felt like questioning every one, but did not dare to stop anybody. From the doors of the houses, the people would turn to look at that poor, ragged and dusty boy, whose appearance showed that he had come from a great distance. He looked among the people for a face that would inspire him with confidence enough to ask that tremendous question, when his eyes fell upon the sign of a store, upon which he read an Italian name. He saw a man and two women inside. He slowly approached and summoning a resolute courage and calmness said: "Will you tell me, sir, where the family of Mequinez lives?"

"The *ingeniero* Mequinez?" asked the shopkeeper in his turn.

"The engineer Mequinez," replied the boy in a despairing voice.

"The Mequinez family," said the shopkeeper, "is not in Tucuman."

A desperate outburst of pain, like that of a person who has been stabbed, rang as the echo of those words.

The shop-keeper and the women arose, and some of the neighbors ran to him. "What is the matter, boy," said the shop-keeper, drawing him inside of the store and putting him on a chair. "There is no use despairing. The Mequinez family is not here, but at a short distance, only a few hours' walk from Tucuman."

"Whereabouts? Whereabouts?" cried Marco, springing up as if restored to life again.

"About fifteen miles from here," pursued the man, "on the shore of the Saladillo river, in a place where they are building a large sugar factory, a cluster of houses, one of which is the home of signor Mequinez. Everybody knows it, and you can reach there in a few hours."

"I was there a month ago," said a young man who had run forward at that cry.

Marco looked at him with wide open eyes, and, growing pale, he impatiently asked, "Have you seen the woman in the service of signor Mequinez—the Italian woman?"

"The Genovesa? Yes; I have seen her."

Marco burst into convulsive sobbing, half laughing, half crying.

Then with a sudden resolution he impetuously asked: "Which way must I go? Quick; show me the way, and I will leave at once."

"But it is a day's walk," they all said together. "You are tired; you must rest; you can start in the morning.

"Impossible! Impossible!" cried the boy. "Tell me which way to go. I cannot wait a moment, I want to go at once, even if I have to die on the way."

Seeing how inflexible he was, they opposed him no longer. "May God be with you," they said. "Look out on your way through the forest." "Pleasant trip to you, Italianito."

The man escorted him outside the door and showed him the way, giving him some instructions about the road, and waiting to see him go. After a few minutes the boy disappeared behind the thick trees which lined the road.

That very night was a terrible one for the poor sick woman who suffered excruciating pains which wrung shrieks from her almost enough to burst her veins, and rendered her delirious at times. The women who waited upon her were at a loss. The mistress ran in from time to time affrighted. They all commenced to fear that even if the operation were decided upon, the physician who would have to come the day after would arrive too late. In the intervals in which she was not delirious one could see that she suffered more terrible torture from the thought of her distant family than from her bodily pains. With an agonized look on her distorted face, she would thrust her hands into her hair in a desperate gesture, which was heart-rending, and cry:

"Oh, my God! My God! To die and so far away! To die without seeing them again! My poor children who will be without a mother, my young creatures, my dearest ones! My little Marco, who is still so small, only tall as this, and so affectionate! You do not know what kind of a boy he was! Oh, my mistress, if you only knew! I could scarcely tear him away from my neck when I departed, he sobbed enough to move any one to pity; it seemed as though he apprehended that he would never see his mother again! My poor Marco! My poor child. I thought my heart would burst! Ah, if I had only died then, when he was bidding me farewell. It would have been far better if I had dropped dead then! Without a mother, poor child, he who loved me so much, who wanted me so badly, without a mother, reduced to misery, he will have to go and beg, he, my Marco, to be obliged to stretch out his hand in hunger——Oh! Eternal God! No, I do not wish to die! Call the doctor! Call him at once! Let him come! Let him cleave my breast! Let him drive me mad, only let my life be saved! I wish to recover, I wish to live, I want to go away to-morrow, at once. The doctor! Help! Help!"—The women around her seized her by the hands, caressingly and begging her to calm herself, speaking to her of God and of hope. Then she would fall back in a mortal dejection, weeping, with her hands on her grey hair, moaning like a child, uttering deep lamentations, and murmuring from time to time: "Oh! my Genoa! My home! All that sea! Oh! my Marco, my poor Marco! Where is he now, that poor child of mine?"

It was midnight, and poor Marco, exhausted with fatigue, having spent many hours upon the bank of a stream, was then walking through a vast forest of gigantic trees, monsters of vegetation, whose huge trunks, similar to the pillars of a cathedral, interlaced their enormous silvery branches at a lofty height under the light of the moon. Through that semi-obscurity, he dimly perceived myriads of trunks of all shapes, upright, inclined, contorted, crossing each other in strange positions of menace, and some of them overthrown on the ground like towers that had fallen down a long time ago, covered with a thick and confused mass of vegetation which looked like a throng of people who were disputing, inch by inch, the possession of the forest. Others collected in groups stood vertically bound together like trophies of Titanic lances, whose tops touched the clouds; a superb grandeur, a prodigious disorder of colossal forms, the most majestic, terrible spectacle that vegetation had ever offered to him. At times a great stupor overtook him. But at once his soul took flight toward his mother. He was totally worn out. His feet were bleeding. He was alone in the midst of that formidable forest, where he only saw at long intervals some small human dwellings, which looked like ant hills in comparison with those enormous trees. He passed some sleeping buffaloes by the side of the road. He was tired out, but did not feel his weariness; he was alone, but did not feel afraid. The grandeur of the forest enlarged his soul. The nearness of his mother infused in him the strength and boldness of a man; the remembrance of the ocean, of the sufferings, of the struggles which he had undergone, all the fatigues he had endured, the iron constancy which he had displayed, caused him to uplift his head. All the strong and noble Genoese blood flowed back to his heart like a warm tide of joy and audacity. A new feeling arose in his mind. Up to that time he had borne in his brain a dark and faded image of his mother, dimmed by the two years of separation, but in this moment her image grew clear; he saw her wholesome and open face as he had not seen it for a long time. He saw her near him, illuminated and speaking; he saw again the most fleeting motions of her eyes and of her lips, all her attitudes, all her gestures, the very shadow of her thoughts; and, urged on by these remembrances, he hastened his step, while a new affection and an indescribable tenderness was becoming stronger and stronger in his heart, causing some sweet and quiet tears to flow down his cheeks. Going along in the darkness, it seemed that he spoke to her, that he whispered words to her, that he would murmur in her ear, before long: "I am here, mother; here I am; I will never leave you again; we shall return home together; I shall always be near you upon the boat, close beside you, and no one shall ever take me from you, nevermore, till you shall leave this world!" And he did not perceive that from the tops of the gigantic trees, the silvery light of the moon was dying out in the delicate whiteness of the dawn.

At eight o'clock on that same morning, the physician of Tucuman, a young Argentine gentleman, was already at the bedside of the poor sick woman, accompanied by the surgeon, trying for the last time to persuade her to allow the operation to be performed, and the engineer Mequinez and his wife were adding their persuasions to that of the others. But it was all in vain. The woman, feeling that she was exhausted, had no longer any confidence in the operation; she was certain that she would either die under it or would only survive half an hour after suffering more terrible pains than those which would naturally kill her. The physician was repeating that the operation was a sure one, that her safety was certain if she would only exercise a little courage, and he added that her death was equally certain if she refused. These were words thrown to the winds. "No," she answered in a faint voice. "I still have courage to die, but I have none left to suffer uselessly; thanks, doctor! It is my destiny! Let me die quietly."

The doctor discouraged, desisted. No one dared to speak

again. Then the woman turned her head toward her mistress, and, with a dying voice, made her last request. "My good mistress," she said, sobbing and speaking with great effort, "you will send the little money that I have and my poor effects to my family through the Consul. I hope that they are all alive. My heart presages me good in this last moment. You will do me the favor to write that I have always thought of them; that I have always worked for them, for my children; that my only sorrow is never to see them again; but that I died with courage, resigned, and blessing them—my husband, my eldest son, and my poor Marco, whom I have borne in my heart up to this last moment——" Becoming suddenly excited, she cried, clasping her hands: "My Marco, my little child! My life!"—and raising her eyes filled with tears she perceived that her mistress was no longer beside her; they had secretly called her away. She looked for the master; he had also disappeared. No one but the two nurses and the surgeon were in the room.

She could hear in the adjoining room a great noise of steps, a murmur of hasty and subdued voices and repressed exclamations. The sick woman fixed her eyes upon the door and waited. After a few minutes, the physician appeared with an unusual expression upon his countenance; then her master and mistress, each with an altered face, entered the room. The three persons looked at her with a singular expression, and exchanged a few words in a low tone. It seemed to her that the physician said to the mistress: "It would be better at once!"

"Iosefa," said the mistress with a trembling voice, "I have some good news for you. Prepare your heart for good news."

The woman looked at her attentively.

"News," continued the lady, growing more agitated, "that will cause you great joy."

The sick woman's eyes dilated.

"Prepare yourself," pursued the mistress, "to see a person to whom you are very much attached."

The woman raised her head with a start and rapidly began to observe alternately her mistress and the door, with flashing eyes.

The mistress, growing pale, added, "A person has just arrived unexpected to you."

"Who is it?" cried the woman in a strange, choking voice like that of a frightened person.

A moment later she gave vent to a shrill scream, and, raising herself to a sitting posture on the bed, remained motionless, with her eyes staring, and her hands on her temples as though confronted by a superhuman apparition.

Marco, dirty and tattered, was standing there on the threshold of the door, held back by the doctor's arm.

The woman cried: "My God! My God! My God!"

Marco ran forward, she raised her fleshless arms, and pressing him to her heart with the strength of a tiger, burst into a violent laugh broken by deep sobs, without shedding any tears. Then she fell back suffocating on her pillow.

But she soon recovered, and, crazy with joy, covering the head of her boy with kisses, crying· "How is it that you are here?—How is it possible?—Is it you?—How you have grown!—Who brought you here?—Are you alone?—Are you not ill?—Is it you, Marco?—This is not a dream is it, great God?—Speak to me."

Then suddenly changing her manner, she said: "No! Be silent! Wait!"—And, turning hastily to the surgeon: "Quick, quick, doctor. I wish to recover. I am ready. Do not lose a moment. Take Marco away so that he cannot hear.—My Marco, it is nothing; I will tell you everything.—Another kiss, go.—I am ready for you, doctor."

They took Marco away. The master and mistress and the women quietly left the room, only the doctor and the surgeon remained. They closed the door.

Signor Mequinez tried to draw Marco into a distant room, but it was impossible; he seemed rooted to the floor.

"What is the matter?" he asked. "What is the matter with my mother? What are they doing with her?"

And then Mequinez said softly, trying to pull him away "Listen, I will tell you; your mother is ill; it is necessary to perform a simple operation; I will explain everything to you; come with me."

"No," replied the boy resisting, "I wish to stay here; explain it to me here."

The engineer heaped words upon words, trying to pull him away. The lad began to get frightened and trembled.

Suddenly a sharp and shrill scream, like the cry of a person hurt to death, resounded through the whole house.

The lad answered with another desperate cry, saying, "My mother is dead!"

The doctor came to the door and said, "Your mother is saved!"

The boy looked at him for a moment and then threw himself at his feet, and sobbing exclaimed: "Thanks, doctor, thanks!"

But the doctor lifted him up saying: "Get up, stand up! You are an heroic child. You have saved your mother's life!"

SUMMER

Wednesday the 24th.

The Genoese boy Marco is the next to the last little hero with whom we will form an acquaintance this year. Only one remains for the month of June. There are only two more monthly examinations, twenty-six school days, six Thursdays, and five Sundays. One already feels the end of the year approaching. The pupils are already dressed in their summer clothes. It is a fine sight to see them as they come out of the school room. They look so different from what they did last month; the curls which touched their shoulders have been cut off; all the heads are shorn; and we can see the bare calves of the boys, and their bare necks. Straw hats of every shape with ribbons which fall down upon the back; blouses and neckties of all colors. The smallest ones all wear red or blue, a border sewed on, or a tassel, something of a bright color, put on by their mothers, no matter how, in order to make them showy, even among the poorest of them. Many come to school without a hat, as if they had run away from home. Some wear their white gymnastic suits. There is a boy in Mistress Delcati's room who is dressed in red from head to foot, like a lobster. Some wear sailor suits; but the handsomest of all is the Little Mason, who now wears a large straw hat which makes him look like a small candle with a shade over it. It is very laughable to see him make the hare face beneath it.

Coretti has put aside his cat-skin cap and wears an old grey silk traveling cap. Votini has a sort of a Scotch suit, close fitting; Crossi displays his bare breast; Precossi is lost inside of the blue blouse of the blacksmith. And Garoffi?—Now that he has been obliged to lay aside his cloak which hid all his wares, all his pockets remain visible, filled with every kind of bric-a-brac, which forces itself out with the lottery lists. Every one knows what he carries; fans made of half a newspaper, knobs of canes, and arrows to throw at birds, and some May bugs, that crawl out of his pockets and go slowly over his jacket.

Many of the little ones carry bouquets to the teachers. The teachers are also dressed in summer attire of bright colors, except the "Little Nun" who is always dressed in black, and the teacher with the red feather who still wears her red feather and a knot of red ribbon on her neck. The ribbon is all tumbled by the hands of the pupils, who always make her laugh and then they run away. It is the season of cherries, of butterflies, of open air music on the avenue, of excursions into the country. Some of the Fourth Elementary boys already run away to bathe in the River Po. Every boy has his heart set upon vacation time; every day we come out of school more impatient and happier than the day before. The only thing which pains me is to see Garrone dressed in mourning and to notice that my poor teacher of the first upper is whiter and more emaciated than ever, her cough growing worse and worse. She walks bent over and salutes me in a very sad way.

POETRY

Friday the 26th.

Thou dost begin to understand the poetry of school, Enrico, but for the present thou only seest the inside of it. It will appear to thee more beautiful and more poetic in thirty years from now, when thou wilt come here to accompany thy children and behold it from the outside, as I do now. At the close I stroll through the silent streets around the building, and listen at the windows of the ground floor, close by the window blinds. Through one of the windows I hear the voice of a mistress who says: "Ah, that bar on the 't,' that is not right, my child, what would your father say?" At another window near, I hear the full voice of the master, who is slowly dictating: "I will buy fifty meters of cloth for four and *one-half lire a meter. You will sell these———."* Further ahead it is the voice of the mistress with the red feather, who reads in a loud voice: "At that moment Pietro Micca, with a lighted fuse—" From a neighboring class comes a sound like the sharp twittering of a hundred birds, which means that the teacher has left the room for a moment. I move ahead, and at the corner I hear a pupil crying and the voice of the mistress who reproves and consoles him. From other windows issue verses, the names of great men, fragments of sentences which advise virtue, love of country and courage. A few moments' silence ensue, during which one would think that the building is empty, and it does not seem possible that there are seven hundred boys inside; then one hears hilarious outbursts, provoked by the jest of a teacher in good humor———and the people passing by stop to listen. They all cast a look of sympathy at that kind building which contains so much youthful vigor and so many hopes. Then one hears a sudden deafening sound and clapping of books and satchels, a rustling of feet, a sort of buzzing which spreads from class to class, from the top to the bottom, like the sudden diffusing of good news; the janitor is making his rounds to announce that the session is over. At that noise, a crowd of men, women, girls and youths are rushing here and there in front of the door, awaiting, some their brothers, some their nephews, while from the doors of the class rooms come forth, as if poured out into the large hall, the smallest children to take their little cloaks and hats, creating a confusion upon the floor, dancing all around till the janitor drives them out, one by one; finally, they leave in long rows, stamping their feet. Then all the relatives begin a shower of questions: "Did you know your lesson? How much work has he given you? What do you have for to-morrow? When will the monthly examination take place?" Even the poor who do not know how to read open the books, look at the problems and ask how many points their children had. "Only eight?" "Commendation and ten points?" "Nine on the lesson?" And they grow angry or rejoice, and question the teachers in regard to the prospects of the examination.*

How beautiful it all is! How great, and what a noble promise for the world!

Thy Father.

THE DEAF AND DUMB GIRL

Sunday the 28th.

The best way to finish the month of May was with that visit which I made this morning. We were about to go out when the bell rang, and we all went to see who it was. I heard my father exclaim in astonishment:

"You here, Giorgio?" It was Giorgio, our gardener of Chieri, whose family is now at Condove.

He had just come from Genoa, where he had landed the day before upon his return from Greece, after having worked there for three years on a railroad. He looks a little older than when I saw him last, but has a rosy and jovial face.

My father wished him to come in but he refused to do so; and becoming very serious, inquired at once: "How is my family? How is my Gigia?"

"She was well a few days ago," answered my mother.

Giorgio drew a deep sigh and said: "Let the Lord be praised! I did not have the courage to present myself at the Deaf and Dumb Asylum without first hearing something about her. I beg permission to leave my valise here and hasten to go after her. It is three years since I have seen her, my poor daughter! Three years since I have seen any of my people!"

My father told me to accompany him.

"Another word, please," said the gardener upon the landing. But my father interrupted him: "And how is it about your business?"

"Quite good," he replied, "thanks to God. I have brought home a few soldi. But I was about to inquire how the education of the little deaf and dumb one is progressing; tell me a little about it. When I left her she was like a little animal, poor creature. I do not put much confidence in those institutions. Has she learned to make signs? My wife wrote me that she learns to speak and is making progress? But I was saying to myself: 'What does it matter if she does learn to speak if I do not know how to make the signs? How can we understand each other, poor child!' It is all right enough for the deaf and dumb to understand each other, one unfortunate with another unfortunate. How then is she getting along? How is she?"

My father smiled and replied: "I will not tell you anything; you will see for yourself; go, go; and do not rob her of one minute more of your presence."

We left the house. The asylum is quite near. On the way, walking with long strides, the gardener was talking to me and all the time growing sadder. "Oh, my poor Gigia, to be born with that misfortune! To think that I have never heard her call me *father* and she has never heard herself called *daughter* by me, and that she has never heard or spoken a word in this world! It is fortunate that we found a charitable gentleman to pay her expenses at the asylum. But she could not go there before she was eight years old. She has been away from home for three years now. She is fully eleven. Has she grown, tell me, has she grown much? Is she in good spirits?"

"You will soon see," I said to him, hastening my steps.

"But where is this building?" he asked. "My wife took her to that place after I had gone away. It seems to me it must be in this direction."

We had just arrived. We immediately entered the parlor and one of the janitors came to meet us.

"I am the father of Gigia Voggi," said the gardener; "send for my daughter instantly."

"They are having their recreation," replied the janitor, "I will go and notify the teacher," and he went away.

The gardener was no longer able to speak or keep still, and he was looking at the pictures on the wall without seeing any-

anything. The door opened and the teacher, dressed in black, entered, holding a girl by the hand.

Father and daughter looked at each other a moment, and then they fell into each other's arms, uttering a cry.

The girl was dressed in a striped reddish cloth gown and a white apron. She is taller than I am. She wept and pressed her father's neck with both arms.

Her father disengaged himself and began to look at her from head to foot with tears in his eyes; and, panting as though he had been running a distance, he exclaimed: "How she has grown! How handsome she has become! Oh, my dear, my poor Gigia! My poor deaf and dumb girl! And you, Signora mistress? Tell her to make some signs for me that I may see if I can understand, and then after awhile I will also learn. Tell her to make me understand something by gestures."

The teacher smiled and said in a low voice to the girl, "who is this man who has come to see you?"

And the girl with a thick, strange, dissonant voice like that of a savage who speaks our language for the first time, but pronouncing distinctly and smiling all the time — "It is —— my fa-ther."

The gardener fell back and uttered a cry like a lunatic: "She speaks! But is it possible! How can it be! She speaks! You speak, my child! Do tell me, do you really speak?" and he embraced and kissed her on the forehead three times. "But is it not with signs that they speak, signora teacher? Is it not with the fingers like this?"

"No," replied the mistress, "it is not with gestures. That was the old method; here they use the new method, the oral. How is it that you do not know it?"

"I knew nothing about it," replied the gardener, amazed. "I have been away for three years. Perhaps they have written it to me but I have not understood it: I am a sort of a blockhead. Oh, my little girl, you understand me then? You hear my voice? Answer, do you hear? Do you hear what I say?"

"No, my good man," replied the mistress, "she cannot hear your voice because she is deaf; she understands from the movements of your lips what you are saying, but she does not hear your words, and not even those which she speaks to you; she pronounces them because we have taught her letter by letter how to place the lips and move the tongue, and what an effort she must make with her chest and throat to throw out the voice."

The gardener did not understand, and stood with his mouth wide open; he did not believe it possible.

"Tell me, Gigia," he said to the daughter, speaking in her ear, "are you glad your father has returned?" and raising his head he waited for the answer.

The girl looked at him thoughtfully but said nothing.

Her father was perturbed.

The mistress laughed. Then she said: "My good man, she does not answer you because she has not seen the movement of your lips — you have spoken in her ear. Repeat the question, keeping your face in front of hers."

Looking sharply in her face, her father repeated: "Are you glad that your father has returned? That he will never go away again?"

The girl who had looked attentively at his lips, trying to see inside of his mouth, at once replied: "Yes, I am gla-d that you have re-turn-ed, that you will not go away again."

The father embraced her impetuously, and then in great haste, in order to assure himself still further, he overwhelmed her with questions.

"What is mamma's name?"

"An-tonia."

"What do you call your little sister?"

"A-de-laide."

"What is the name of this asylum?"

"The Deaf and Dumb."

"How much is two times ten?"

"Twenty."

We thought that he was laughing for joy, but all of a sudden he began to weep. That was also on account of his joy.

"Have courage," said the mistress, "you have reason to rejoice and not to weep. Do you see, you will make your daughter cry also. Be cheerful." The gardener grasped the teacher's hand and kissed it two or three times, saying: "Thanks, thanks, a hundred times thanks. Thanks a thousand times, my dear signora mistress! And do forgive me that I do not know how to express myself better!"

"She not only knows how to speak, but she can write also. She knows how to calculate. She knows the name of all the ordinary objects. She knows a little history and has some knowledge of geography. She now belongs to the normal class; when she has gone through two more classes she will know a great deal more. When she leaves this place she will be in a condition to take up some profession. We have some of our deaf and dumb in stores, waiting upon customers, and who know how to do business like other people."

The gardener was again astonished. He acted as though his ideas were again becoming confused; he looked at his daughter and rubbed his forehead. His face showed that he wished to ask another question.

Then the mistress turned to the janitor and told him to call a girl from the preparatory class.

The janitor came back in a short time with a deaf and dumb girl about eight or nine years old, who had entered the asylum a few days before.

"This girl," said the teacher, "is one of those to whom we teach the first elements. This is the way we go about it. I wish to have her say *ah*. Pay attention." The teacher opened her mouth as we open it to pronounce the open *a*, and she motioned to the girl to open her mouth in the same way. The child obeyed. Then the mistress made a sign to her to throw out her voice: the girl emitted her voice but instead of saying *a* pronounced *o*. "No," said the mistress, "that is not right." And taking the girl by both hands, put one of them on her throat and the other on her chest and repeated *a*. The child, feeling with her hand the movements of the throat and chest of the mistress, opened her mouth as before and pronounced *a* very correctly. Then the mistress made her say *c*, *l*, *d*, always holding the two small hands upon her chest and throat. "Do you understand now?" she asked.

The father understood, but seemed more surprised than when he did not understand. "Do you teach them all to speak in that same way?" he inquired, after a moment's reflection, looking at the teacher. "Have you the patience to teach them to speak in that way, little by little, all of them, one by one, year after year? You are saints! You are like the angels of paradise! And now, please, leave me alone with my daughter; leave her with me for five minutes."

Pulling her on a side seat, he began to question her while the child would answer and he laughed with tears in his eyes, striking his knee with his fists, grasping the girl with his hand, looking at her, beside himself with hearing her as though it were a voice from heaven. Then he asked the mistress: "Am I allowed to go and thank the director of the asylum?"

"The director is not here," replied the teacher. "But there is another person whom you ought to thank. Here, every girl is entrusted to the care of an older companion, who acts as a sister, or a mother to her. Your daughter has been entrusted to a deaf and dumb girl of seventeen, the daughter of a baker; she is truly kind and very fond of her. Every morning for the last two years she has helped her to dress; she combs her hair, teaches her to sew, mends her clothes and keeps her company. Luigia, what do you call your asylum mamma?"

The girl smiled and replied: "Cate-rina Gior-dano." Then she said to her father: "Very, very kind."

The janitor having gone out at a motion from the teacher returned with a deaf and dumb girl, blonde and robust, with a jovial face, also dressed in a reddish striped dress and a gray apron, who stopped at the door blushing; then she bowed and smiled; she had the figure of a woman but the expression of a child.

The daughter of Giorgio ran to her, took her by the arm like a child and dragged her to her father, saying with her thick voice: "Ca-te-rina Gior-dano."

"Oh, what a good girl!" exclaimed the father, and he stretched out his hand to caress her, but immediately drew it back, saying: "Ah, you dear, good girl, may God bless you, may He grant you much happiness and consolation, may He make you happier than all your people. Such a kind girl she has been to my poor Gigia; it is an honest workman, a poor father of a family who wishes all this to you with all his heart."

The older girl caressed the little one, all the time smiling, and the gardener continued to look at her as he would gaze at a Madonna.

"Now you may take your daughter with you," said the mistress.

"Of course, I will take her," replied the gardener. "I will take her to Condove and bring her back to-morrow morning!" —The daughter ran away to dress—"Three years that I have not seen her," repeated the gardener, "and now she speaks! I will take her to Condove immediately, but first I want to make a tour around Turin with my little deaf and dumb daughter on my arm, that they may all see her, and I will take her to see my few acquaintances, that they may hear her! Oh, what a beautiful day! This is what you may call a consolation! Here, give me your arm; give your arm to your father, my Gigia!"

The girl who had returned with a little cloak and cap, gave him her arm.

"Thanks to all," said her father at the door. "Thanks to all with my whole soul! I shall return again, thanks to all!"

He stood thinking for a moment, then he took his arm from his daughter's and turned back, feeling in his waist-coat pocket, and shouted like a furious man: "You see I am a poor fellow, but here, I leave these twenty lire for the asylum, a nice bright new gold piece!" and he threw it upon the table with a bang.

"No, no, my good man," said the mistress, moved, "take back your money. I cannot accept it. Take it back; we do not need it. You will come when the director is here. But he will not accept it either, you may be sure. You have worked too hard to earn your money, poor man. They will all be grateful to you just the same."

"No, I wish to leave it," said the gardener obstinately: "and then later—we will see."

But the mistress replaced the coin in his pocket without giving him time to push her back.

Then he gave it up, shrugging his shoulders, and throwing a kiss to the teacher and the older girl, he again took his daughter's arm and rushed out of the door, saying: "Come, come, my daughter, my poor deaf and dumb, my treasure!"

And the deaf and dumb girl exclaimed with a thick voice: "What a beau-ti-ful sun-shine."

JUNE

GARIBALDI

To-morrow is the National Feast Day

June the 3rd.

This is a day of national mourning. Garibaldi died last night. Dost thou know who he was? It was he who delivered ten millions of Italians from the tyranny of the Bourbons. He died at the age of seventy-five. He was born in Nizza, a son of the captain of a sailing vessel. At the age of eight, he saved the life of a woman; when he was thirteen, he dragged to safety a boat loaded with his companions who were about to be shipwrecked; at twenty, he rescued a youth who was drowning in the waters of Marseilles; at forty-one, he saved a ship from a fire on the ocean. He fought for ten years in South America for the liberty of a foreign people. He fought in three wars against the Austrians for the liberation of Lombardy and Trent. He defended Rome against the French in 1849. He liberated Palermo and Naples in 1860. He fought again for Rome in '67. Combatted against the Germans, in 1870, for the defense of France. He bore the flame of heroism and the genius of war. He was engaged in forty battles and won thirty-seven of them. When he was not engaged in war, he worked for his living; he found seclusion upon a solitary island and tilled the land. During his life he was a teacher, a sailor, a workman, a merchant, a soldier, a general, a dictator. He was great, simple and good, he hated all the oppressors, and loved all the people. He always protected the weak ones; he refused honor, despised death, adored Italy. When he uttered a war cry, a legion of valorous men would run to him from every side. Gentlemen would leave their palaces, workmen their shops, and youths their schools, in order to go and fight under the sunshine of his glory. In war time, he wore a red shirt. He was a blonde, handsome and strong. Upon the field of battle he was like lightning; in his affection like a child; in his sorrow like a saint. Thousands of Italians have died for their country, glad while dying to see him pass at a distance, victorious. Thousands would have died for him; millions have blessed him; and millions will continue to bless him. He is dead. The whole world mourns for him. Thou canst not yet comprehend it. But thou wilt read of his deeds, thou wilt hear him spoken of continually during thy life; and as thou growest, his image will grow before thee; when thou art a man, thou wilt behold him as a giant; and when thou art no longer in this world, the children of thy children, and the thousands to be born of the coming generations, will see on high his radiant image glorifying him as the redeemer of the people, crowned with the names of his victories as with a circle of stars, and the brow and soul of every Italian will beam as he pronounces his name.

Thy Father.

THE ARMY

Sunday the 11th, the National Holiday having been postponed for seven days on account of the death of Garibaldi.

We went into the piazza Castello to see the military parade, which filed in front of the Chief Commander of the Army Corps, between two rows of people While the soldiers were marching past, at the sound of the trumpets and the music of the bands, my father pointed out to me the different corps and the glories of the flags. At the head of the line came the cadets of the academy, who will become officers in the engineering and the artillery corps; about three hundred of them dressed in black, passed by with the dashing and easy elegance of the soldier and student. After them, the infantry passed: first the Aosta brigade which fought at Goito and at San Martino, next the Bergamo brigade which fought at Castelfidardo, four regiments, company after company, thousands of red tassels that looked like a double and very long crown of flowers of a blood red color, extended and fluttering at the ends, and carried across the crowd. After the infantry, marched the battalions of the Engineer's Corps, with their black plumes and crimson stripes, and while they were filing past, we could see coming in front and back of them hundreds of straight long plumes, which rose above the heads of the spectators. These were the Alpine soldiers, the defenders of the gates of Italy, all of them tall, rosy, and strongly built, wearing Calabrian hats and lapels of a vivid green, the color of the grass of their mountains. The Alpine soldiers were still filing by when a quiver ran through the crowd, and the "Bersaglieri," the old twelfth battalion, the first ones who entered Rome through the breach of Porta Pia, their faces bronzed, alert, quick, with their feathers floating in the wind, passed like a wave in a black sea, making the piazza ring with the sharp tones of their trumpets which sounded like cries of joy. But that sound was deafened by a rumble which announced the field artillery, and they passed proudly, seated upon their caissons, drawn by three hundred spans of fiery horses, the handsome soldiers with the yellow lacings, and the long bronze and steel cannons glittering upon their carriages which were rattling and making such a noise that the earth trembled beneath our feet. Then came slowly, grave and beautiful in their heavy and solid appearance, the stalwart soldiers of the mountain artillery with their powerful mules, that mountain artillery, which carries dismay and death as high as the foot of man can climb. The last to pass was the beautiful regiment of Genoa cavalry, which wheeled down like a whirlwind upon ten fields and fought scores of battles from Santa Lucia to Villafranca, galloping, with their helmets shining in the sun, with their lances erect, their pennons floating in the wind, glittering with silver and gold, filling the air with jingling and neighing.

"How beautiful!" I exclaimed.—But my father almost reproached me for those words, and said:

"You must not look upon the army as an amusing performance. All those young men, full of vigor and hope, may be called upon at any time to defend our country and be crushed to pieces in a half hour by bullets or grape-shot. Every time you hear the cry at a feast, 'Long live the army! long live Italy!'—just think of the regiment passing over a field covered with corpses and flooded with blood, and then the hurrahs to the army will come out of the most profound depths of your heart, and the image of Italy will appear greater and more severe."

ITALY

Tuesday the 14th.

Thus thou must salute thy country in the days of festivity: "Italy, my noble and beloved land, where my father and my mother were born and will be buried—where I hope to live and die, where my children will grow up and die: Beautiful Italy, grand and glorious for many centuries, united and free for the last few years; who hast scattered so much light and divine intellect throughout the world! Italy, for whom so many valorous men have died upon the field of battle and so many heroes upon the scaffold; august mother of three hundred cities and thirty millions of children! I, a child who cannot understand thee, for I am still unable to fully know thee, I venerate and love thee with all my soul, and am proud to be born of thee, to be able to call myself thy son! I love thy beautiful seas, thy sublime Alps; I love thy solemn monuments and thy immortal memories; I love thy glory and thy beauty; I love and venerate thy whole country as I do that most beloved part where for the first time I saw the sun and heard thy name. I love every portion of thee with devoted affection and with equal gratitude:— Turin, the valiant; Genoa, the superb; Bologna, the learned; Venice, the enchanting; Milan, the powerful. I love you all with the equal reverence of a child. Florence, the gentle, and Palermo, the terrible; Naples, great and beautiful; Rome, marvelous and eternal. I love thee, sacred country! And I swear that I shall love all thy children like brothers; that I will always honor in my heart thy great, illustrious men and thy noble dead; that I will be an industrious and honest citizen, constantly intent upon elevating myself, to render myself worthy of thee, to assist with my small powers to cause to disappear from thy face all misery, ignorance and crime, that thou mayest live and expand tranquilly in the majesty of thy justice and thy strength. I swear that I will serve thee as it is granted to me, with my talent, with my arm, and with my heart, humbly and boldly; and if the day comes in which I shall have to shed my blood and give my life for thee, I will shed my blood and die crying—crying to the sky thy holy name and sending my last kiss to thy blessed flag!"

Thy Father.

THIRTY-TWO DEGREES CENTIGRADE

Friday the 16th.

In the five days which have passed since the national feast, the heat has increased three degrees. We are now in full summer, every one begins to feel tired; the boys have all lost their rosy color; the heads droop, the legs grow thin, and the eyes close. Poor Nelli, who suffers so much from the heat, has now a face the color of wax. Sometimes he falls asleep with his head upon his copybook, but Garrone is always prompt to put in front of him an open reader, standing it upright, so that the teacher cannot see him. Crossi leans his large head upon the desk in such a way that it looks detached from the shoulders and placed there. Nobis complains that there are too many in the room and that we corrupt the air. We have to make a great effort to study. I see from the window those beautiful trees which cast a dark shadow, where I would like to go and run, and I feel impatient because I am obliged to shut myself up among the benches. But then I take courage again, seeing that my good mother always looks at me when I come out of school to see if I am pale; and asks me, while going over every page of the lesson:

"Do you feel bad?" Every morning when she wakes me at six to do my lessons, she exclaims:

"Courage! there are only so many more days; after that you will be at liberty to rest, and you will be able to go under the shade of the trees."

She is right to remind me of the boys who work in the fields, beneath the extreme heat of the sun, or on the white gravel of the river, where they are blinded by the reflection and scorched by the heat, and of all those who are employed in glass factories, who stand motionless the whole day with their faces held over a gas flame. They all get up sooner than we do and have no vacations. Let us have courage then! Derossi is the first in this as in everything else; he suffers neither from heat nor drowsiness; he is always alive and merry, with his blonde curls in summer as well as in winter. He studies without tiring and keeps every one around him awake, as if refreshing the air with his voice. There are two others who always keep awake and are attentive to the lesson: first, that stubborn boy, Stardi, who pricks his face in order not to fall asleep, and the warmer and more tired he gets, the closer he shuts his teeth, and he opens his eyes wide as though he were going to devour the teacher; and after him that trafficking lad Garoffi, who keeps busy manufacturing fans out of red paper, ornamented with borders taken from match-box pictures, which he sells for a centesimo each. But the bravest of all is Coretti, poor Coretti, who gets up at five to help his father carry wood. By eleven o'clock, he can scarcely keep his eyes open and his head falls upon his chest. Nevertheless, he shakes himself, strikes himself upon the back of the neck, and asks permission to go out and wash his face, and tells the others to shake him and to pinch him.

In spite of all that, this morning, not being able to fight his drowsiness any longer, he fell into a deep sleep. The teacher called him loudly: "Coretti!" He did not hear. The teacher, irritated, repeated: "Coretti!"

Then the son of the charcoal dealer, who lives next door to Coretti, arose and said:

"He worked from five until seven, carrying fagots." The teacher let him sleep and continued the lesson for another half hour. Then he moved softly in front of Coretti's bench, and blowing in his face, woke him up. The latter, seeing the teacher before him, drew back frightened. But the teacher took his head in his hands and told him, kissing his hair:

"I do not reprove you, my child, your sleep is not one of laziness; it is the sleep of fatigue."

MY FATHER

Saturday the 17th.

Certainly neither thy companion Coretti nor Garrone would answer their father as thou hast answered thine this evening. How is it possible, Enrico? Thou must promise me that this will never occur again as long as I live. Every time that thy father reproaches thee a bad answer flies to thy lips. Think of that day which will inevitably come when he will call thee to his bedside to tell thee: "Enrico, I leave thee." Oh, my child, when thou wilt hear his voice for the last time, and also for a long time after when thou wilt weep in thy solitary room, in the midst of those books which he will never open again; then thou wilt remember that at times thou hast failed in respect to him, and thou wilt ask of thyself: "How is it possible?" Then thou wilt understand that he has always been thy best friend, and that when he was forced to punish thee, he suffered from it more than thou didst; that he has never caused thee sorrow but has always done thee good. Then thou wilt repent; weeping, thou wilt kiss that table upon which he has worked so hard, upon which he has worn out his health for his children. Now thou canst not comprehend, because he hides everything from thee except his kindness and his love. Thou dost not know that at times he is so weary that he thinks he has only a few days more to live, and in those moments he only speaks of thee; he has no other care in his heart than that he may not leave thee poor and without protection! And how often, thinking of this, he enters thy room when thou art asleep and remains there with a light in his hand, looking at thee, and then, sad and tired as he is, he returns to work! Thou dost not even know that he looks for thee and stays with thee because he has a bitterness in his heart; certain sorrows which attack every man in the world, and looks for thee as for a friend to find comfort and forgetfulness; and he feels the necessity of finding refuge in thy affection to recuperate his serenity and courage. Think, then, what a sorrow it must be for him when instead of finding affection in thee, he finds coldness and irreverence! Never stain thyself again with that horrible ingratitude! Think that if thou wert as good as a saint, thou wouldst never be able sufficiently to repay him for all that he has done and is continually doing for thee. Think also that one cannot rely upon one's life, that a misfortune may deprive thee of thy father when thou art still a boy, in two years, in three months, to-morrow. Then, my poor Enrico, what a change thou wouldst see in everything around thee; how empty and desolate would thy home appear, with thy poor mother dressed in black! Go, my child, go to thy father; he is in his room at work; go on tip-toe that he may not hear thee enter; go and place thy brow upon his knees, that he may forgive and bless thee.

Thy Mother.

IN THE COUNTRY

Monday the 19th.

My good father forgave me this time also, and allowed me to go on the excursion into the country, which had been planned ever since Wednesday with Coretti's father, the wood-huckster. We all felt the need of the fresh air on the hills. It was a regular feast. Yesterday at half-past two, we all met in the Piazza dello Statuto; Derossi, Garrone, Garoffi, Precossi, Coretti and his father, and I, with our provisions of fruit, sausages, bread and hard boiled eggs; we also had some leather cups and some tin cups. We rode in the omnibus as far as La Gran Madre di Dio, and then off quickly to the hills. Everything was green, shady and fresh; we rolled upon the grass, put our faces over streams, and jumped over hedges. Coretti's father followed us at a distance with his jacket on his shoulder, smoking his clay pipe; from time to time he would admonish us with his hand that we should not tear our trousers. Precossi whistled; I had never heard him whistle before. Coretti was doing a little of everything with his jack-knife on the way; he knows everything, that little man. He makes small mill wheels, forks and squirts. He wanted to carry the things of the others, and he was laden, wet with perspiration, but as nimble as a goat. Derossi was stopping every moment to tell the names of the plants and insects. I do not know how he manages to know so many things. Garrone ate his bread in silence, but he no longer eats his bread with such mischievous bites, poor Garrone, since he has lost his mother. However, he is always the same, always as good as he can be. When one of us took a start to leap over a ditch, he would run from the other side and reach out his hand, and because Precossi was afraid of the cows, having been tossed by one when a little boy, every time that one passed Garrone placed himself before him.

We went up to Santa Margherita, and then down the incline in leaps, rolling in such a way that we ran the risk of hurting ourselves. Precossi, tumbling into a thorn-bush, tore his blouse and stood there shamefaced with the strip dangling; but Garoffi, who always has pins in his jacket, pinned it up so that it scarcely showed, while Precossi was saying to him: "Excuse me, excuse me." Then he started to run again. Garoffi was not losing his time on the way; he was picking herbs to make salads, with some snails; and every shining stone that he found he put in his pocket, thinking there might be gold or silver in it. We went along, running and rolling, climbing in the shade and in the sunshine, up and down through all the lanes and paths, until we came panting and breathless to the top of the hill, where we stopped to eat our lunch on the grass. From this place we could see an immense plain and the azure Alps with their white peaks. We were almost dying of hunger, and the bread seemed to melt in our mouths. Coretti's father gave us each a portion of sausage upon a pumpkin leaf instead of a plate. We all began to talk at once about our teachers, about our companions who were not able to come on the excursion, and about the examinations. Precossi seemed to be a little ashamed to eat, and Garrone forced the best of his share into his mouth. Coretti sat next to his father with his legs crossed. They looked more like brothers than like father and son when you gazed at them so near to each other; both red and smiling with those white teeth. Coretti's father drank with pleasure and emptied the leather and tin cups which we left half finished, saying:

"You, who study do not need to drink so much; it is the wood-huckster who needs it!"

Then he grasped the nose of his child, saying:—"Boys, you must like this fellow here, he is the flower of an upright man; it is I who say this!" And all except Garrone laughed.—Coretti's father continued to drink.

"What a pity! now you are all together as good comrades and in a few years from now, who knows where you will be; Enrico and Derossi will be lawyers or professors, how do I know,—and you other four will probably be in some shop working at a trade. And then 'Good bye, comrades.'"

"What?" said Derossi, "so far as myself am concerned, Garrone will always be Garrone, Precossi will always be Precossi, and the others the same, even though I should become the Emperor of Russia; where they are, I will go."

"Bless thee, my child!"—exclaimed Coretti's father, raising the flask,—"that is the way to talk! Touch! Long live the good companions, and long live the school which makes you all of the same family, those who are rich and those who are poor!"

We all touched his flask with our cups and drank for the last time. He added:

"Hurrah for the squad of the 49th!" rising upon his feet

and swallowing the last drop; "and if ever you have anything to do with squads, be careful to be steady as we were!'

It was already late; we descended running and singing, walking for long distances arm in arm, and we reached the River Po as it was growing dark, and thousands of fire-flies were darting through the air, We did not separate until we reached the Piazza dello Statuto, where we agreed to meet next Sunday in order to go to the Vittorio Emanuele Theater, to attend the distribution of prizes to the pupils of the evening schools.

What a fine day! How joyfully I would have returned home if I had not met my poor teacher. I met her as she was coming down the stairs of our house, almost in the dark, and as soon as she saw me she took me by both hands and whispered in my ear:

"Good bye, Enrico, remember me!"—I noticed that she was weeping. I mounted the stairs and said to my mother:

"I have met my school mistress."—"She was just going to bed," replied my mother, whose eyes were red. Then she added with sadness, looking at me:

"Thy poor mistress is very, very low."

THE DISTRIBUTION OF PRIZES TO THE WORKMEN

Sunday the 25th.

As it had been agreed, we all went together to the theatre Vittorio Emanuele, to attend the distribution of prizes to the workmen. The theatre was decorated as on the 14th of March, and it was thronged; but almost entirely with workingmen's families, and the pit was occupied by the pupils of both sexes of the Choral Singing School, who sang a hymn, "To the Dead Soldiers in the Crimea," which was so beautiful that when it was over, the audience arose, clapping their hands and shouting, and they were obliged to sing it over again.

Soon after, those who were to receive the prizes began to file in front of the Mayor, the Prefect, and many others, who gave them small books of the Savings Bank, diplomas, and medals. In a corner of the pit, I saw the Little Mason sitting next to his father; on the other side was our principal, and behind him I saw the red head of my teacher of the second class.

The first to file out were the pupils of the evening schools for drawing, then the engravers, the stone cutters, lithographers and some carpenters and masons. Next those of the commercial school; then those of the musical Lyceum, among whom were many girls, working girls, all in gala dress, who were greeted with great applause and who laughed. At last, the pupils of the evening elementary schools passed by; it was a beautiful spectacle. They were of all ages, of all trades, and dressed in all sorts of ways. Men with grey hair, boys from the work-shops, and workmen with long black beards. The young ones looked at their ease, the grown men were a little embarrassed. The people clapped their hands at the youngest and the oldest. But no one among the spectators applauded as they did at our celebration. One could see that they were all attentive and serious.

The wives and children of many of those who received prizes were in the pit. There were some little children, who, when their father passed upon the stage, would call him loudly by name and point their finger at him, laughing. Some farmers and some porters passed by, who belonged to the Boncompagni school. There was a bootblack from the Citadella school, whom my father knows and who received a diploma. After him, we saw a large man, who looked like a giant and whom I thought I had seen before. It was the father of the Little Mason. He received the second prize. It came back to my mind when I had seen him in a garret at the bedside of his sick child, and I sought with my eyes the "Little Mason" in the pit, poor child! He was gazing at his father with tears in his eyes, and in order to hide his emotion he was making the hare face.

At that moment I heard a crash of applause, and looking upon the stage I saw a little chimney sweep, with a clean face but in working clothes, and the Mayor spoke to him holding him by the hand. A cook came next after the chimney sweep.

Then one of the municipal chimney sweeps received his medal; he belongs to the Rainieri school. I was feeling something inexplicable in my heart, something like a great affection and a great respect, thinking how many efforts those prizes had cost those workmen who had families and were loaded with cares; how many fatigues were added to their ordinary fatigues; how many hours were snatched from the sleep they needed so much; and also of how they must have taxed their intellects which were not accustomed to study, and I thought of all those hands roughened and calloused by work!

A boy from a factory passed, and it was evident that his father had loaned him a jacket for the occasion, as the sleeves hung down so far that he was obliged to turn them up there upon the stage to enable him to take his prize, which caused a great many to laugh, but the laughing was stifled by the clapping of hands. Then came an old man with a bald head and white beard. Some of the artillery soldiers who came to the evening class of our school passed by. Then some municipal guards and some guards who watch the schools. At last, the pupils of the Evening Choral School sang again the hymn, " To The Dead in the Crimea," and with so much spirit this time and with such powerful effect, that it was clear it came direct from their hearts. There was scarcely any applause, and all retired slowly in deep emotion and without making any noise. In a few moments, the wide street was crowded. In front of the door of the theater, there was the chimney sweep with his prize book bound in red, and all around him stood gentlemen speaking to him. Many saluted each other from opposite sides of the street; workmen, boys, guards, and teachers; my teacher of the second class came out between two artillery soldiers. You could see wives of workmen with little children in their arms, who were holding in their small hands the diplomas of their fathers, and were proudly showing them to the people.

MY DEAD SCHOOL MISTRESS

Tuesday the 27th.

While we were at the theatre Vittorio Emanuele, my poor school mistress died. She died at two o'clock in the afternoon, seven days after she made her visit to my mother. The principal came to tell us of her death this morning, saying:

"Those among you who have been her pupils know how good she was, how fond she was of her boys. She was like a mother to them. She is no longer here below. A terrible sickness has consumed her for some time. Had she not been obliged to work to earn her living, she might have been able to take care of herself and perhaps would have recovered; at least, she might have prolonged her life for some months if she had asked for a leave of absence; but she wished to remain with her boys up to the last day. Saturday evening, the 17th, she took leave of them with the certainty that she would not see them again; she gave them some good advice, then kissed each one and left sobbing. Now no one will ever see her again in this world. Remember her, boys."

Little Precossi, who had been one of her pupils in the first primary, leaned his head on the desk and began to weep.

Last evening, after school, we all went together to the house of the dead to escort her body to the church. The hearse, drawn by two horses, was already in front of the house, and many people were waiting, talking in a subdued voice. The principal was there, all the teachers and school mistresses of our school, and also several from other schools where she had taught before she came to our school All the children of her class were there, led by their mothers, carrying tapers, and a great many who belonged to other classes, and about fifty girls from the Baretti school, some holding wreaths in their hands, and others, roses.

A number of wreaths had already been placed upon the hearse, upon which was hanging a large acacia crown, bearing this inscription in black letters: "*To their school mistress—the scholars of the fourth class.*" Below this large crown hung a smaller one which had been carried there by her own boys. You could see in the crowd servant girls, sent by their mistresses with candles, and there were two domestics in livery, holding lighted torches; a rich gentleman, the father of one of her pupils had sent his carriage lined in blue silk. They were all thronging in front of the door. Many of the girls were wiping away their tears.

We waited very silently for a long time. Finally, the casket was brought down. Several of the little children began to weep loudly when they saw the coffin put into the hearse, and one started to cry as though he understood for the first time that his mistress was dead, and he was so convulsed by sobbing that they had to take nim away. The procession set out slowly and in order. First came the daughters of the Ritiro della Concezione, dressed in green; then came the daughters of Maria, all dressed in white with blue ribbons; after these came the priest; and behind the hearse came the teachers and school mistresses, the little pupils of the first upper and all the others, and finally the crowd. People looked from the windows and doors to see all those children and the floral crown. They were saying: "It is a school mistress."

There were ladies who were escorting the smallest boys and some of them were weeping. As soon as we reached the church, they took the casket from the hearse and carried it into the middle of the nave in front of the altar. The school mistresses laid the wreath upon it, the children covered it with flowers and all the people, with their lighted candles, began to chant hymns in that large dark church. Then all of a sudden, when the priest said his last Amen; the candles were put out and all left hastily, and the poor mistress was left there alone. Poor mistress, who was so good to me, who had so much patience, who had toiled for so many years.

She left a few books to her pupils; to one an inkstand, to another a little picture, all she possessed. Two days before dying she told the principal not to allow the smallest boys to attend her funeral, she did not wish them to cry. She has done much good, she has suffered, she has died. Poor mistress, to be thus left alone in that dark church! Good bye, forever, my good friend! Sweet and sad remembrance of my infancy!

THANKS

Wednesday the 28th.

My poor school mistress wished to finish her year at school, and she left only three days before the lessons came to an end. After to-morrow, we will come together but once more to hear the reading of the monthly story, "*A Shipwreck*," and then it is all over. Saturday, the first day of July, will be examination day. Another year, and then the fourth elementary course is finished. If my mistress had not died, the year would have passed well. I think of what I knew last October, and it seems to me that I know much more now; that I have so many new ideas in my mind; I am now able to speak and to write better what I think than I could then; I am also able to figure like many adults who are not rapid in calculations and could assist them in their business; I understand a great deal more; I comprehend nearly everything I read. I am happy, but how many have pushed me forward and helped me to learn, in one way or another, at home, at school, in the street, and everywhere I have gone, and in all places where I have seen anything! I thank them all now. I thank, above all my companions, you my good teacher, who have been so indulgent, so affectionate toward me, and for whom every acquisition of mine, for which I rejoice and feel proud, has been such a fatigue. I thank you, Derossi; you helped me several times to understand difficult subjects and to overcome the obstacles at the examination. And you too, Stardi, good and strong, who have shown me with your iron will how one can succeed in everything; and you, Garrone, kind and generous, who make all who associate with you love you; and thanks to both of you, Precossi and Coretti, who have always given me an example of courage in sufferings and serenity in work; I thank you all, and I say thanks to all the others, too. But above all, I thank you, my father, my first teacher, my first friend, who have given me so much good advice and taught me so many things, while you were working for me, concealing your worries, and seeking in every way to render my study easy and my life beautiful. You also, my sweet mother, my guardian, beloved and blessed angel, who have rejoiced over all my joys and suffered all my bitterness, who have studied, struggled and wept with me, with one hand caressing my head, the other pointing to heaven. I kneel before you as when a little child, and I thank you with all the tenderness you have infused into my soul for twelve years; I thank you for all your sacrifices and love.

A SHIPWRECK

(THE LAST MONTHLY STORY)

One December morning, several years ago, there sailed from the port of Liverpool a large steamship, which was carrying on board two hundred persons, of whom seventy were men of the crew. The captain and almost all the sailors were English. Among the passengers, there were several Italians: three ladies, a priest, and a company of musicians. The steamer was bound for the island of Malta. The weather was menacing.

Among the third class passengers in the forecastle, there was an Italian boy about twelve years old, rather small for his age, but robust, with the fine, bold and severe face of a Sicilian lad. He was sitting on a coil of rope close to the foremast, and he kept his hand on a worn out valise which contained all his effects. He had a brown face and black wavy hair which fell upon his shoulders. He was poorly clad, wearing a torn blanket on his shoulders and an old leather bag on his belt. He was pensive and gazed about him at the passengers, the ship, the sailors who were running past, and at the restless sea. He had the appearance of a boy who had suffered some great family sorrow. He had the face of a child and the appearance of a man.

After the departure, one of the sailors, an Italian with grey hair, appeared forward, leading by the hand a little girl, and stopping in front of the little Sicilian, he said to him:

"Here is a companion for your voyage, Mario."

And he left.

The girl sat down on the coil of rope beside the boy.

They looked at each other.

"Where are you going?" asked the Sicilian.

The girl replied: "To Malta and then to Naples."

Then she added: "I am going to meet my father and mother who are expecting me. I am called Giulietta Faggiani."

The boy said nothing.

After a few moments, he drew some bread and some dried fruit out of the bag; the girl had some cakes, and they ate together.

"We will have some fun!" cried the Italian sailor, passing by in haste. "We are already beginning to toss!"

The wind was increasing and the ship rolled heavily. But the two children did not suffer from seasickness and did not mind it. The little girl smiled. She was about the age of her companion, although rather taller; she was slim, dark complexioned, and looked somewhat sickly; she was dressed in a very plain way. Her hair, which was curly, was cut short. She wore a red handkerchief on her head and two little silver rings in her ears.

While eating together they told each other their story. The boy had no longer any father or mother; his father, a workman, had died in Liverpool a few days before, leaving him alone, and the Italian Consul had sent him back to his native place, to Palermo, where some distant relatives lived. The little girl had been taken to London the year before by a widowed aunt, who was very fond of her, and to whom her parents, being poor, had confided her for some time, trusting in the promise that she should be heir to her aunt's estate. But, a few months after, the aunt was crushed under an omnibus and died without leaving a penny. The girl had had recourse to the Consul, who had put her on this steamer bound for Italy. Both children had been recommended to the Italian sailor on board.—"Thus," concluded the girl, "my father and mother thought I would return home rich, and instead I return poor.—But they love me just the same.—And so do my brothers, I have four of them; they are all small.—I am the oldest of the family.—I dress them.—They will make a great deal of me when they see me.—I will enter on tip-toe.——How ugly the sea is!" Then she inquired of the boy: "Are you going to stay with your relatives?"

"Yes, if they wish to have me," replied the boy.

"Don't they care for you?"

"I do not know."

"I will be thirteen years old on Christmas," said the girl.

Then they began to talk about the sea and about the people they had met. They remained together during the whole day, exchanging a few words from time to time. The passengers believed them to be brother and sister. The girl was knitting a stocking, the boy was thinking. The sea continued to grow rougher. At the moment of separation, that evening, before going to sleep, the girl said to Mario: "Sleep well."

"No one will sleep well, poor children!" exclaimed the Italian sailor, as he passed on a run, having been called by the captain. The boy was about to answer his friend: "Good night," when an unexpected rush of water dealt him such a blow that it flung him against a bench.

"Dear me, he is bleeding," cried the little girl, kneeling beside him. The passengers who were running below paid no attention to them. Mario was stunned by the blow and she wiped his forehead, which was bleeding Taking the red handkerchief from her head, she tied it around his head, then she pressed his head upon her breast in order to knot the ends, and in this way she got a blood stain upon her yellow dress just above the waist. Mario shook himself and rose to his feet.

"Are you better," inquired the girl.

"It is all over," he replied.

"Sleep well," said Giulietta. "Good night."

"Good night," replied Mario. And they descended the stairs into their respective dormitories.

The sailor had predicted aright. They had not yet fallen asleep, when a frightful tempest broke upon them. It was a sudden onslaught of furious waves, and in a few moments a mast was broken, and three of the boats, as well as four oxen which were on deck, were carried away like the leaves of a tree. A frightful confusion arose on board the ship. Everything was crashing and there was a terrible uproar of cries and sobs and prayers, enough to make one's hair stand on end. The tempest grew in fury during the night, and at day-break it was still increasing. The formidable waves dashed transversely against the craft and were breaking over the deck, smashing, sweeping, and washing everything into the sea. The platform which covered the machinery was burst open, and the water rushed in with a terrible roar; the fires went out and the stokers fled. Huge, raging streams of water were pouring into the steamer from every side, and a thundering voice cried;

"To the pumps!" It was the voice of the captain.

The sailors rushed to the pumps.

A sudden wave struck the ship on the stern, demolishing the bulwarks and the glass in the port holes and letting in a flood of water.

All the passengers, more dead than alive, had found refuge in the large state room.

At that moment, the captain appeared.

"Captain! Captain!" they all cried at once. "What is the matter? What is going on? Is there any hope for us? Are we safe?"

The captain waited until they were all silent, and then said impressively: "Let us resign ourselves to our fate."

One woman shrieked: "Mercy!" None of the others were able to utter a sound. All were frozen with terror. Some time passed in this way. The silence was like that of a tomb. They all looked at one another with deathly faces. The sea was growing more and more furious, and the breakers were dashing against the ship. The captain attempted to launch a life boat; five sailors entered it and the boat was lowered, but the waves overturned it and two of the sailors were drowned, one of whom was the Italian; the others with great difficulty succeeded in grasping the ropes and got on board again.

After this the sailors lost their courage. Two hours later the ship was submerged in water to the height of the portholes.

A tremendous spectacle then presented itself on deck. Mothers were desperately pressing their children upon their breasts; friends were embracing each other, and saying: "Good bye." Some were going down to their cabins to die out of sight of the sea. One of the passengers shot himself in the head with a pistol and fell headlong upon the stairs of the dormitory, where he expired. Some clung frantically to each other; some of the women writhed in horrible convulsions, and a number of them were kneeling around the priest. You could hear a chorus of sobbings and childish lamentations in shrill and strange voices, and you could see here and there some who were motionless like statues, stupefied, with their eyes dilated and without sight, as you see them on corpses or lunatics. The two children, Mario and Giulietta, clinging to a mast of the ship, were gazing fixedly at the sea as though insane.

The sea had quieted a little, but the steamer was sinking slowly; only a few moments remained.

"Launch the long boat!" cried the captain.

The boat, the last one remaining, was launched and fourteen sailors and three of the passengers went into it. The captain remained on board.

"Come down with us!" they all cried.

"I must die at my post!" replied the captain.

"We will meet some ship," cried the sailors to him. "We will be saved. Come down or you are lost."

"I remain!"

The sailors then cried: "There is place for one more," and turning toward the other passengers, "a woman!"

A woman came forward supported by the captain, but seeing the distance between the ship and the life boat, she had not the courage to take the jump and fell back upon the deck. The other women were all in a faint or almost dying.

"A child!" cried the sailors.

At that cry, the Sicilian boy and his girl companion, who had so far stood as though petrified in an extraordinary stupor, suddenly awakened by the violent instinct of self preservation, let go of the mast at once and rushed to the side of the ship, shouting together: "I!—Save me!" and tried to drive each other back in turn like two furious beasts.

"The smaller of the two!" cried the sailors, "the boat is already overloaded! The smaller of the two!"

Hearing those words, the girl, as though struck by lightning, let her arms fall and stood motionless looking at Mario with eyes filled with the anguish of death. Mario looked at her a moment, he saw the blood stain upon her waist, recalled everything, and a divine idea flashed through his mind.

"The smaller of the two!" the sailors were crying together with imperious impatience! "We are going!"

Then Mario in a voice which did not seem his own shouted: "She is the lighter of the two.—You go, Giulietta! You have a father and mother! I am alone! I give you my place! Go now!"

"Throw her over!" cried the sailors.

Mario grasped Giulietta round the waist and threw her to them. The girl uttered a cry as she took the plunge, a sailor caught her by the arm and pulled her inside the boat.

The lad remained standing on the side of the ship, with his head held high, his hair flying in the wind, motionless, tranquil, sublime!

The boat moved away but was hardly able to pull out of the whirlpool of the waters, produced by the sinking of the steamer, and which threatened to overturn it.

The girl almost lost her senses, but at last raising her eyes to the boy, she broke into an outburst of weeping.

"Good bye, Mario," she cried to him between her sobs, and with her hands stretched towards him: "Good bye! Good bye! Good bye!"

"Good bye," cried the lad raising his hand above his head.

The boat moved swiftly away upon the troubled sea under that dark sky.—No one was any longer crying on the steamer. The water was already lapping the edge of the deck.

Suddenly the boy fell on his knees with his hands joined together and his eyes turned to the sky.

The girl covered her face.

When she raised her head and looked again upon the sea, the ship was no longer there.

JULY

THE LAST PAGE FROM MY MOTHER

Saturday the 1st.

The year is finished, Enrico, and it is a nice thing that the image of the sublime child, who sacrificed his life for his little friend, will remain with thee as a remembrance of the last day. Now that thou art about to separate from thy teachers and thy companions, I have sad news to communicate to thee. The separation will last not only three months, but forever. Thy father, for reasons concerning his profession, is obliged to leave Turin and we must go with him. We will move next autumn. Thou wilt have to enter a new school. Thou art sorry for this, art thou not? For I am sure that thou carest for thy old school, where for four years, twice a day, thou hast experienced the pleasure of toiling, where thou hast seen for a long time, for so many hours each day, the same boys, the same teachers, the same parents, and thy mother who was waiting with a smile for thee; thy old school, where thy talents were developed, where thou hast found so many good companions, where every word that thou hast heard had a purport of something for thy good, and where thou hast not experienced any sorrow without its being beneficial to thee! Thou wilt carry this affection with thee, and say farewell from the bottom of thy heart to all those boys. Some of them will meet with misfortunes, several may soon lose their father and mother; others will die young; some will probably shed their blood nobly upon the field of battle; others will become good and upright workmen, fathers of industrious families such as their own. And who knows that there might not be some one of them who will render some very great service to his country and make his name glorious! Thou wilt separate from them with affection, leaving a little of thy soul in that great family in which thou didst enter as a child and from which thou comest out a youth, and which thy father and thy *mother love because there thou hast been loved so much. The school is like a mother. My Enrico, it snatched thee out of my arms when thou couldst scarcely talk, and now it returns thee to me, tall, strong, good, and studious; may it be blessed, and thou must never forget it, my child. It will be impossible for thee to forget it; thou wilt go about the world, and thou wilt see large cities and marvelous monuments; thou wilt forget many of these, but that modest, white building with those closed blinds, and the little garden where sprouted the first flower of thy intelligence, thou wilt always behold it to the last day of thy life, as I will see the house where I first heard thy voice!*

Thy Mother.

THE EXAMINATION

Tuesday the 4th.

The examination day has come at last. Around the streets and about the school, we hear nothing else spoken of, by the boys, by the fathers and mothers, even by the teachers: every one talks about examinations, points, problems, average, remanded, promoted; every one repeats the same words. Yesterday morning we had the examination in composition, this morning in arithmetic. It was affecting to see the parents taking their boys to school, bestowing the last advice on the way. Some of the mothers would accompany their children as far as the benches in the school room to see if there was ink in the inkstand and to try the pen, and turning around at the door to say: "Have courage! Pay attention! I beseech you!"

Our assistant teacher was Coatti, the one with that rough black beard, who has a voice like a lion and who never punishes any one. Some of the boys on the benches were afraid. When the teacher unsealed the letter from the school board and took out the problem, not a breath could be heard.

He read the problem in a loud voice, looking first at one and then at another with terrible eyes, but we could see that if he had been able to dictate the solution also and have us all promoted, he would have experienced much pleasure.

After an hour's work, a great many began to grow tired, as the problem was difficult, and one of the boys cried. Crossi was beating his head with his fist. It was not the fault of some, that they were unable to solve it, as they had not had time to study, having been neglected by their parents. However, a providence was at hand. You ought to have seen how much pains Derossi took to help them out, how he tried to pass his figures and to suggest the operation without being noticed, anxious for all as if he had been our own teacher. Garrone, who is strong in arithmetic, also helped all those that he could, and even assisted Nobis, who, finding himself in a quandary, was unusually kind. Stardi remained motionless for more than an hour, with his eyes on the problem and his fist at his temples, and then he put down his work in five minutes.

The teacher was walking between the benches, saying: "Be calm! Be calm! I advise you to be calm!" And when he saw some one who was discouraged, in order to make him laugh and restore his spirits, he opened his mouth as if to devour him, imitating a lion.

Looking through the blinds about eleven o'clock, I noticed many of the parents coming and going in the street, looking rather impatient. There was Precossi's father, wearing a blue jacket, having just come out of the workshop with his face still black. Crossi's mother, the vegetable vender, was there, as well as Nelli's mother, all dressed in black; she was not able to keep still. A little before noon, my father came and raised his eyes toward my window: my dear father! At noon we were all through. There was quite a performance at the exit. The parents all ran to meet the boys and ask them questions, and they looked over the leaves of the copy-books, comparing them with the lessons of their companions: "How many operations?" "What is the total?" "How is it about the subtraction?" "What is the answer?" "How is it about the point in the decimal?" All the teachers were going here and there. called by a hundred voices. My father took the rough draft from my hand, looked at it and said: "It is well done." Next to us was the blacksmith Precossi, who was looking at the problem of his son, rather uneasily, not comprehending it. He turned toward my father and exclaimed: "Would you favor me by telling me the total?" My father read the figure. The blacksmith looked at the book—it agreed. "Bravo, little fellow!" he joyfully exclaimed, while my father and he looked at each other with a pleasant smile like two friends; my father reached out his hand, and the other shook it and they separated, saying: "Until the oral examination"— "Until the oral examination." After walking a few steps, we heard a falsetto voice which caused us to turn around. It was the blacksmith singing.

THE LAST EXAMINATION

Friday the 7th.

This morning we had the oral examination. We were all in the class room at eight o'clock, and at a quarter past eight they began to call us, four at a time, into the large hall, where there was a large table covered with a green cloth, and around it sat the principal and four teachers, among whom was our own. How well I then perceived that he is really fond of us. While the others were questioning, his eyes were constantly fixed upon us; he grew uneasy when we were uncertain in our replies and serene when we gave a good answer; feeling everything, and was making us signs a thousand times with the hands and with the head, as if saying:—" That is right—no—pay attention—slower—courage!"

Had he been allowed to speak, I believe he would have prompted us in everything. If one after the other our fathers could have been put in his place, they could not have done any better. Ten times I felt like crying "Thanks" to him in the presence of them all. When the other teachers told me: "That is right, you may go," his eyes beamed with happiness

I returned to the class and waited for my father. Nearly all of the pupils were there. I sat next to Garrone. I was not a bit happy. I was thinking that it was the last time that we should sit so near each other! I had not yet told Garrone that I should not be able to go through the fourth elementary with him, that I had to leave Turin with my father; ne knew nothing about it. He was sitting there bent double, with his thick head leaning upon the desk, drawing some ornamental figures around a photograph of his father, dressed as a machinist. His father is a big tall fellow with a head like an ox, and has a serious and honest look like his boy. While he was bent down thus, with his shirt a little open in front, I spied on his bare and robust chest the golden cross which Nelli's mother had given him when she learned that he had protected her son. However, it was necessary that I should tell him that I was going to leave, and I said to him:

"Garrone, next autumn my father will leave Turin forever."

He asked me if I were also going, and I answered that I was.

"Will you not go through the fourth elementary with us?" he asked.

I answered, "No."

He remained quiet for a short time, continuing to draw. Then he asked, without raising his head: "Will you ever think of your companions of the third elementary?"

"Yes," I replied, "I will remember all of them, but I will think more of you than of the others. How could I forget you?"

He cast at me a serious glance, which expressed a thousand things, and said nothing; but he reached out his left hand, pretending to draw with the other, and I grasped it between both of my hands, that strong and loyal hand!

At that moment, our teacher rushed in with a red face and said hastily in a low and merry tone of voice: "Good boys, so far everything goes well, I hope those who remain will do as well, my good boys! Courage! I feel very well satisfied."

And in order to show us his content and to exhilarate us, leaving the room quickly, he feigned a stumbling movement, catching the wall to prevent his falling; he, whom we had never seen laugh! It seemed so strange that instead of laughing we were all dumfounded· we all smiled, but no one laughed.—I cannot explain the pain mingled with tenderness that that childish act of joy caused me. That moment of cheerfulness was his whole reward, the reward of nine months of goodness, of patience, and of worries! It was for that he had wearied himself so much, and that he had come so many times to teach when sick, our poor master! That was all, and nothing else did he ask in exchange for·so much affection and so many cares!

And it seems to me now that I shall always see again that joy of his when I remember him for many years, and when I am a man, if he be still alive and we meet, I will tell him about that outburst which touched my heart, and I will kiss him on his white hair.

FAREWELL

Monday the 10th.

At one o'clock we gathered for the last time in the school room to listen to the result of the examination and to receive our books of promotion. The streets were thronged with people. They had also invaded the large hall, and a great many of them had entered the class room pushing themselves as far as the teacher's desk. In our class room, they were filling all the vacant space between the wall and the first bench. There was the father of Garrone, the mother of Derossi, the blacksmith Precossi, Mrs. Nelli, the vegetable vender, the father of the Little Mason, the father of Stardi, besides many others whom I had never seen before. One could hear from every side a buzzing and hum, as though we were in a square. Our teacher entered; a profound silence ensued.

He was holding in his hand the catalogue and commenced to read it at once. Abatucci, promoted, sixty-sixtieths; Archini, promoted, fifty-five sixtieths; the Little Mason, promoted, Crossi promoted. Then he read loudly: "Ernesto Derossi, promoted, seventy-seventieths, and first prize."

All the parents who were there and who knew him exclaimed: "Bravo, bravo, Derossi!"

He shook his blonde locks with an easy and beautiful smile, looking at his mother, who saluted him with her hand. Garoffi, Garrone, and the Calabrian boy, promoted. Then three or four names in succession, remanded; one of them began to weep as his father who stood near the door made him a sign of menace. But the teacher said to the father: "No, sir, allow me; it is not always the pupil's fault, it is sometimes hard luck, and this is the case with your son." Then he read: "Nelli, promoted, sixty-two-seventieths." His mother sent him a kiss with a fan. "Stardi, promoted with sixty-seven-seventieths;" but hearing that fine point, he did not even smile, nor did he take his fist from his temple. The last of all was Votini, who had come there finely dressed and with his hair well brushed; promoted. Having read the last name, the teacher arose and said:

"Boys, this is the last time we will meet together. We have been together a year, now we separate as good friends, do we not? I regret to separate from you, dear children."-- He hesitated and then resumed: "If at times I have lost my patience, if at times I have been unjust or too severe, forgive me."

"No, no," said the parents of many of the pupils, "no, signor maestro, never, never."

"Forgive me," repeated the teacher, "and remember me. Next year you will no longer be with me, but I will see you all again, and you will remain forever in my heart. Farewell, boys!" Immediately he came forward into our midst, and we all reached our hands to him, rising from the benches; some kissed him, and fifty voices cried together:

"Until we meet again, master! Thanks, signor maestro; may happiness follow you! Do remember us!"—When he went out he looked as though oppressed by emotion.

We all came out in confusion. From class rooms on every side the others were coming out, and they were all mingled together. There was a great noise; the boys and parents were saying farewells to the teachers and to the school mistresses, and were saluting one another. The mistress with the red feather had four or five little children on top of her and about twenty around, who were almost taking her breath away. They had torn the hat of the "Little Nun," and they had stuck a dozen bouquets between the buttons of her black dress and in her pockets. A number of them were greeting Robetti, who that day had laid aside for the first time his crutches From every side, one could hear: "Till next year!" "Till the twentieth of October?" "To meet again at All-Saints Day!" We also greeted one another. How we forgot all the disagreements of the past in that moment! Votini, who had always been so jealous of Derossi, was the first to rush towards him and throw his arms around him. I saluted the Little Mason and kissed him just at the moment he was making to me for the last time the hare face, that dear lad! I saluted Precossi and Garoffi who told me the date of the drawing of his last lottery and presented me with a little majolica paper weight which was broken in one corner. I said good-bye to all the others. It was nice to see how poor Nelli clung to Garrone, so that they could not take him away; they all crowded around Garrone and said: "Good-bye, Garrone, good-bye till we meet again." And some were touching him and pressing him to say good-bye, that brave, noble boy! His father stood there in amazement; he looked at us and smiled. Garrone was the last one whom I embraced in the street, and I stifled a sob in my heart; he kissed me on the forehead. Then I ran to my father and mother. My father asked me: "Have you bade farewell to all your school-mates?"—I replied: "I have."—"If there is any one whom you have wronged, go and ask his forgiveness. Is there any one?"—"No one," I replied.—"Then, good-bye!" said my father with emotion, casting a last glance at the school.—And my mother repeated: "Good bye!"—I was not able to speak.

www.ingramcontent.com/pod-product-compliance
Lightning Source LLC
Chambersburg PA
CBHW031337230426
43670CB00006B/352